Flowering
House Plants

THE TIME-LIFE ENCYCLOPEDIA OF GARDENING

Flowering House Plants

by

JAMES UNDERWOOD CROCKETT

and

the Editors of TIME-LIFE BOOKS

Watercolor Illustrations by

Allianora Rosse

An Owl Book

HENRY HOLT AND COMPANY

NEW YORK

THE TIME-LIFE ENCYCLOPEDIA OF GARDENING

EDITORIAL STAFF FOR FLOWERING HOUSE PLANTS:
EDITOR: Robert M. Jones
Assistant Editor: Carlotta Kerwin
Picture Editor: Kathleen Shortall
Designer: Leonard Wolfe
Staff Writers: Marian Gordon Goldman,
Paula Pierce, Kelly Tasker
Chief Researcher: Joan Mebane
Researchers: Diane Asselin, Muriel Clarke,
Evelyn Constable, Helen Fennell, Gail Hansberry,
Sandra Streepey, Mollie Webster, Gretchen Wessels
Design Assistant: Anne B. Landry
Staff Illustrator: Vincent Lewis

Library of Congress Cataloging-in-Publication Data
Crockett, James Underwood.
Flowering house plants.
(The Time-Life encyclopedia of gardening)
"An Owl book."
Reprint. Originally published: New York: Time-Life
Books, 1972.
Bibliography: p.
Includes index.
1. House plants.   2. Flowers.   3. Indoor gardening.
I. Time-Life Books.   II. Title.   III. Series.
SB419.C68 1986   635.9'65   86-12045
ISBN 0-8050-0122-0 (pbk.)

First published by Time-Life Books in 1972.
First Owl Book Edition—1986
Printed in the United States of America
10 9 8 7 6 5 4 3 2 1

ISBN 0-8050-0122-0

THE AUTHOR: Author of 13 of the volumes in the Encyclopedia, co-author of two additional volumes and consultant on other books in the series, James Underwood Crockett has been a lover of the earth and its good things since his boyhood on a Massachusetts fruit farm. He was graduated from the Stockbridge School of Agriculture at the University of Massachusetts and has worked ever since in horticulture. A perennial contributor to leading gardening magazines, he also writes a monthly bulletin, *Flowery Talks,* that is widely distributed through retail florists. His television program, "Crockett's Victory Garden," shown all over the United States, is constantly winning new converts to the Crockett approach to growing things.

THE ILLUSTRATOR: Allianora Rosse, who provided the more than 125 delicate, precise watercolors of house plants beginning on page 100, is a specialist in flower painting. Trained at the Art Academy of The Hague in The Netherlands, Miss Rosse worked for 16 years as staff artist for *Flower Grower* magazine. Her illustrations of shrubs, trees and flowers have appeared in many gardening books.

GENERAL CONSULTANTS: Dr. O. W. Davidson, Professor of Horticulture Emeritus, Rutgers University, New Brunswick, New Jersey. Staff of the Brooklyn Botanic Garden: Robert S. Tomson, Assistant Director; Thomas R. Hofmann, Plant Propagator; George A. Kalmbacher, Plant Taxonomist; Edmund O. Moulin, Horticulturist. Mrs. Joy Logee Martin, Logee's Greenhouses, Danielson, Conn. Albert P. Nordheden, Morganville, New Jersey.

THE COVER: Three of the thousands of varieties of America's most popular flowering house plant, the African violet, grace a living room in New York City. From front to back, they are Ruth, Annette and Sophie of the Rhapsodie group of hybrids, notable for bearing quantities of long-lasting flowers.

CONTENTS

1 The pleasures of gardening indoors

7

Picture essay: DECORATING WITH HOUSE PLANTS

16

2 Providing light and water

25

3 Soils, pots and potting

45

Picture essay: ORCHIDS YOU CAN GROW AS HOUSE PLANTS

54

4 The basics of day-to-day care

67

Picture essay: THE EXPERTS SHARE THEIR SECRETS

80

5 Growing new plants from old ones

89

6 An encyclopedia of flowering house plants

101

APPENDIX

Characteristics of 149 house plants   152

Bibliography   155

Credits and acknowledgments   155

Index   156

The pleasures of gardening indoors

1

"My family lives in a jungle," one of my daughters once warned a visitor. She exaggerated. But it is true that I share my office at home with a fragrant orchid, a dwarf pomegranate tree, a primrose, a fern, several pots of pink and white African violets that blossom tirelessly, a huge white poinsettia in season and a number of colorful, exotic specimens with Latin names a yard long. It is also true that until the painters arrived, some handsome vines framed the great window in the living room.

My plants surround me with beauty and satisfy my need for having growing things close by. Almost everyone, whether country-born or city-bred, has that need. You can satisfy it no matter where you live, even if you lack so much as a tiny window sill. My own indoor garden, which includes plants from all over the world, thrives in many rooms of my home in Massachusetts. Some extraordinarily beautiful African violets that I saw recently had been raised in a cellar in Plymouth, New Hampshire. The florist who was selling them told me that a local nurse grew them under artificial light—a technique that more and more gardeners employ each year. Even the concrete forests of cities are coming to look a little like the Hanging Gardens of Babylon. Towering tropical plants reach upward in skyscraper lobbies and reception rooms. Flowers blossom in office windows, and all kinds of potted plants contribute cheer to desks tucked in corners that never see sunlight.

Just as people grow potted plants almost everywhere, so do they grow almost every kind of plant in pots. Nearly every type of plant that does not need a rest period in winter cold can be cultivated in some form indoors with a reasonable expectation of success. True, the indoor plant must adjust to a lower level of light than it would receive outside, to the high winter temperatures that people demand indoors, to low levels of humidity and confined quarters for its roots. But to compensate, the plant does not have to stand up to wind, driving rain and wide-ranging temperature fluctuations. Disease and insects are less of a threat, and a plant-loving

In the conservatory of Mark Twain's house in Hartford, Connecticut, a low fountain is surrounded by rosy purple cyclamens, blue hyacinths, red gloxinias and pink begonias. In the right foreground is a pink hydrangea.

owner can generally be counted on for a regular supply of food and water. Plants as diverse as ferns and vines, bushes and miniature trees flourish indoors, but the plants that add the brightest note to a home, distilling the essence of the beauty of nature, are those that flower. Such plants are themselves a huge group, and this book will deal specifically with them, describing in detail more than 140 in the encyclopedia section, beginning on page 101.

THE BEGINNINGS

The pleasures to be gained from growing plants indoors have attracted—and challenged—people for a long time. The Minoans, whose civilization thrived on Crete thousands of years before Christ, seem to have had flowerpots. At least, when the Minoans disappeared, about 1100 B.C., they left behind beautifully decorated potting containers with holes in the bottoms. The Greeks, the Indians and the Chinese all raised potted plants, and ancient Egyptian friezes show slaves carrying some in processions. The Romans of the Caesars' days went earlier civilizations one better. They shaved huge chunks of mica into thin sheets and used them to make translucent roofs for heated greenhouses where they produced out-of-season lilies and roses. Seneca, the First Century philosopher-statesman, who was a Stoic and therefore somewhat puritanical, thought his countrymen were going too far. "Do not those live contrary to nature," he asked, "who require a rose in winter and who, by the excitement of hot water and an appropriate modification of heat, force from winter the later blooms of spring?"

Whether people in what used to be called the Dark Ages grew plants inside their gloomy homes, nobody knows. A painting of a legendary martyr of those times, Saint Ursula, shows two house plants on her bedroom window sill, but the historical reliability of that picture is rather doubtful since it was made by the Venetian artist Vittore Carpaccio more than 1,000 years after Saint Ursula's death. By Renaissance times, however, there were palatial indoor gardens that rivaled those of the Romans. The great Scholastic philosopher Saint Albertus Magnus built an artificially heated indoor fruit and flower garden in which he entertained a nobleman, William of Holland, in 1259.

A little later, Venetian and Genoese merchants began using their ships to import such exotic plants as hibiscus from Syria and jasmine from Persia to sell to wealthy Europeans. Semitropical fruits particularly caught the fancy of people who lived where it was too cold to grow such trees outdoors. The French, the Dutch, the Germans and the English all wanted oranges and lemons, and began wintering tubbed trees in heated sheds. The sheds gave way to greenhouses that grew ever bigger and better, and eventually such plants as camellias shared the warmth and space with the cit-

A CALENDAR OF FRAGRANCE

Many indoor gardeners overlook the fact that it is possible not only to have house plants that blossom in sequence but ones that smell in sequence as well. The following provide fragrance at different times of the year.
September to December: *clerodendrum (Clerodendrum fragrans pleniflorum)*
Christmas: *flowering tobacco (Nicotiana alata grandiflora)*
December to March: *nasturtium (Tropaeolum majus)*
December to May: *hyacinth (Hyacinthus orientalis albulus)*
January to June: *gardenia (Gardenia jasminoides veitchii), butterfly gardenia (Ervatamia coronaria plena), Carolina jasmine (Gelsemium sempervirens)*
February to July: *star jasmine (Trachelospermum jasminoides)*
March: *walking iris (Neomarica gracilis)*
March into Summer: *wax plant (Hoya carnosa), yellow star jasmine (Trachelospermum asiaticum)*
Easter: *Easter lily (Lilium longiflorum)*
May to October: *Madagascar jasmine (Stephanotis floribunda)*

rus trees. If the favorable conditions of a specially built greenhouse were lacking, a gardener made do with whatever warm place he could find for his plants. An English glass manufacturer named Jacobs won a measure of fame in 1660 when Sir Hugh Platt, in a book entitled *Garden of Eden,* wrote about him: "I have known Mr. Jacobs of the Glassehouse to have carnations all the winter by benefit of a room that was near his glassehouse fire."

From such beginnings came the conservatory, the pride and pleasure of the 19th century. (The conservatory differs from the greenhouse in that it is a place to display plants as well as to raise them, and unlike most greenhouses it usually is within a dwelling instead of apart from it.) It achieved its maximum splendor in the Victorian decades, when parlors and bay windows were lush with palms, heliotropes, ferns, ivies, begonias, camellias, fuchsia, geraniums, carnations, cinerarias, calceolarias and aspidistras—all seeming to be carefully placed to intimidate rambunctious small boys. But elaborate conservatories were the vogue even early in the century. One was described by Bory de Saint-Vincent, who entered Vienna with Napoleon's army in 1803. He wrote:

"It was a novel and enchanting circumstance, so far as I am concerned, to find the apartments of most ladies adorned with conservatories and perfumed in winter with the pleasantest of flowers. I recall among others, with a kind of intoxicated delight, the boudoir of the Countess of C., whose couch was surrounded with jasmine climbing up daturas [shrubs of the nightshade family] . . . and all this on the first story. You repaired from it to the sleeping chamber through clusters of African heaths, hortensias, camellias —then very little known—and other precious shrubs planted in well-kept borders, which, moreover, were ornamented with violets, crocuses of every color, hyacinths and other flowers, growing in the green turf. On the opposite side was the bathroom, likewise placed in a conservatory where papyrus and iris grew around the marble basin and the water conduits. The double corridors were not less plentifully garnished with beautiful flowering plants; you might readily, in this enchanted recess, leave open the doors and windows as if an eternal spring had prevailed—the hot-water pipes which promoted and preserved the freshness of the vegetation securing in every department an equality of temperature. Yet all these marvels were kept up at no very great expense."

Your own indoor garden may never rival that of the Countess of C., whoever she was, but that remark about "no very great expense" still holds true. And in most other ways, the modern indoor gardener has advantages that 19th Century Viennese who were not countesses never enjoyed. Central heating permits you to grow exotic flowering plants native to the tropics. The big windows of today's houses admit more light than ever penetrated old-fashioned farmsteads and city brownstones, and electricity supplements it with artificial light. Even the cooking gas now used in American kitchens favors house plants. In the past it was manufactured from coal and gave off fumes that—whether anyone noticed them or not—pervaded much of the house and poisoned plants; natural gas, which has generally supplanted coal gas, is nontoxic to plants.

The materials employed for indoor gardening have also been improved. Soils and fertilizers are compounded to suit specific plants in the way that a pediatrician's formula suits a specific infant. The plants themselves may be purchased at nurseries, florists' shops and garden centers. And the variety now available is astonishing, thanks in part to air freight, which quickly brings from remote corners of the world exotic species that could not survive an extended trip. Before you buy anything, though, you had better decide what plants will please you most and what plants among them will do well in the conditions that you can provide.

SELECTING PLANTS   Consider first what a flowering house plant is. The definition is not so simple as "a plant that flowers in the house." Besides bearing flowers, it must be suitable in size for indoor living; you do not want to be crowded out of the house even by the most beautiful of plants. It must tolerate the generally low levels of winter light (even with those big windows) or be a kind that will prosper under artificial light. It must withstand both the generally high level of heat and the low humidity in most houses. And it should grow well enough under ordinary care to delight you.

But flowers are the primary goal, and you should know what to expect of a plant before you choose one. First there are those that blossom incessantly and, when given proper treatment, live for years. Among them are the African violets, whose profuse quarter-size blossoms of white, pink, blue or purple have made them an outstanding favorite; the wax begonias, sparkling with pink, white or red flowers about as big as a man's thumbnail; and the Chinese hibiscus, which is no small plant from the forest floor, but a tropical shrub—it bears white, pink, yellow, red or orange single or double blossoms, 4 to 5 inches across, and would grow to the ceiling if you gave it a chance. I keep mine down to 3 feet in height by pruning the roots and tops *(page 53)*, and it has been bearing blossoms the year round for nearly 25 years.

A second category of house plants embraces those that bloom only part time in the house, but bear attractive foliage when not in blossom. Among such plants is the Christmas cactus, which sends

A ROLL-AROUND PLANT BOX

An inexpensive wooden container on casters displays house plants off the floor and allows the plants to be moved about according to their light and temperature needs. The inside is waterproofed with heavy-gauge plastic sheeting or silver asphalt paint. A 2- or 3-inch bed of gravel or perlite steadies the pots and keeps the plants above any water that reaches the bottom. Plants in large pots are set directly in the gravel; smaller ones are raised to the same level by being set on top of inverted empty pots. Sphagnum moss stuffed around the pots provides stability and is kept moist to maintain needed humidity around the plants.

out sprawling chains of inch-long, dark green, elliptical leaves linked together and suddenly, at Christmastime, produces 2½-inch blossoms at the end of each chain. I have one that must have been 20 years old when I inherited it from my grandmother 30 years ago, and it still dresses itself up with hundreds of pink blossoms every winter. The rest of the year its unique greenery earns its keep.

In a third category are such lovely plants as the gloxinia—a relative of the African violet but one bearing bigger blossoms. These types thrive for 20 years or more, but bloom for only a few months at a time, and need careful storage during their rest periods.

And finally, there are exceedingly beautiful house plants that are short-term but welcome guests. Grown in greenhouses by professionals and acquired by indoor gardeners at the peak of their glamour, they last but for a while. A pot of crisp tulips blooming in midwinter can bring instant spring into the house for a week, or for several weeks, depending on the temperature; the colder the room, the longer the tulips will last, but the ideal temperature for the plant would prove far too low for you. Usually such plants fade and land in the garbage can because they are not truly suited to household life, though the knowing gardener will check first to see if they can be moved outdoors.

The flowering habits of the popular house plants are described in the encyclopedia section, Chapter 6. These characteristics have nothing to do with the botanical classifications of the plants—the everblooming African violet is related to the intermittently blooming gloxinias but not to the free-flowering wax begonias. But an unusual number of house plants are drawn from just three of the 300 families in the plant kingdom: the orchids, the gesneriads and the bromeliads; they account for more than a quarter of the plants in the encyclopedia.

Orchids, of which there are thousands of varieties that come from climates as disparate as Alaska's and Brazil's, share the distinction of having the most highly evolved reproductive system of all plants: the pistil and stamen are fused in a single column. A few orchids grown as house plants are terrestrial; that is, like most plants they require soil in which to grow. Most, however, are epiphytes, or air plants; in the wild they grow mainly on trees. They are not parasites, but simply use the trees as living places, gathering their nutrients from the air, from rain water and from bits of decaying leaves caught in the crotches of branches. Most orchids grown as house plants thrive in the warm temperatures we maintain in our homes, and although special attention is required to provide them with enough humidity, the species recommended in the encyclopedia are as easy to grow as many other indoor plants.

The gesneriads, which count among their 85 genera such flowering plants as African violets, gloxinias and achimenes, are mostly herbs of tropical or subtropical origin, whose family ties derive from similarities in the structure of their flowers. The bromeliads, of which there are 51 genera and perhaps 1,000 species, include such seemingly different plants as pineapple and Spanish moss; many have stiff leaves in the form of rosettes, and bear bright flowers on spikes. Some are epiphytic; that is, like many of the orchids, they are air plants.

The biological relationships that connect so many house plants have led a few indoor gardeners to specialize. Some concentrate on orchids, and there are also bromeliad and gesneriad fanciers (and national societies devoted to the culture of each of these plant families). The family connection is indicated in the encyclopedia (which lists plants by genus) for those plants that belong to the orchid, bromeliad or gesneriad families.

MICROCLIMATES AT HOME When you have decided what kinds of plants you would like to grow, take stock of the conditions you can provide for them. Since house plants come from many different parts of the world, their needs for light, temperature and humidity vary greatly. But plants are adaptable, and many neophyte gardeners do not realize that their houses also are adaptable, that is, that each house offers a broad range of microclimates within itself. Even with central heating, different sections of a house will be far from uniform in temperature. A window sill on the north side is usually far cooler than one on the south. A window on the south generally gets more light than one on the north. Kitchens and bathrooms are usually more humid than other rooms.

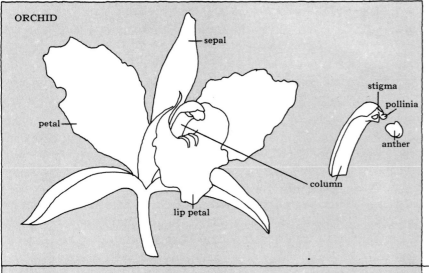

ORCHID

sepal

stigma
pollinia
anther

petal

column

lip petal

THREE DISTINCTIVE FAMILIES OF FLOWERS

Despite their spectacular range of configurations, sizes and colors, the flowers of all orchids have the same basic structure: three sepals, or petallike outer leaves, and three petals. One petal, called the lip, assumes a variety of shapes, often curling around a fleshy column formed of the fused male and female organs, a unique characteristic of the orchid. Insects that are attracted to the orchid's nectar easily knock the anthers off the column (inset) and deposit pollen picked up from another orchid on the exposed stigma, fertilizing the flower.

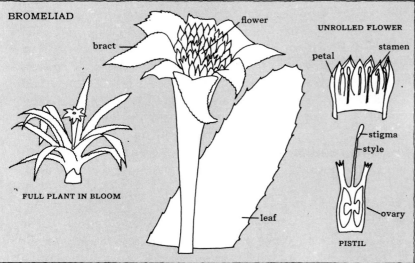

BROMELIAD

flower

UNROLLED FLOWER

bract

stamen

petal

stigma
style

ovary

FULL PLANT IN BLOOM

leaf

PISTIL

The tiny flowers of the bromeliad family of plants come in clusters, some spread out along a tall central spike, some in compact clumps like the one at the left in the drawing, which is shown enlarged in the center view. The flowers are usually overshadowed by brilliantly colored, scalelike leaves, or bracts, attached in various ways to the flower clump. The flowers ripen a few at a time, the petals opening to disclose male stamens (upper inset at right) and female pistils (lower inset). Pollen deposited on the pistils finds its way down to the ovary, fertilizing the ovules to produce seeds.

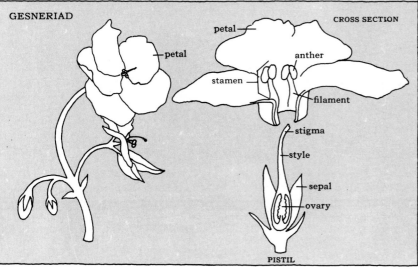

GESNERIAD

CROSS SECTION

petal

petal

anther

stamen

filament

stigma

style

sepal
ovary

PISTIL

The flowers of African violets appear to have five petals, but these sections are actually deeply cut lobes of the single trumpet-shaped petal that distinguishes the gesneriad family. Each flower has but two male stamens topped by large pollen-bearing anthers (upper inset). The female pistil thrusts far above the anthers, a design that favors cross-fertilization over self-fertilization —the stigma at the pistil tip (lower inset) is more likely to trap pollen that has previously been picked up by a visiting bee than pollen the bee gathers from this flower as it pokes down past the low-set anthers.

In determining the locations where your plants will do best, you will find a maximum-minimum thermometer and a hygrometer *(Chapter 2)* almost indispensable. The first records the extremes of temperature that are a principal factor influencing the growth of house plants, the second measures relative humidity. With them, you can discover many microclimates within your house and capitalize on them to grow a variety of plants.

HOW TO BUY PLANTS   Since the choice is so wide, the principal problem in selecting plants to grow may be making up your mind. More objective standards apply when you come to buy individual specimens. The first rule is: acquire them from a reputable source and be prepared to pay a fair price. I am skeptical of bargains and you should be too, for horticulture, I must admit with sorrow, has its full share of marginal operators who are long on promises and short on performance. Even when you know your nurseryman or florist is reliable, examine your plants carefully before you buy. Choose those that are of peasant build, that is, short and stocky, rather than tall and spindly, and that have abundant foliage growing right down to the top of the pot *(drawings below);* such characteristics indicate vigorous health and promise prolific blooms. Plants on which the first buds are about to open are preferable to those with full-blown blossoms because

WHAT TO LOOK FOR IN BUYING A HOUSE PLANT

This plant is a poor buy: it has only three flower stems, two past their blossoming prime and only one that promises any future flowers; the plant's main stalk is gangly and off center, and the leaves are sparse.

A near-perfect plant has a thick and well-balanced array of leaves on a straight, sturdy central stalk. Only one stem is in bloom, but many buds at different stages of maturity indicate a long flowering to come.

you will be able to enjoy their beauty from the beginning. And, of course, pass over plants with symptoms of pest infestation. Look at the undersides of the leaves for tiny spots that are lighter than the rest of the leaf: if you find any, you know that insects have been sucking the plant's juices, to its detriment. Examine leaf surfaces near the tip of new growth for the minute green, yellow, pink, black or brown insects called aphids, or plant lice. Check for evidence of spider mites, or red spiders, as they are commonly called; the mites are too small to be seen without a magnifying glass but the damage they cause is not: they manifest their presence with speckled, whitish discoloration of the leaves. Look at the leaf axils—the points where leaves and stems join—for a white, cottonlike substance that is really a community of mealy bugs.

Once you are satisfied that all is well with the plants that you have chosen, make sure they are properly wrapped if the weather is chill. Many house plants suffer quickly from cold, and even if your car is only three steps from the greenhouse door, your purchases will require protection in subfreezing temperatures.

After you have a few healthy plants growing, I predict that you will want more. Fortunately, plants are easy to multiply (Chapter 5) and you will find that other indoor gardeners are eager to share experiences and swap cuttings. One example of such generosity can be seen in a New York skyscraper that enjoys the beauty of several dozen pots of angel wing begonia—a lovely plant with canes that thrust out as much as 5 feet in every direction, 5-inch-long speckled copper-green leaves and grapelike clusters of pink flowers. All the building's specimens are children or grandchildren of a single plant with a Cinderella-like history. The parent plant —which was a descendant of a plant imported long ago from the jungles of South America—was given to an acquaintance of mine by two friends who had found it on a trash heap. It was in a sorry state. It did not even have a pot. Its long canes were shriveled, and its roots were dry and almost devoid of soil. The recipient of the plant responded to the challenge. He potted the orphan in good soil, trimmed it of dead wood, watered it cautiously while it convalesced, and set it in a cool, shaded window. It soon recovered and began to grow so vigorously that it became too large for his house and he had to move it to his office, where visitors, only half in jest, expressed fear that it would strangle them. But those who were pressed into accepting cuttings to grow for themselves soon became converts to house-plant gardening. In a surprisingly short time they were growing other kinds of plants as well, enthusiastically committed to the "green revolution" indoors and worthy successors to the Minoans, the Greeks, the Romans, the Countess of C. and Mr. Jacobs of the Glassehouse.

WRAPPING A PLANT

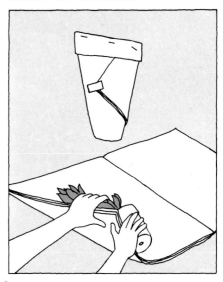

If you have to carry a house plant outdoors in winter, wrap it in three or four layers of newspaper to prevent harm from cold. Set the pot on its side in one corner of the outspread sheets and roll it diagonally so that the paper forms a cone around the pot. Then fold the paper under the bottom of the pot, fasten the side with tape and staple across the top (inset). Such protection is essential, even for the short walk from a florist's shop to the car on a cold day; otherwise the abrupt change in temperature can shock a plant enough to cause it to lose leaves or even die.

Decorating with house plants

Whether you fill every room in your home with flowering plants or limit your indoor garden to a window sill here and there, the plants you choose and how you arrange them can make all the difference in the satisfaction they provide. While foliage plants such as philodendrons and rubber plants will thrive in an inside corner, most flowering plants need light in which to flourish and blossom well. This generally means putting them close to windows, and window gardens can be handled in many attractive ways. A striking effect can be achieved simply by placing a single trailing plant like a clerodendrum or ivy geranium in a hanging container in the center of the window. Two or three glass shelves or adjustable metal shelves across a window will hold an entire collection of small- to medium-sized plants, doubling or tripling the window-sill space. Or a whole cascade of flowers can be banked to provide a stunning and useful "greenhouse" effect (overleaf).

Other parts of the house can serve as plant settings. Plants brought to blossom at a bright window, or outdoors in mild weather, can be moved to interior locations and enjoyed for days or even weeks before being moved back; many plants can be used this way as the need suggests itself—placed inside the front door to greet visitors, on the dining table as a centerpiece for a dinner party, or in an upstairs bedroom to welcome weekend guests. And today window light is not essential. Artificially lighted plant boxes like the one in the picture opposite dramatically demonstrate possibilities of indoor gardening that did not exist a few decades ago.

These indoor gardeners have immeasurably enhanced a conventional window display with another under artificial light just below it, a bright focal point that shows off pink phalaenopsis orchids, red laeliocattleya orchids and ferns in front of tall-leaved red-flowered aechmeas. The owners made the cabinet themselves, tailoring it to the style of the bookcases on either side, and fitting it with fluorescent plant-growing lights. For the window above it they selected mainly nonflowering varieties, whose leafy forms can be enjoyed in silhouette.

Orchids, aechmeas and ferns in a lighted cabinet provide a day and night display in the library of a house in Connecticut.

Gardening in the window

The traditional placement of flowering house plants—next to windows where they can thrive in natural light—need not be a cliché, as the imaginative treatments shown here demonstrate. In the high-ceilinged room at left below, a window corner is made into a garden spot by a grouping of low flowering plants around a tall acacia tree in a tub. The yellow flowers of the acacia add a touch of warm sunny color even on the grayest winter day and help tie the room to the terrace and trees outside.

In the bay window below, several tricks have been used to avoid the monotony of a line of pots and to keep plants at their flowering best. The cyclamens are all about the same size, but they virtually fill the

A bright corner in a dining room in Dover, Massachusetts, is created by red azaleas and begonias displayed next to large and small acacias.

window because they are staged, or set on various levels rising from front to back. The staging in this case is not shelving but hollow cylinders of plastic set into a bed of pebbles, with the pots placed on top.

The bay window has also been equipped to help the plants grow vigorously. Fluorescent lights above the window, not visible in the photograph, are used to supplement the plants' light needs. A transparent screen of flexible plastic, attached to a roller in the manner of a pull-down window blind, turns the bay window into an instant greenhouse when wanted, protecting the plants from the warmth and dryness of the house and giving them the cooler night temperatures that allow them to produce beautiful flowers.

Pink and white cyclamens, banked against a living-room window in Newton, Massachusetts, are set on translucent plastic tubes, allowing sunlight to filter through. In the foreground are fairy primroses.

A winter window sill in New England is brought to life by an array of polyanthus primroses. Together with a pink cyclamen on

the large coffee table, their bright yellow and purple blossoms harmonize with, yet enliven, the room's restrained color scheme.

*Well placed on tables, red azaleas and
purple cinerarias complement the
striking accents of paintings, fabrics and
accessories around the living room.*

22

A bold blend of colors

The vivid decor of this house and garden in San Diego shows how stunningly flowering plants can be integrated into an overall design. Blossoms are placed all over the living room, their colors and shapes chosen to complement the owners' collection of abstract American paintings, Mexican sculpture and hand-woven fabrics from Guatemala, India and Morocco. The plants are also chosen to provide a succession of bright blooms year round. Annuals such as the cinerarias are bought from the florist when in flower and discarded when they wither; others, such as the gerberas and azaleas, are brought into the house from the garden as they near their peak, and replanted outdoors when they fade, to flower again next year.

Red gerbera daisies, green-centered yellow chrysanthemums and a purplish red azalea highlight the hues of pillows and a painting on a fireplace.

The patio glows with white and purple cinerarias (foreground), red gerbera daisies, red and white azaleas and pink, yellow and red chrysanthemums.

Providing light and water 2

Like people, plants need to feel at home. Otherwise they go into a decline and eventually pine away. Yet those African violets mentioned in the preceding chapter were, in their Plymouth, New Hampshire, cellar, a long way from their fatherland in East Africa's mountains, where Baron Adalbert Emil Walter Radcliffe Le Tonneux von Saint Paul-Illaire found them in 1892 and gave them their official name, *Saintpaulia*. The most popular geraniums, those with scalloped leaves and clusters of coral or pink flowers, originated in South Africa. Begonias, of which there may be as many as 1,000 species, range in their free state throughout the tropics and subtropics of the world. In the Western Hemisphere, they are found from Brazil north to the Caribbean islands and Mexico. But like hundreds of other plant immigrants from all over the planet, the begonias, the geraniums and the African violets can flourish here as long as they are made to feel at home.

To feel at home, they demand appropriate temperatures, light, water and humidity, similar to those they were accustomed to in the old country. Plants are adaptable, but the closer you can come to creating the environment that each finds ideal, the more they will flourish and bloom. Because they come from such diverse places as deserts and jungles, their preferences differ widely, but they all share one need—light. Without light, plants starve to death, no matter how well they are fed otherwise. In fact, a fertilized plant without light will die—of indigestion—sooner than an unfertilized plant without light.

The reason plants need light is simple and mysteriously wonderful. All plants—that is, all green, chlorophyll-pigmented plants, not such fungus growths as mushrooms—depend on photosynthesis for their lives. So do many plants that do not *look* green, even those that have red or copper leaves; the green is there, but obscured by the dominant colors. Photosynthesis gets its name from the Greek words for *light* and *putting together* and it is a process that does just that. Light striking a green leaf activates the chlo-

The seven flowering house plants most frequently sold as gifts make a multicolor display in a San Francisco florist's. The plants, keyed in the drawing at right, are poinsettias (1), chrysanthemums (2), an Easter lily (3), a geranium (4), a begonia (5), azaleas (6) and African violets (7). At top left and in the rear are sprays of peach branches in blossom.

rophyll within the leaf. The chlorophyll sets the plant to work combining water and carbon dioxide from the air to produce the sugars and starches that provide energy for the plant's life processes; as a waste product from water and carbon dioxide, plants give off oxygen vital to man. (You may have heard that plants thrive in human company. They do, but it is not your presence that they enjoy, I suspect, but the carbon dioxide that you exhale.) When the light fades, the synthesizing process gradually stops and the plant has to draw energy by consuming the stored-up supplies of sugars and starches. If the light does not return before the supply runs out, the plant dies. Although all flowering house plants need light to survive, each species has its idiosyncrasies about how much and what kind it needs when. Some, such as geraniums and chrysanthemums, require plenty of strong, straight-from-the-source sunlight. Camellias also like bright light, but not the sun's direct rays; they do better if set a bit away from a bright window. Others prefer their light in even more moderate doses: cyclamens, primroses and African violets, for example, will tolerate the weak sun of northern winters from November through February but need partial shade during the rest of the year. The African violets, however, exemplify the adaptability of plants and will also blossom quite handsomely on a north-facing window sill where they never see the sun. So will wax begonias and patient Lucy.

The strength of light varies of course—as any camera buff with a light meter knows—by latitude, by season, by the weather and by the time of day. These variations, and the preferences of plants in the matter of light, present together one of the challenges that make indoor gardening so fascinating—at least to me.

HOW TO PICK THE SPOT

To cope with the challenge, it is necessary to know, not to guess at, the needs of each plant, and this information is detailed in the encyclopedia *(Chapter 6)*. Where climate and weather are variables, you will not always be able to provide the optimum conditions, such as at least five hours of winter sunlight for gardenias, crossandras and lantanas, which will make them produce abundant flowers. To come closest to this ideal, put your gardenias, crossandras and lantanas in the brightest, south-facing window in your house, and if the room is painted white—which reflects light—so much the better. Make sure that the window you choose *is* the brightest—a tree or an overhanging roof may make one window less desirable than another that seems less bright but is unobstructed. (The alternatives, chopping down the tree or removing the roof overhang, are not necessarily recommended.) A light meter, if you have one, will help you determine which windows offer your plants the lighting that is actually the brightest.

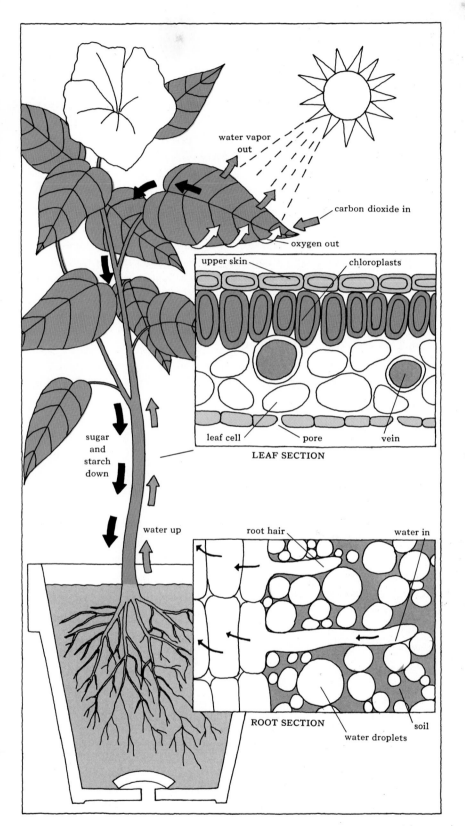

water vapor out

carbon dioxide in

oxygen out

upper skin   chloroplasts

leaf cell   pore   vein

LEAF SECTION

sugar and starch down

water up

root hair   water in

ROOT SECTION

water droplets   soil

MAKING FOOD FROM AIR, WATER AND SUNLIGHT

Photosynthesis, the process by which plants convert light into food, is especially crucial to house plants, because they rarely have access to as much light energy as outdoor plants do. The process starts as tiny root hairs draw moisture from the soil and pass it on to the root cells, as indicated in the lower inset, which shows the magnified cross section of a typical root. From the roots the water moves through an intricate system of tiny pipelines up the stem and into the leaves. At the same time carbon dioxide is absorbed from the air through the pores in the undersides of the leaves, as shown in the upper inset, an enlarged cross section of a leaf. Light striking the leaf activates the light-sensitive green pigment, chlorophyll, which is contained in cells called chloroplasts just beneath the leaf's translucent skin. The chlorophyll splits the water molecules into hydrogen and oxygen; the carbon dioxide and hydrogen engage in reactions to form sugar and starch. This food is conducted through the veins and eventually to the other parts of the plant. Cells in the leaves and the rest of the plant convert the food into energy and new growth. Oxygen, a waste product of the process, and excess water vapor not used by the plant are given off into the atmosphere by the leaves.

*Charles Dickens, whose love for flowers
and gardens is apparent in his novels,
always had a small cup of fresh blooms
on his desk when he wrote, and in 1869,
the year before he died, he realized
a long-held ambition: to have his own
conservatory where he could raise
living plants. Built as an addition to his
country retreat in Kent, largely with the
proceeds from reading his works on a
lecture tour of America, this "brilliant
but expensive" glass and iron structure,
as Dickens described it, opened onto
both the drawing room and the dining
room. Dickens loved to linger there
after dinner, admiring his blue lobelias
and scarlet geraniums, which he
sometimes lighted at night with Chinese
lanterns strung below the glass roof.*

But suppose all your windows are bright and the plants you choose are lady's-slipper orchids and African violets, which do not need much sun. Place the plants far enough back from the window to keep them out of the direct rays of the sun, or draw a sheer curtain across the window. Dark walls may help in a situation like this, for the darker the paint, the less light it reflects. But conditions differ so much in each house that in the end you will have to do the best you can for each plant, and then rely on pragmatism. If a plant does well, leave it where it is. If it does not do well, try another place, keeping in mind the plant's needs. You can determine whether or not the plant is doing well by looking at the distance between leaves on new stems and comparing it with the distance between leaves on older parts of the plant that grew in a greenhouse before you purchased it. If the distance has increased, the plant is—in effect, though not in truly scientific terms—stretching itself to seek more light. The same test applies to plants that you have raised yourself from infancy: if there seems to be too much stalk and not enough leaf, the light is insufficient. Move the plant closer to the window glass (but, during the winter, do not let it touch the pane, which will chill it at night), or put it in a sunnier spot. If it is getting too much light, drooping leaves will warn you. Move it to a shadier place, or draw the curtain across the window for part of the day.

Despite all the variables and the dangers of generalization in indoor gardening, one rule holds true for almost all plants: the more light that a plant can be given without causing damage to its foliage and without depriving it of its nightly rest in the dark—which is just as vital to plants as it is to human beings—the more likely it is to produce a rewarding abundance of flowers.

USING ARTIFICIAL LIGHT

Thus far, we have been talking in terms of natural light, which in northern parts of the country, in winter, often falls short of the optimum. Artificial light offers a solution: it improves the health of plants and increases the production of flowers so markedly that it has become one of the most useful tools of the indoor gardener. I discovered this myself during World War II. I was serving on a naval ship in the Pacific late in 1941, and I became all too aware—for the first time—how much I needed contact with the world of flowers and forests and the earth itself. I desperately desired a green, living plant to counter the gray of the ship and the ocean's mists. But I was not the captain with a sunny cabin; I was a seaman living below the water line.

I did, however, have an electric light over my desk in the storeroom where I both worked and slept. And on my last shore leave at Pearl Harbor before the ship sailed on a long voyage, Dr. Harold St. John, who was then head of the Botany Department at the University of Hawaii, had given me a "ti log," a small piece of stem of *Cordyline terminalis,* which is a foliage plant. I set it in a shallow dish of water under my lone light bulb, and within weeks I had a beautiful, healthy plant with long, graceful, cornlike leaves. No white-gloved officer on Saturday morning inspection ever ordered it banished as not covered by Navy Regulations, and when I went to Midshipmen's School almost 18 months later it was still thriving. I left the plant behind to brighten the below-decks life of my successor in the storeroom.

My shipboard light bulb was of the old-fashioned incandescent variety, not sufficiently bright to bring a flowering plant into bloom without daylight; but artificial lighting for plants has developed tremendously since those days. There are fluorescent lamps that emphasize certain parts of the spectrum, fostering plant growth and giving off light with much more beneficial rays than did the yellow glow in my cubbyhole. Fluorescent lamps that emit both blue and red rays promote photosynthesis, encouraging the development of foliage and promoting the production of flowers. A similar effect can be achieved by combining ordinary cool-white tubes that are strong in blue rays with warm-white tubes that are strong in red.

Artificial light can also provide supplemental illumination for plants that already get some, but not enough, sunshine. An ac-

GROWING PLANTS UNDER ARTIFICIAL LIGHT

African violets, gloxinias and other low-growing plants will bloom healthily even in a dark cellar if kept under fluorescent lights of a type made especially for growing plants. The standard unit shown here, two 48-inch tubes set in a reflector, is adequate for two rows of pots. Cords led through ceiling-mounted pulleys and fastened to the wall by means of cleats allow the unit to be adjusted to the proper height for the plants.

quaintance of mine has a deep window sill that looks east and is darkened by an overhanging roof, so the plants that crowd it receive considerably less than the natural light they need. But they flourish because, amidst them, an heirloom kerosene lamp that has been electrified glows every night from dusk to 9 or 10 p.m. The lamp's bulb is a 100-watter of the incandescent variety, and the sill and nearby walls are painted white. My acquaintance's plants might produce even more blossoms if he turned on the light before breakfast, for it is a good rule of thumb that supplemental lighting proves most effective when, added to daylight, it provides a total of 12 to 16 hours of light a day, depending on the plant's needs.

There is a successful commercial grower of carnations who used that rule most profitably. He supplemented the natural light in his greenhouses with fluorescent lighting—to provide 15 hours a day of illumination—and tripled his output of blossoms. A supermarket operator in Alaska saves the high cost of importing tomatoes by growing his own in a greenhouse under fluorescent lights that lengthen the short subarctic winter days.

But it is the second use of artificial lighting—to replace sunshine completely—that many gardeners find most challenging and rewarding. Using it 14 to 16 hours a day, they grow such plants as African violets, gloxinias and wax begonias even in closets—or like the Plymouth, New Hampshire, nurse, in cellars.

LIGHTED PLANTERS   Most beginners experimenting with artificial lighting find it more practicable to buy ready-made planters, complete with lamps and almost everything else except plants. They come in a variety of models: one resembles a white-enameled three-tiered tea cart with a canopy; another looks like a child's free-standing garden swing, a third like a set of bookshelves, a fourth like a desk lamp and still another like a miniature greenhouse. The price range is tremendous: a simple lamp might cost less than $20, the elaborate tea-cart type about $50, a glass-enclosed completely controlled environment more than $1,000. For simple models, an automatic-timer light switch will cost you only a few dollars more and will pay for itself many times over in convenience by turning the lights on and off without your having to remember this chore.

In choosing a planter, you will find that most are of reliable quality, and that the decisive factors must be the use to which you will put your planter and the amount you wish to spend. The three-tier cart, for example, is showy and permits you to grow on its different levels plants with widely varying light preferences, since each level has its individual fluorescent tubes that can be of differing wattage. But a planter of the three-tier or bookshelf variety will accommodate tall plants only on the top shelf; the space between tiers will limit the lower levels to shorter plants such as African violets and gloxinias. The free-standing child's-swing type is adjustable; the canopy and its lighting tubes can be raised or lowered, depending on the size of the plants below.

Some gardeners-by-artificial-light prefer to build their own equipment and purchase only the fluorescent tubes and perhaps the canopy fixture. If you follow that course, be sure to make the height of the canopy adjustable; one way is to suspend it from the ceiling on chains that can be shortened or lengthened at will as the growth of the plants requires.

But whether you buy the ready-made kind or build your own, the general rules for their use are the same: use at least two tubes, allow 15 to 20 watts for each square foot of foliage, and keep the tubes 6 to 12 inches from the tops of your plants. And remember that almost all flowering plants need their rest, so they should be exposed to light for no more than 12 to 16 hours. Otherwise they will die of fatigue or never blossom. The importance of uninterrupted darkness, as well as of light, becomes evident when an indoor gardener keeps a poinsettia and tries to make it blossom the second year. Under natural conditions, the plant would have complete darkness from sundown until dawn. Indoors, even the ordinary house lights, turned on in the plant's vicinity after dark, will inhibit the plant from producing flowers. I once saw a single-stem poinsettia at the U.S. Department of Agriculture greenhouses in Beltsville, Maryland, that has been grown for several seasons with artificially induced very long days and very short nights. It was at least 12 feet tall, and almost touched the greenhouse roof, but it had yet to sprout a single bud.

Artificial lighting is not yet the perfect substitute for sunlight, for its rays lack the intensity and some of the life-giving qualities of the sun's. Nevertheless, most plants will at least survive under electric light, and some will do much better than others. The types of plants that thrive best, producing rich foliage and an abundance of flowers, are those that in nature prefer subdued light—a category that includes African violets, gloxinias and wax begonias.

While the proper amount of light is indispensable to a healthy plant, equally critical is the amount of water it receives. Years ago when I was a retail florist, I found that every customer waiting for me to finish wrapping his purchase asked the same question, "How often should I water it?" It was easy enough to specify the needs of any given plant, but when the question is applied to house plants in general, the reply has to be, "It all depends."

Before I explain, I want to warn you that, in my opinion, over-watering is the No. 1 killer of house plants, and inexperienced

FRUITFUL HOUSE PLANTS

Some house plants are raised as much for their edible fruit as for their blooms: Several varieties of capsicum bear colorful peppers; the plums of carissas can be eaten right off the bush and a species of kumquat, Fortunella margarita, can be made into a delicious preserve. Perhaps the most spectacular fruiting house plant, however, is the ponderosa lemon (Citrus limonia ponderosa, page 112), sometimes called the "American wonder lemon." In addition to abundant, fragrant blooms, it bears lemons the size of grapefruits. One Boston housewife, who has had a ponderosa lemon tree growing next to her dining room window for years, bakes several lemon pies every time one of the oversize fruits ripens.

WHEN TO WATER

gardeners are its well-meaning but dangerous accomplices. One of my daughters, for example, refuses to allow a certain big-hearted member of our household to enter her room. "She'll kill my plants with kindness," she explains. Some people are so afraid that their plants will die of thirst that they keep their soil saturated. Plants cannot grow in waterlogged soil because the overabundant water drives out air, which is vital to root growth and to the activity of beneficial soil organisms. Roots rot. The soil becomes foul smelling. When this happens to a house plant, it is usually beyond salvation. Throw the victim away, start over with a healthy young plant—and do not repeat the crime.

Watering correctly is so important that there is a saying among professional greenhouse horticulturists that "the profit depends on the man with the hose," who can tell at a glance whether or not to shower a given plant.

So—how often to water? The generally accepted advice that a plant should be allowed to become moderately dry between thorough waterings is sound, to a point, but not entirely accurate. There are some exceptions, which I have noted in the encyclopedia (*Chapter 6*). And there is another important exception to the rule, which is to spare the water in the case of a dormant, or "resting," plant. Just as they rest at night, many plants also rest between their flow-

THREE WAYS TO WATER HOUSE PLANTS

Watering from the bottom, by filling the saucer under the pot, allows the soil to draw up through the drainage hole as much moisture as it can absorb. To avoid root rot, empty the saucer half an hour after watering.

Top watering is best done with a long-spouted can, which allows you to reach in without wetting the leaves or dripping water on the floor. Occasional top watering flushes away accumulated fertilizer salts.

To give a very dry plant a thorough soaking, immerse the pot in a bucket or sink filled with water to a level that barely covers the top of the pot. Remove the plant from the water when bubbles stop rising, and drain.

ering periods. An otherwise healthy plant that is getting enough light and warmth and still shows no new growth is probably dormant; gloxinias, for example, actually shrivel up like old crones during this period. A dormant plant needs less frequent watering than one that is blossoming. Those that become completely dormant and lose all their top growth should not be watered at all until they start to grow again.

The best watering time of day for all plants is in the morning, so they can utilize the nourishment during the hours of daylight. Any excess water should be removed from their saucers or trays within a half hour or so to prevent waterlogging of the soil.

How to water is nearly as important as *when*. The first rule is: do not use cold water, which will set back many plants severely—especially in winter. African violets are so sensitive to cold water, in fact, that if water below room temperature is spilled on their leaves, the leaves will develop ugly yellow blotches. This characteristic has given rise to the widespread belief that African violets cannot stand water on their foliage. Not so. It is just water of the wrong temperature that they detest: in commercial greenhouses, African violets get water as warm as the greenhouses themselves. For my house plants I use water at a temperature of about 90°F. You don't

HOW TO WATER

(continued on page 37)

VACATION CARE OF HOUSE PLANTS

For a few weeks during the summer, most house plants can take care of themselves if placed outside in light shade in a bed of gravel to keep them cool and moist. In dry climates, use peat moss with, or instead of, gravel.

To tide plants over vacations at any time, set them out of direct sun in a tray of moist gravel or perlite, water them and cover with clear plastic. Support the plastic on stakes in the pots; tuck the ends under the tray.

Notables who shared their names with plants

JEAN NICOT

The genus *Nicotiana*, which includes the fragrant flowering tobacco plant as well as leaf tobacco, is named for the scholar and diplomat Jean Nicot, French ambassador to Portugal from 1559 to 1561. While at the court in Lisbon, he was introduced to tobacco, which had been brought back from the New World in 1558. Intrigued with the new plant, he sent seeds to the Queen Mother Catherine de Médicis of France, to whom he owed his position. After his return home, Nicot also raised tobacco himself on his country estate and promoted the fashionable new custom of smoking among the members of the elegant French court, as Sir Walter Raleigh later did in London.

NICOTIANA

BEGONIA

Begonias are named for an amateur botanist who was a patron of the science, the French magistrate and administrator Michel Bégon. Posted to the French Antilles in 1681 to introduce legal reforms after a series of civil disorders there, Bégon brought begonias back with him and introduced them to the botanists of Europe. His large collection of botanical books, illustrated with original paintings, was open to any interested student or amateur.

MICHEL BÉGON

JOEL ROBERTS POINSETT

Joel Poinsett, whose name the familiar Christmas plants bear, served as the first U.S. Minister to Mexico from 1825 to 1829. His indiscreet support of local revolutionaries had previously led to his recall from posts in South America, and his brash enthusiasm for Mexican politics finally resulted in his being asked to leave that country as well. On his return to his South Carolina home, he brought back cuttings of poinsettias and of the similar Mexican fireplant, which grow wild in the Mexican countryside. At first thought to be two species of a new genus, which was named in Poinsett's honor, these plants were later found to be members of the genus *Euphorbia*, so he is remembered only in the poinsettia's common name.

POINSETTIA

VRIESIA

The genus of bright tropical plants known as *Vriesia* is named in honor of a brilliant 19th Century Dutch botanist Willem Hendrik de Vriese. By painstaking experiments he proved that plants, like animals, absorb oxygen and use it in converting food into heat energy. He spent some time in Batavia in the Dutch East Indies and sent a collection of native plants to the British Royal Gardens at Kew.

W. H. DE VRIESE

CARL PETER THUNBERG

Thunbergia, the lovely clock vine, is named for the 18th Century Swedish botanist and explorer Carl Peter Thunberg. A pupil of the famed classifier of plants and animals, Carl Linnaeus, at Uppsala University, and like his teacher a doctor of medicine as well as botany, he joined the Dutch East India Company as a physician so he could study the plant life of Japan, a land closed to all Europeans except the Dutch. He landed in 1775, the first botanist to visit the country in nearly a hundred years and the last one for almost half a century after he left in 1776. During his trip he stopped off in Java, Ceylon and South Africa, exploring and collecting plants. His career was crowned by his appointment as Linnaeus' successor at Uppsala in 1781.

THUNBERGIA

COLUMNEA

The bright-flowered tropical columnea commemorates in Latin the name of Fabio Colonna, the botanical star of a talented and noble Roman family that included statesmen, generals, cardinals, popes (Nicholas IV, Martin V) and a poetess to whom Michelangelo wrote love sonnets. Fabio is noted mainly for compiling in 1592 all the botanical data then known; he also was a member of the exclusive Society of Lynxes, a club of about 30 eminent early scientists, including the astronomer Galileo.

FABIO COLONNA

L. A. DE BOUGAINVILLE

The name of the brilliant-blooming bougainvillea commemorates the French navigator and commander Louis Antoine de Bougainville, who explored much of the world for King Louis XV during a globe-circling voyage in 1766-1769. The man who named the genus was the naturalist on board, Philibert Commerson, who undoubtedly saw the plants when the ship put in along the coast of South America, where they are native. On the Pacific leg of the voyage, Bougainville, Commerson and their crew touched at Samoa and Tahiti, the New Hebrides, the Solomon Islands, the Moluccas and the Tuamotus, charting the unfamiliar waters, studying native populations and making further botanical observations. The largest of the Solomons and two straits also bear Bougainville's name.

BOUGAINVILLEA

BRUNFELSIA

The chameleon plant, whose showy flowers turn color from deep purple to white as they mature, was named brunfelsia by an unknown botanist after Otto Brunfels, a 16th Century botanist—a wry tribute, for Brunfels had himself turned color: a Catholic monk, he became a Protestant early in the Reformation. In 1530 Brunfels published the first German herbal, an illustrated study of Rhineland plants. In it he included some of the earliest botanical renderings of lifelike quality done directly from nature, in hopes of starting his own small reformation in the world of plants.

OTTO BRUNFELS

MALPIGHI

The delicate-flowered, bright-fruited plants of the genus *Malpighia* honor the 17th Century Italian physician Malpighi, who in a day of ruthless and drastic medical practices was known as the "gentle doctor." Best known for his pioneering use of the microscope to study anatomy and physiology, Malpighi also explored the world of plants. In 1662, two years after he discovered the principle of capillary circulation in the lungs, his probing microscope and analytical mind made a valuable contribution to botany: he was the first to prove that a tree's age can be determined by counting the number of rings in a cross section of its trunk.

MALPIGHIA

FUCHSIA

The dainty-blossomed plants of the *Fuchsia* genus were named in honor of the German physician Leonhard Fuchs, author of a handsome 1542 herbal that contained woodcuts of over 500 specimens gathered near Tübingen, where Fuchs taught medicine. The herbal is still used as a reference work by botanists and horticultural historians.

LEONHARD FUCHS

QUEEN CHARLOTTE SOPHIA

Strelitzias, the flamboyant South African plants known as "bird-of-paradise flowers," commemorate the maiden name of a Queen of England whose happiest hours were spent among the flowers of the Royal Gardens at Kew. Charlotte Sophia of Mecklenburg-Strelitz was only 17 when she left her family's tiny duchy to marry George III and dutifully bear him 15 children. In 1771, when she was 27, Sir Joseph Banks, the British naturalist traveling with Captain Cook on his voyage around the world, came across specimens of the bright-flowered bird-of-paradise plants near the Cape of Good Hope and named them after his Queen. On Banks' recommendation Charlotte later sent an official plant collector to seek out other exotic plants for Kew Gardens, soon turning it into one of the most famous collections of horticultural specimens in the world.

STRELITZIA

GAZANIA

The colorful South African genus *Gazania* is named in honor of a Greek-born scholar of the 15th Century, Teodoro Gaza, who translated into Latin the ancient Greek of *Theoretical Botany* and *History of Plants,* two Third Century B.C. works by Aristotle's pupil Theophrastus. These versions of Theophrastus, prepared while Gaza was a refugee in Italy from the Turkish invasion of his homeland, remained the only books on botanical theory for nearly two centuries.

TEODORO GAZA

need a thermometer to test it. Just put your finger in it. If it feels pleasantly tepid, it will do.

Of less importance than the water's temperature, but of concern to some gardeners, is the chemical content of the water. Plants are highly adaptable in this respect, and despite the wide variations in water around the country, excellent house plants grow all over. But if water is highly chlorinated—as your tongue and nose will warn you—it is a good idea to let it stand in a shallow pan for a day so that the chlorine will evaporate before you pour it on your plants. The very qualities that make chlorine a disinfectant make it somewhat injurious to vegetation. Highly saline water also has a deleterious effect—and if by chance you have any doubt about your water's salinity, check with your local water department. Where salinity is a problem, and the air is relatively clean, you would do well to use rain water, collected in a rain barrel set beneath a rainspout. Some of the finest plants I have ever seen drank only rain water—just like the flowers that bloom in meadows and forests. But rain water in many big cities and small but heavily industrialized towns is far from pure; in fact it can be so heavy with the floating filth in the air that it may be harmful to plants. If you live in such a place, let it rain for a few minutes to wash the air clean before you collect the rain water for your plants.

The perfect water for plants is the kind that is low in soluble salts. Water that has passed through certain—but not most—kinds of water-softening devices also is excellent. Most softening units work by substituting sodium for the calcium or magnesium that makes the water hard. If the sodium is not removed, it draws water out of plants and thus proves more harmful to them than the calcium or magnesium of the hard water would be. Some of the more expensive softening devices are equipped with deionizing units that do eliminate the sodium and other harmful salts, and the water that they produce is almost the equivalent of distilled water and is fine for plants. But if you have a water softener without the deionizer, your plants should get rain water or untreated hard water, perhaps from an outside tap that serves the garden hose.

Now, to the actual watering of your plants: there are three common methods—watering from the top of the pot, placing water in the saucer or tray in which the pot stands, and immersing the whole pot. It is generally poor advice to suggest that any plant should always be watered the same way. A combination of methods is preferable, for reasons that calceolarias and cyclamens, for example, demonstrate. If you water them from the top when there is not enough sunshine to dry them, the crowns of the plants—which have dense foliage close to the top of the pot—become wet and it is not uncommon for decay to set in close to the surface of the soil.

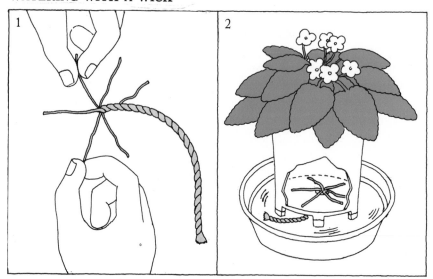

Plants such as African violets, which thrive with constant moisture, can be watered by a glass-fiber wick, which draws water up into the soil. Prepare the wick by unraveling one end so it will cover the bottom of the pot.

Before potting the plant, insert the wick through the drainage hole of a raised wick-watering pot and spread the unraveled ends flat on the inside. The water in the saucer should cover the wick but not touch the pot.

But if they—or other plants—obtain all their moisture by soaking up water from saucers, fertilizer salts in the soil will rise to the top, accumulating on the soil's surface and on the top edges of the pots, where they will burn the nearby growth. This occurs commonly in African violets, with injury to leaf stems. Although I usually water my African violets by the saucer method, I occasionally give them copious top-of-the-pot watering to leach away the accretions of fertilizer salts on the surface. But I do so only when the air is dry and the weather bright, so that the plants' crowns will not stay wet for too long. This same approach of alternating watering methods works well with almost all of my house plants.

The third method, immersion of the pot in a pail of tepid water, is time-consuming and laborious, but worth using once in a while because most plants benefit from a thorough soaking occasionally. When you use this method, make sure that the water in the pail rises above the soil level in the pot. Immediately the soil will begin to emit bubbles that gurgle noisily. When the bubbling stops, take the plant out of the pail and let it drain for 20 minutes before putting it back on its saucer on the window sill. Some gardeners use this dip method exclusively. But I still prefer to water my plants from the top with a long-spouted nondrip watering can. Such a watering can does not have to be followed around with a mop. (A can like that makes a fine house gift for a friend who wants to become an indoor gardener.)

Whatever method you are using at the moment, do the job thoroughly. Do not apply only a little water at a time, because much of the soil deep in the pot is apt to remain dry—and so will some of the roots. But remember that a plant's need for water varies not only with its life cycle—as in the waning gloxinia I mentioned—but with external conditions: on sunny days plants need more water than they do on cloudy days and even on a curtained window sill they respond to the weather. Plants that have just been moved to larger pots need less moisture than they will when they have settled down in their new homes and their roots have filled the balls of soil.

Because the demand for water varies so much, some gardeners use self-watering devices that reduce the frequency of watering and keep the soil uniformly moist for long periods. One simple method, called wick watering, involves installation of a wick, preferably of fiberglass, during potting or repotting. The usual drainage material (pebbles or shards from a broken flower pot) is omitted from the bottom of the pot. The wick is spread out on the pot's bottom (*drawings, opposite*) and one end is drawn through the drainage hole and allowed to rest in a tray, saucer or other container of water below the pot. (The pot does not sit in the water, but is raised on legs or a little platform.) The wick, by capillary action, draws water from the container up into the pot. Some plants that need to be kept constantly moist—azaleas, for example—benefit from wick watering. But the water requirements of most plants vary so much that the wick may provide an excess of water on dull, cloudy days, and too little on bright, sunny ones, and even experts have had difficulty determining just what size wick will serve what plant best. If you are in an experimental mood, however, you may want to try. There are also several commercial devices that provide a steady supply of moisture, including at least one that senses how dry the soil is and waters accordingly.

Moisture in the air is quite as important to plants as moisture in their soil. Except for kitchens and bathrooms, most houses in winter frequently are as dry as deserts, and in such arid air house plants never attain the full beauty for which they have the potential. Indeed, many of them get brown around the edges of the leaves; if dry air draws off enough moisture the leaves will simply shrivel away. So to increase the humidity—which human beings need as much as plants do—I keep many of my potted plants sitting in large trays. These should be about 2 inches deep and can be made of plastic or any painted or nonrusting metal; a tinsmith will make

HOW TO INCREASE HUMIDITY

them for you if you cannot find them in the right size or shape. Cover the bottoms with at least an inch of perlite, sand, pebbles or pea-sized granules of charcoal, and add water, keeping the water level below the surface of the material selected. The material on which the pots rest serves as a reservoir of moisture and will raise the humidity in the immediate vicinity, depending on the hour and the room temperature, by 100 to 500 per cent. If you doubt my word, measure the humidity around your plants with a hygrometer—the cheaper models cost only a few dollars —and find out for yourself.

Plants themselves contribute generously to raising the humidity level. Every plant exhales moisture constantly through its leaves. When a number of plants grow together in one part of a room, they constitute an informal mutual-aid society: the moisture that each gives off serves to raise the humidity and benefits them all. (Come to think of it, I have never seen a lonely plant—the only one in the room or house—that was doing more than barely surviving.) Consider how much water you provide your plants in a week. After they have used it, the moisture they give off hangs suspended in the air. You can add to it by misting your plants with a bottle-type atomizer that emits a fine vapor. Use water of at least room temperature and spray the plants' leaves lightly—not so

MISTING PLANTS WITH AN ATOMIZER

In a heated house in winter, and in dry weather year round, plants will benefit from daily sprays of mist provided by an atomizer. The type used by florists, shown above, produces a volume of fine spray when the lever handle is squeezed (a simple squeeze-plastic atomizer or an old spray-cleaner container of the plunger type will also do the job). Fill it with lukewarm water and keep the nozzle 18 inches from the plants.

CONTROLLING HUMIDITY

To provide constant humidity around indoor plants, group several together on 1 or 2 inches of gravel or perlite in a tray of plastic or nonrusting metal. Keep water in the tray to a level that is below the bottom of the pots; evaporation, along with the moisture transpiring through the plants' leaves, should keep the relative humidity around the plants at the desired levels— about 50 per cent for African violets and other gesneriads, 60 per cent or more for orchids. To make exact measurements, use a hygrometer; in the type shown, a moisture-sensitive coil turns a pointer on a dial marked in per cent relative humidity.

much that moisture will form beads on the foliage. The aim is not to wet the plants, but to increase the humidity of the air around them. Try it and see how much better your plants will grow.

THE PROPER TEMPERATURES

Air temperature, especially at night, is as important to house plants as the temperature of the water you pour in their pots or spray on their leaves. Most people, I suspect, keep their thermostats set in winter at from 68° to 72°F., day and night. That is much too warm for potted tulips, for example, but fine for African violets. But no matter how much people may cherish their plants, they quite rightly cherish their own comfort more. And even if they were willing to forgo it for the sake of their plants, they could hardly reconcile the preferences of the African violets with those of the tulips. But thermostat or no thermostat, the thermometer in the living room does not really reflect the temperatures of different parts of the house. The exposure, the presence or absence of storm windows, and the position of heating ducts and radiators cause surprising variations. On an enclosed but unheated sun porch or in a spare bedroom where the radiator is kept off, you will be able to grow many plants that cannot stand the heat of the kitchen. In my house, the temperature on a wide window ledge in a guest bedroom upstairs drops to 46° on winter nights with the heat turned low—in the absence of a guest, I had better add. The ledge is bright with cyclamens, primroses, azaleas and winter-flowering bulbs. (Once, when I complimented a hostess on her cyclamen, she replied, "It lives in the bedroom and comes downstairs only for company.")

All plants, indoors or out, grow better if they have cooler temperatures at night than by day, and before central heating, indoor

THE HIGH-LOW THERMOMETER

A maximum-minimum thermometer, which many indoor gardeners find to be an invaluable aid, records not only the temperature of the moment but the high for the day (right side) and the nighttime low (left side). As the temperature changes, a clear liquid in the ball and tube at the left expands or contracts, moving the mercury, visible as a dark column in the U-shaped tube. The mercury, in turn, pushes ahead of it two small metal bars, which stick inside the tube until dislodged once more by the mercury. The thermometer is reset by means of a small magnet, which is used to draw the metal bars back to the level of the mercury.

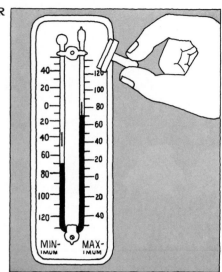

temperatures fell at night as they do outside. Now, too often, we set the thermostat dial and forget it. Many plants will adapt to average house temperatures, but others will not: fuchsias, poinsettias, calceolarias and many other plants will not set flower buds, and camellias will drop theirs if night temperatures are above 65°; they prefer rooms much cooler than that. On the other hand, African violets and gloxinias and their relatives will come close to perishing if night temperatures fall to 50° or 55°. So to some extent it depends on which plants you prefer.

A tale to the point was recounted to me recently by a friend. He owns a large garden center and maintains a "hot line" for gardeners with questions. He got a phone call from a man who said that his philodendron did not look quite right—in fact, he insisted, it was turning blue. The plant was in a big tub, and repotting it would have been difficult, so my friend advised the inquirer to dig out some of the old soil and replace it with rich, fresh potting soil. About five minutes later the man called back. He could not dig out the old soil because it was frozen. He had neglected to mention in his first call that the plant was located in his bedroom—and that he slept with the window wide open. It was midwinter and the thermometer had hovered around zero for a week.

THE USEFUL THERMOMETER

In the encyclopedia, I specify the ideal night temperatures, as well as the recommended day temperatures, for each plant. When you go looking for these ideal temperatures—and there are many microclimates in our houses—you will find the maximum-minimum thermometer *(drawing, top)* helpful. As a matter of fact, I consider it one of the greatest boons to indoor gardening. This device is not always easy to come by; you may have to ask your hardware dealer to order one for you, but it will prove well worth the trouble and the price. A maximum-minimum thermometer differs from ordinary thermometers in that its column of mercury is U-shaped rather than vertical and records the day's highest temperature on one side of the U and the lowest on the other. (Tiny slivers of metal remain in place at the high and low temperature marks until the thermometer is reset with a magnet that comes with the device.) It was with a thermometer of this sort that I discovered the chilly window ledge in the guest bedroom.

One temperature problem often encountered by apartment dwellers—and lots of other people—who would like to grow house plants but complain that they cannot, is presented by radiators. The heat and the dryness around radiators make their immediate vicinity inhospitable to most vegetation. But if the radiator is beneath a window, or anywhere that has sufficient light for plants, its presence need not defeat you. The solution is to deflect the heat. Install a shelf, using a board at least 6 inches wider than the radiator, about 6 inches above it. Cover the top of the shelf with a layer of asbestos insulating board (available at building supply centers) or any other nonconductor of heat. Put a tray on top of this, with the usual inch-thick layer of pebbles, perlite or sand on the bottom. Use your maximum-minimum thermometer to determine the range of temperatures on the shelf, day and night, and then find suitable plants for the tray in the encyclopedia. But be sure to keep water in the pan always, and except when watering your plants, never let the water level rise to the bottom of the pots.

One final word about environment. Plants need some circulation of air; even in wintertime, greenhouse operators keep their ventilators ajar. Plants do not, however, like drafts—that is, cold air blowing on them suddenly from an open window or door nearby. When you want to freshen a room, open a window at the top, and choose one that is farthest from your plants, even the hardiest ones. But do not worry that plants such as cyclamens and primroses on a sill of a closed window will suffer from cold at night, for they can tolerate 40° temperatures without damage, so long as their foliage does not touch the cold glass. Tropical plants such as African violets and gloxinias, however, should not be chilled. Move them away from the cold at night.

Now you know (I hope) how to create the proper environment for growing green flowering things. This is not so complicated as it may sound. All it takes, really, is a degree of dedication, a reasonable amount of intelligence, a watering can—and a careful eye on temperature and light.

PLANTS AND COLD DRAFTS

Soils, pots and potting 3

Of all the near miracles of gardening that we take for granted, one of the most impressive is the ability of plants to thrive in containers —a variety of pots, boxes, trays, wooden tubs, tin cans, virtually anything that will hold soil. It seems so unnatural. Out of doors, plants can pick and choose their preferred growing conditions —coniferous trees the sandy, acid earth of a hillside, flowering annuals a sunny meadow rich with manure, saw grass a swamp. But indoors we toss a few cupfuls of soil into a container, embed a plant's roots in it, and say "Now grow." The marvel is that the plant usually does grow. And if it does not flourish, it will at least survive, for plants possess a determination to live that enables them to make the best of even the poorest soil—and in the case of so-called air plants, no soil at all.

But you want your plants to do more than survive. You want them to thrive, and whether they thrive depends on the kinds of soil and containers they live in. Although some plants have unique requirements, most will do well in any container in which water does not collect and remain unused to drown the plants or rot their roots. But they will need better than average soil if they are to bear husky foliage and masses of bright flowers. Your garden soil, no matter how rich it looks, is not well suited to potted plants. For one thing, it may contain insect eggs, weed seeds or disease spores; more important, it lacks sufficient organic matter to make it porous enough for proper drainage in the confines of a pot under frequent watering. The lack of porosity also blocks air, which the roots of plants need just as much as they do moisture. The soil is soon compacted into a hard, impenetrable mass.

So when growing house plants, your first concern should be to make sure that you have the right kind of growing medium for each kind of plant. Generally speaking, orchids raised as house plants are air loving and require a special medium, a porous fibrous mixture, and many bromeliads and gesneriads flourish in a mixture including twice as much peat moss or leaf mold as you would give

The ancient Greeks used potted plants as tokens of yearly rebirth. In this detail from a Fifth Century B.C. vase, Eros, god of love, hands seedlings to a girl celebrating rites for Adonis, symbol of plant fertility.

most house plants, approximating the natural environment in which they grew wild. But the majority of house plants will do well in a more or less standard mixture. You can make such a mixture by pasteurizing ordinary garden soil in the kitchen oven (heating it for half an hour at a temperature of 180°) to get rid of weeds, insects and diseases, and then mixing it with various supplements. But most indoor gardeners buy prepackaged potting soil, available at garden centers, florists' shops and many supermarkets. Packaged potting soil has been pasteurized and packed with enough moisture to make handling and potting easy. It comes in airtight plastic bags that retain moisture; any leftover soil will not dry out if the bag is resealed. Many potting soils also contain soil-loosening agents such as peat moss, and enough nutrients to start plants off well.

IMPROVING POTTING SOIL   If I have any complaint about packaged potting soils, it is only that they have been screened too finely; perhaps the packers do that to forestall complaints from misguided gardeners about twigs, pebbles or clumps of peat moss in the product. The truth is that plants, except for very tiny seedlings, benefit from a little roughage in their soil. So although most packaged soils can be used as sold, I prefer to add coarse organic matter, which opens up the soil structure, and also some gritty material, which facilitates drainage. The most wide-

HOW MUCH SOIL TO PUT IN A POT

If the soil level in a pot is too high (left), water will spill over the side of the pot and the plant will not get enough moisture when you water it. A low level (center) presents an almost irresistible temptation to *fill up the empty space, and too much water may cause the plant's roots to rot. The correct level (right), which makes adequate watering easy to gauge, is about ½ inch from the top (1 inch in pots 6 inches or larger).*

ly available organic material is peat moss, the partially decayed fibers of bog mosses. (The best kind of peat moss for potting mixtures is sphagnum peat moss; this material should not be confused with sphagnum moss, the dried but undecayed form of the moss used for packing plants, holding moisture in hanging baskets and rooting cuttings.) Another good organic material is leaf mold, which consists of decayed, compacted leaves. Whichever you use, make sure it is coarse. The best kind of peat moss is the poultry grade, so called because it used to be spread on the floors of chicken coops to absorb droppings. Unlike the finer garden variety of peat moss, it comes in chunks ¼ to ½ inch in diameter, and this rough texture makes an ideal addition to the packaged potting soil.

For gritty material, many professional growers use the mineral called perlite, an expanded volcanic glass that is light in weight and spongy; it not only loosens the soil so that air can enter but absorbs and stores moisture. I happen to dislike its color—white —which seems out of place in a pot of soil, but the plants do not seem to mind in the slightest. Cheaper than perlite is coarse, or "sharp," sand, the kind that builders use; it can be bought at most building supply centers and local lumberyards. (Ocean sand will not do; its salt content is harmful to plants and the grains are too fine to provide good drainage.)

To prepare a potting mixture that contains the essentials for most house plants, start with a bag of packaged soil, a similar quantity (by volume) of coarse peat moss or leaf mold, a like amount of perlite or coarse sand, a trowel or small shovel and a tightly woven bushel basket or a large pail.

Using the trowel or shovel, place some of the soil in the basket or pail, then add equal quantities of the peat moss or leaf mold and the perlite or sand, and mix them together thoroughly. Repeat the procedure several times until you have enough for the job at hand. Then add ground limestone, at the rate of 3 to 5 ounces per bushel, and mix thoroughly again. The limestone will counter the mixture's acidity, giving it a suitable pH of about 5.5 to 7.0, which approaches the neutral middle of the scale between extreme acidity (pH 0) and extreme alkalinity (pH 14). If the mixture is intended for acid-loving plants such as azaleas or gardenias, use 2 parts peat moss to 1 part potting soil and 1 part perlite or sand to provide the acidity these plants need, and do not add limestone.

With properly mixed soil, almost any type of container can be adapted to any kind of plant. The most common containers, of course, are pots—but pots come not only in many sizes but in different materials and in several different shapes that are designed for different uses.

LILIES FOR EASTER

The great trumpet blossoms of the pure white, sweet-scented Easter lily seem as much a part of Easter as bunnies and colored eggs. Yet Lilium longiflorum is a comparative newcomer to the Christian world. The Madonna lily of Europe, Lilium candidum, was long the Easter flower but it has one disadvantage: it is difficult to be sure of bringing it to blossom in time for the holiday. About a hundred years ago, a missionary returning from the Orient stopped off in Bermuda and presented a friend there with some early flowering wild lily bulbs he had gathered. They thrived in the island's mild climate. Soon their similarity to the Madonna lily—and their more convenient blossoming season—attracted U.S. florists. They promptly adopted the "Bermuda" lily, and the importation of longiflorum bulbs, from both Bermuda and the Orient, became big business.

SELECTING THE POTS

DISPLAYING PLANTS IN DECORATIVE CONTAINERS

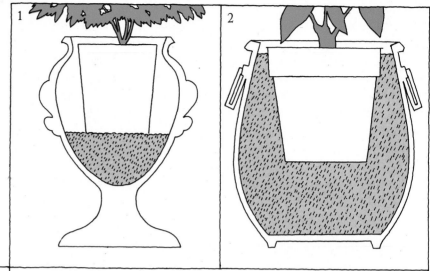

1. *Plants in clay or plastic pots can be set inside many kinds of ornamental containers to display them to advantage. A formal urn suits well-pruned, symmetrical plants such as hydrangeas. To reduce weight, use a plastic pot set in a bed of perlite, which will keep it above drainage water.*

2. *A heavy brass tub on the floor makes a suitable base for a tall, substantial plant such as a hibiscus. The plant is potted solidly in a heavy clay pot that has been surrounded by perlite.*

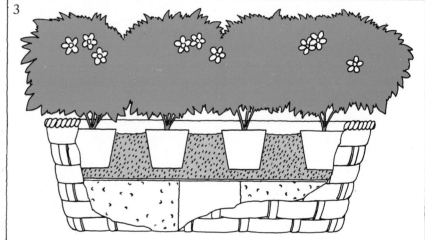

3. *A shallow round basket of woven wood can be filled with several small pots of profusely blooming plants such as cinerarias, giving a room a focal point and a massive splash of color. To provide an attractive, unifying background for the plants as you look down at them, place the pots in a metal liner made for you by a tinsmith and filled with gravel or perlite up to the pots' rims; if the basket is too high for the plants, prop the liner up on blocks. Sprinkling the gravel occasionally will provide a reservoir of moisture to raise the humidity around the plants.*

4. *A tall wicker basket can be used for displaying large, bushy plants such as gardenias. Push a deep metal liner into the top of the basket; a cake or biscuit tin may fit, or you can have a tinsmith make one for you. Set the potted plant into the tin, or use the tin itself as a pot, but put a 2-inch layer of shards or coarse gravel on the bottom for drainage.*

5. *A pewter or silver pitcher holding a delicate plant such as a lantana makes a charming table centerpiece. If necessary, elevate the potted plant on perlite.*

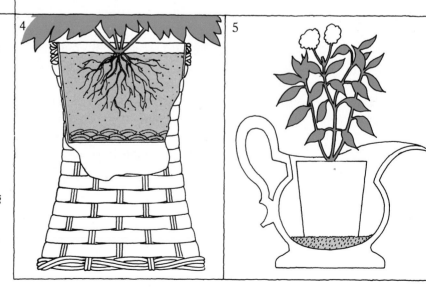

Whatever its use, a pot's size is described by its top diameter. The smallest pot in common use is 2 inches across and the largest 12 inches, although some can be found in larger sizes. In shape, regular flowerpots are as tall as they are broad across the top, and are used for most plants from African violets and begonias to geraniums and primroses. Three-quarter pots, often called azalea pots, are three fourths as tall as their diameter and are used for azaleas and other large plants, to provide stability and to suit their bushy proportions. Pans, which are half as high as they are wide, are used for bulbs because bulbs are planted close to the soil's surface and have a short growing season; they do not need the depth of soil required by other plants.

Most pots are made of clay or plastic, and both have advantages and disadvantages. Clay pots are heavy and thus do not tip over easily. More important, they are porous, so that moisture moves through their walls; this transpiration lessens the danger that waterlogging may rot plant roots, and it adds humidity to the air, which helps most plants. On the other hand, the moisture a clay pot loses through its sides—about as much as its plant uses—is so great that plants in clay pots must be watered more frequently than those in plastic and other nonporous containers. Moreover, with the transpired moisture go dissolved nutrients from the soil; these accumulate on the pots' outside walls, sometimes leading to an unsightly encrustation of fertilizer salts, but more often simply providing a comfortable moist place for unsightly green algae to develop. (The saying that successful gardeners are those with green thumbs may have originated with the handling of algae-covered clay pots.) Some manufacturers prevent transpiration—and algae —by coating the outsides of their pots with the moisture-resisting substance silicone, and some house-plant enthusiasts achieve the same result by painting their pots a decorative color. Most just scrub them clean. Though relatively durable, clay pots do occasionally break, but even the shards can be useful in achieving proper drainage at the bottoms of other pots.

Plastic pots come in most of the sizes that clay pots do, and in most of the shapes; they also come in square and rectangular versions and in various colors. They are light, and thus both easier to carry and more likely to tip over. Because their walls do not permit passage of moisture, they do not collect algae or fertilizer salts on the outside. But the danger of drowning the plant with waterlogging increases; for this reason many plastic pots have four drainage holes in the bottom instead of one. Nevertheless, it is important that plants in plastic pots have well-aerated soil and be watered with great restraint. The same applies to plants in containers of such materials as glazed earthenware, glass and various metals,

THE ORCHID MONKEYS

Part of the almost mystical attraction of the tropical epiphytic, or air-growing, orchids—aside from the rarity of many species—is due to the fact that they make their homes in the tops of giant jungle trees, where they are all but impossible to reach. Orchid hunters solved the problem in Malaysia, where trained berok monkeys have long been employed to collect coconuts, by retraining the monkeys to climb the tall trees and bring the orchids down. The champion, a monkey named Merah, set a record in 1936, when he collected specimens from more than 300 trees.

A DIPSTICK WATER GAUGE

A simple dipstick device, like those used to check the oil level in automobile engines, can help you prevent overwatering a plant set in a decorative container that lacks drainage holes. The dipstick—a thin wooden plant stake or a length of ¼-inch wooden doweling—is contained in a length of thin plastic or aluminum tubing set upright at the side of the pot before the plant is potted; it should reach to the bottom of a layer of coarse gravel 1 to 2 inches deep in smaller pots, 2 to 3 inches deep in larger ones. From time to time insert the dipstick in the tube; do not water the plant unless the stick comes out bone dry.

some of which are handsomer than clay or plastic but otherwise not particularly advantageous.

In choosing pots of any material, select the smallest size that will accommodate your plant without immediately overcrowding the roots, which should extend to within about a half inch of the pot walls, all around (in the case of large plants in large pots, no closer than an inch). Nonporous pots are ready to use as they come from the store. But before using clay pots I recommend that you try a trick that many professional gardeners use—soaking them overnight. If you leave the pots unsoaked, the dry walls will absorb moisture from the potting soil, making it dry out too quickly. It is also a good idea to soak old clay pots every time you reuse them, not only to get them moist but to loosen dirt and old bits of roots so that they can be scrubbed clean easily with a stiff brush or a kitchen scouring pad. After soaking a pot, whether it is an old or a new one, allow it to dry just enough so that soil will not cling to the inside of the pot; then it is ready for use.

GETTING GOOD DRAINAGE   Any pot needs to be filled with more than dirt. First comes material to promote drainage. If the pot is larger than 4 inches, place a shard—a piece of shattered clay pot—over the drainage hole or holes, convex side up, to allow water to drain out while keeping the pot's contents in. In pots that are 6 inches or larger in diameter, a 1-inch layer of shards or pebbles at the bottom is helpful in improving the drainage.

If you are using an ornamental container with no drainage holes in the bottom, special arrangements for drainage should be made. You can set the plant in a slightly smaller pot inside the container, raising the pot on a 1-inch layer of stones if necessary to avoid having the pot stand in water. Or you can plant directly in the container, using a bottom layer of shards, ½-inch pebbles, pea-sized charcoal or perlite to act as a drainage layer. Such a container, if it is 10 inches high or higher, should have 2 to 3 inches of drainage material, which should be lightly covered with a layer of long-strand sphagnum moss, a few autumn leaves, a bit of excelsior or other material to keep the potting soil from sifting down into the drainage area. Care must be taken to avoid overwatering such a closed container, for the only way moisture can leave the container is by evaporation from the soil's surface and from transpiration through the plant's leaves. For the beginner who may be prone to overwater, I suggest the addition of a length of thin pipe reaching from the drainage material to the rim of the pot. Bury this as you

POTTING A PLANT

1. *To pot a plant correctly, hold the plant gently while you put it into the pot, adding enough soil mixture to bring the top of the soil ball to just below the pot's rim. Rest the plant in the pot with one hand and, using the other to add mixture, fill in around the soil ball. The mixture to be used with each type of plant is specified in the encyclopedia, Chapter 6.*

2. *When the mix is at the same level as the base of the stem, press down with your forefinger all around the stem to bring the roots into contact with the mixture.*

3. *Press down with both thumbs around the edge of the pot to firm the mixture; this will eliminate air pockets and will prevent water from draining too rapidly down the sides, bypassing the roots.*

4. *With your forefinger, measure the distance between the top of the pot and the mixture; it should be about a finger's breadth, or half an inch, in pots up to 5 inches wide, up to two fingers, or an inch, in larger ones. If necessary, add or remove mixture. Water thoroughly until water seeps out the bottom drainage hole.*

fill in with soil around the plant. Then by using a dipstick—a thin wooden dowel—be sure that water is not accumulating beneath the plant *(drawing, page 50)*.

Once you have arranged the drainage layer at the bottom of the pot, pick up a handful of your potting soil mixture and make a fist. If the mixture barely holds its shape when you open your hand, crumbles apart at a touch and does not stick to your skin, it is just damp enough for the pot. If it clumps and sticks, it is too damp and needs to dry out a bit. On the other hand, if it is so dry that it will not hold together when squeezed, it should be moistened slightly.

POTTING THE PLANT

Now scoop potting mixture into the pot, and rap the pot on a workbench or table to settle the soil and eliminate air pockets. Hold the plant in the pot to see if the top of the soil ball comes to about ½ inch from the top of the pot (1 inch in larger pots). If the plant is a newly rooted cutting that lacks a ball of soil around its roots, spread the roots gently and sprinkle the mixture in and around them until they are covered. If the plant does have a ball of soil, disturb the ball and the roots as little as possible, using your hands to fill in around the ball with the potting mixture, and firming down as shown in the drawings on page 51.

Having completed the potting, water the plant thoroughly

HOW TO TAKE A PLANT OUT OF A POT

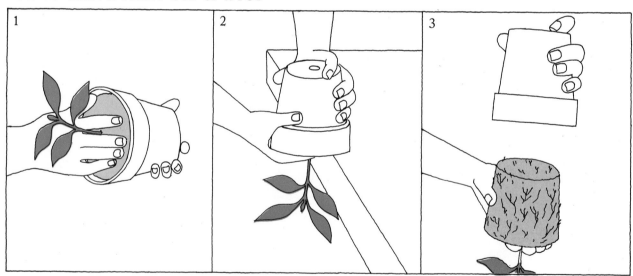

To "knock out" a plant—that is, to remove it from its pot for inspection or repotting—hold the main stem between the fingers of one hand, the pot in the other. Watering an hour in advance will make the job easier.

Without changing your grip on plant or pot, turn them upside down and knock the rim sharply once or twice on the edge of a workbench. The impact will jar the plant loose from the pot, with roots and soil intact.

Pull the pot up and away, allowing the plant to slide out while you hold it in your lower hand. You can now check to see whether the roots have grown enough so that the plant needs a larger pot or root pruning.

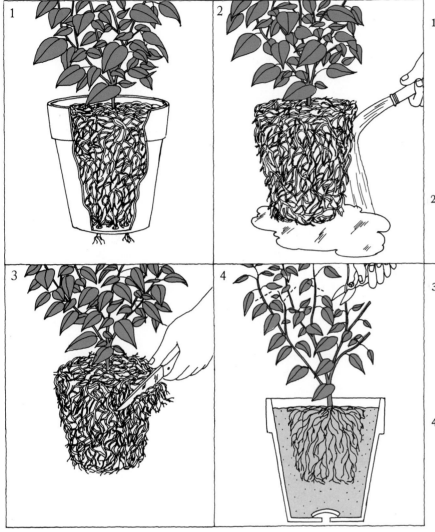

ROOT AND TOP PRUNING

1. *Woody-stemmed flowering plants such as camellias and hibiscuses may become unmanageably large if you use larger pots whenever their growing roots require repotting. When the roots become tightly crowded inside the pot —even cropping out on the surface of the soil and growing down through the bottom drainage holes—pruning of both roots and top growth is in order.*

2. *After knocking the plant out of its pot (opposite page), hose it off to remove as much soil as you can from around the matted roots.*

3. *With a sharp knife, trim the outer roots, shaving down all around the root ball; then turn the plant on its side and slice an equal amount off the bottom. Cut off enough so the roots will be about ½-inch from the edge of a pot 10 inches or less in diameter, 1 inch away in larger pots.*

4. *Repot the plant (page 51), using the old pot scrubbed clean and filled with fresh potting mixture. To keep the plant in healthy balance, prune the stems (dotted lines)—if you cut a third off the roots, cut a third off the stems.*

(Chapter 2) and then do not water again until the soil begins to look dry and crumbly.

A properly potted plant should thrive in its new home for a year, or several years, depending on the speed of its growth. But eventually its roots will outgrow the pot, and it will have to be repotted in a larger container. Only then, when it has more root space, can a healthy plant continue to grow.

Repotting does wonders for plants that seem lethargic, but it cannot restore health to a plant that is already in its last days. Yet many people put all their faith in repotting, as I was reminded not long ago, when I was parking my car close to a florist's shop. I noticed a well-dressed woman carrying into the shop one of the most woebegone plants I have ever seen. My heart went out to the florist for I knew he was going to be asked to repot it, with repot being a euphemism for rejuvenate. The woman obviously did not want the same old straggly plant back in a new pot; she wanted the florist to restore its health and youth—an impossibility at this late stage. But the small disaster might easily have been averted had the plant been repotted when there was still time.

WHEN AND HOW TO REPOT

Repotting is in order when a plant has become pot bound—that is, when its roots have completely filled the ball of soil and the pot. (A few plants, such as agapanthus, basketvines and crinodonnas, blossom more profusely when they are slightly pot bound and for this reason are repotted less frequently; such plants are so noted in the encyclopedia.) Sometimes a plant will signal its need for repotting by wilting between waterings and producing only small new leaves and little growth. Sometimes it will give no signal, and continue to grow actively, but if its roots have filled the pot it is soon going to need new soil and more room in which to flourish. There is only one way to determine with certainty whether or not a plant needs repotting, and that is to slip it out of its pot and examine its roots, a procedure that is not difficult and will not injure the plant if done properly.

A few hours before removing the plant for examination, water it just enough to ensure that the soil is moist throughout; this extra moisture will help hold the soil ball together and will also prevent the tender tips of the roots from clinging to dry spots on the pot walls—they may be damaged when they are pulled away. Then, with the fingers of one hand outstretched over the top of the pot and around the plant's stem or stems, turn the pot upside down and rap it on a wooden bench or table edge (drawings page 52). Plant, earth and roots will drop intact into your hand. If the roots are tight-

(continued on page 59)

Orchids you can grow as house plants

The orchid is something special. Mere mention of the name inspires visions of wondrous beauty in dark jungles, a beauty unattainable by any but the wealthiest or the most adventurous. Yet the orchid, far from being rare, is numerous, varied and ubiquitous. There are at least 25,000 known species, growing on every continent except Antarctica and in nearly every climate from the Congo to Alaska. Despite their seeming fragility, orchids are relatively disease resistant and long lived; despite their aura of exoticism, many are no more expensive than other house plants and take just as comfortably to life in an ordinary living room. Pictured here are some of the many different orchids, from the long-lasting, fragrant Brassavola nodosa to the tawny miniature Cymbidium 'Minuet' (opposite), that have thrived in the author's home without extraordinary care. Instructions for the culture of these and other orchids will be found in Chapters 3 and 4 and in the encyclopedia section, Chapter 6, beginning on page 101.

Brassavola nodosa LADY-OF-THE-NIGHT ORCHID (3- to 4-inch flowers)

Cattleya labiata (5- to 7-inch flowers)

Paphiopedilum callosum 'Balinese Dancer' (4-inch flowers)

Angraecum distichum (¼-inch flowers)

BELOW:
Cymbidium 'Minuet' (2- to 2½-inch flowers)

BELOW:
Oncidium varicosum rogersii DANCING LADY ORCHID
(1½- to 2-inch flowers)

BOTTOM LEFT:
Laelia flava (2- to 2½-inch flowers)

BOTTOM RIGHT:
Sophrolaeliocattleya 'Miami' (5- to 6-inch flowers)

Dendrobium loddigesii
(1½- to 2-inch flowers)

Neofinetia falcata
(1-inch flowers, 1½-inch spurs)

Laeliocattleya 'El Cerrito'
(3- to 4-inch flowers)

Brassia caudata SPIDER ORCHID (2½-inch petals, 5- to 8-inch sepals)

BELOW:
Phalaenopsis amabilis MOTH ORCHID (3½- to 4-inch flowers)

TOP TO BOTTOM:

Epidendrum cochleatum CLAMSHELL
ORCHID (2½- to 3½-inch flowers)

Maxillaria tenuifolia (1½-inch flowers)

Trichocentrum tigrinum (2-inch flowers)

Rodriguezia venusta 'Ann'
(1½-inch flowers)

BELOW:

Odontoglossum pulchellum LILY-OF-THE-VALLEY ORCHID (1½-inch flowers)

ly matted, and resemble the contents of a can of cooked spaghetti, the plant has reached the stage at which it needs repotting. With plants that have a dormant period, repotting should coincide with the start of new growth, which generally occurs in midwinter or early spring; in the case of plants that grow all year round, repotting can be done any time it is necessary.

For repotting a plant that needs more room, choose a pot one size larger; soak the pot if it is new, soak and scrub it if it is not, and let the surface dry. As in original potting, place a shard at the bottom, and in larger pots, add a layer of drainage material. Remove the plant and its ball of soil intact from its old pot, as you did to inspect the roots. Set it in its new pot to try it for size. The ball of soil should be about a half inch away from the new pot's walls, all around (1 inch away in the case of 10-inch or larger pots). Estimate at the same time how much soil the new pot will need at its bottom to raise the ball of soil to the proper level—when you finish, the surface should be half an inch to an inch below the pot's upper rim, depending on the size of the plant (drawings page 46). Raise the plant out of the new pot for a moment, and spread the requisite amount of potting mixture at the bottom. Rap the pot to settle the mixture. Replace the plant and its ball of soil in the pot, and fill the space around the ball with more potting mixture, firming it down with your thumbs. Water thoroughly, and do not water again until the soil begins to dry out.

Sometimes plants need repotting in the same pot, or in a new pot of the same size. This procedure should be followed when a plant needs fresh soil, but must be kept from growing too large for the house—my Chinese hibiscus would reach to the roof if I did not restrain it by keeping it in an undersized pot. The need for fresh soil may be indicated by a diminution in the size of new leaves and by a slackening in the production of blossoms. To carry out this same-size repotting, lift the plant out of the old pot, shake off some of the old soil on the outside of the soil ball or wash it off with a garden hose, then prune the roots and top growth as shown in the drawings on page 53. Replace the plant in the pot in fresh soil mixture with a drainage layer at the bottom. Water thoroughly, and do not water again until the soil is nearly dry.

REPOTTING ORCHIDS

The techniques of potting and repotting orchids differ somewhat from those used for most house plants. Repotting should be undertaken when plants are just starting new roots, which will be visible above the potting medium. Ordinary clay or plastic pots can be used as long as good drainage is provided. The orchids generally grown in the home, being epiphytes, or air plants, require fresh air and excellent drainage.

The most popular potting medium for orchids is the bark of fir trees; it comes in three sizes, finely ground for tiny seedlings, intermediate for larger plants and coarse for mature plants. An equally suitable medium is the shredded fiber of the stalks of Mexican tree ferns. Whether you use fir bark or tree-fern fiber, it should be mixed with coarse or poultry-grade peat moss (at a ratio of 2 parts bark or fiber to 1 part peat moss) to retain moisture. Tree-fern fiber is also sold in the form of chunks, suitable as a growing medium for larger orchids, and in slabs or "logs," on which some of the air-loving orchids, particularly small ones, will grow especially well.

Before potting, consider where your orchids will sit in the pot; some types of orchids should be centered and others planted at one side. Those that require centering are of the so-called monopodial type: they have stems that grow upright like the majority of plants and send out clusters of flowers from the base of each leaf, or opposite each leaf, part way down the stem. A second type of orchid, called sympodial, grows horizontally; the older growth should be set close to the pot wall to permit expansion of the new growth inward. All the orchids listed in the encyclopedia section except *Angraecum* and *Phalaenopsis* are of this type.

Sympodial orchids have nonrigid multiple stems that generally require support to keep from sprawling. Bend one end of a

POTTING AND CARING FOR A MONOPODIAL ORCHID

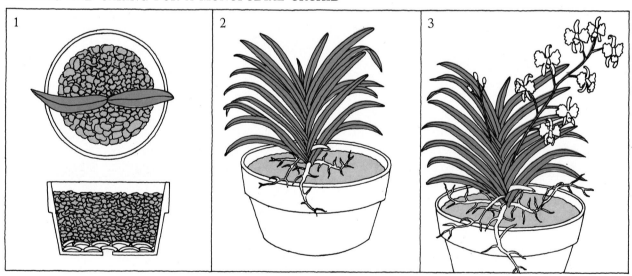

A single-stemmed, or monopodial, orchid should be set in the center of a shallow clay pot 8 or 9 inches in diameter, in fir bark mixed with peat moss. Two layers of shards ensure good drainage (lower drawing).

Properly watered, humidified and fed (see entries in the encyclopedia for Angraecum and Phalaenopsis), the orchid grows steadily, adding new leaves alternately on either side and sending out aerial roots.

When the plant is about five years old, flower stems appear and the flowers themselves finally unfurl. Do not cut flowers until they have reached full firmness and coloring, usually 48 hours after opening.

piece of stiff aluminum or galvanized wire, available at hardware stores, into a semicircle that will fit tightly at the bottom of the pot, and let the rest of the wire rise like a flagpole just to one side of the pot's center *(drawings, below)*. The upright segment of the wire should extend far enough above the pot's top rim so that it will serve to support the vertical stems of a plant that is tied to it—10 to 12 inches should be ample.

From this point on, the potting of monopodial and sympodial orchids is the same. Line the bottom of the pot with one or two layers of shards, then fill the pot halfway with the mixture of bark or fiber and peat moss. Hold the plant over the pot so that the top of its root crown is level with the pot's rim and its roots are dangling lower. Fill the pot almost full with the mix, covering the roots and packing the mix tightly. Water newly potted plants lightly, then mist them twice a day until the new roots become established in the potting medium; at this point follow the watering instructions for the particular species of orchid given in the encyclopedia.

Your orchid is now ready to take its place among your house plants; with a little more experience you will be ready to take your place beside author Rex Stout's famed—though fictional—expert amateur, mystery-story hero Nero Wolfe, in the company of distinguished orchid fanciers.

POTTING AND CARING FOR A SYMPODIAL ORCHID

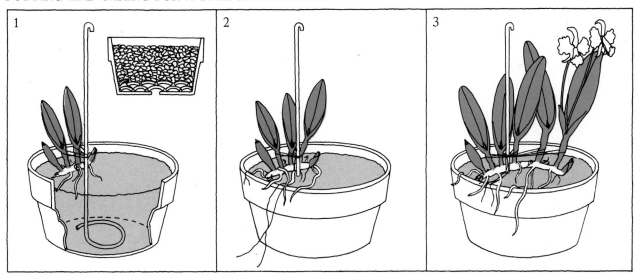

Multiple-stemmed, or sympodial, orchids (including most of the orchids in the encyclopedia) should be planted to one side and supported by a bent wire set in a pot filled with shards, fir bark and peat moss.

As the orchid's ground stem, or rhizome, creeps across the pot, bind each new vertical stem to the wire stake (bent over to prevent accidental injury); use lengths of raffia fiber looped like slings.

A mature sympodial orchid produces flowers when it is about five years old, but only on the lead, or forward, stem. As with other orchids, do not cut off the flowers until they have become firm and fully colored.

What your house plant is trying to tell you

Some people talk to their house plants. In fact, some contend their plants will cringe if they are scolded. There is no evidence that a house plant ever talked back, but if one is feeling poorly it has its own ways of letting you know what is wrong. The leaves may droop, spots may appear, growth may stop. One symptom may mean a plant is getting too little light, another too much water, a third that mealy bugs are attacking. A quick, accurate diagnosis is half the battle in controlling the problem before it gets out of hand.

	SYMPTOMS	CAUSE	WHAT TO DO
1	Stems grow abnormally long, leaves become long and pale, and new leaves are undersized.	Not enough light. Too much nitrogen.	Give plant more sunlight (see encyclopedia, Chapter 6, for specific plants' needs) or move closer to plant-growing lights. Reduce strength of fertilizer or frequency of application.
2	Leaves curl under; new leaves are undersized.	Too much light.	Give plant more shade or move it farther away from plant-growing lights.
3	Stems become mushy, dark in color and rotten; lower leaves curl and wilt; soil at top of pot is constantly wet.	Too much water.	Do not water so much or so frequently; water only when top soil is dry to the touch and reduce watering while plant is dormant. Make sure the pot's drainage hole is not clogged and do not let plant stand in water in its saucer for more than half an hour.
4	Tips of leaves become brown and leaves wilt. Lower leaves turn yellow and fall off.	Not enough water.	Water until the water runs out the bottom of the pot, then do not water again until the soil is dry to the touch.
5	Leaf edges are crinkly and brown.	Lack of humidity.	Increase humidity by placing pots on a bed of moist pebbles in a tray (page 41) or by grouping plants in a planter with moist peat moss around them (page 11). Mist the leaves (page 40). Install a humidifier in the hot-air heating system, if the house has one, or use a cool-vapor room humidifier.
6	Plant bears few or no flowers and an excessive amount of foliage. Stems may be elongated. Green scum may be present on the sides of clay pots.	Too much fertilizer, especially nitrogen.	Fertilize less often, or at half the suggested rate, particularly during winter months when the plant is receiving less light. Do not use high-nitrogen fertilizers during the blooming season. Do not fertilize dormant plants.

Illustrated here and on the following pages are 22 signs that indicate house-plant trouble. A diagnosis and cure for each are also given, but keep in mind that your house is not a plant hospital; discard plants that are obviously in bad shape and replace them with fresh, healthy ones. To forestall problems, wash the leaves regularly *(page 71)* and remove any faded flowers and withered leaves. When you bring new plants into the house, isolate them from other plants for two weeks to make sure they are not carriers of insects or disease.

SYMPTOMS	CAUSE	WHAT TO DO
7 Lower leaves turn pale green and drop off. New leaves are undersized; stems are stunted.	Lack of fertilizer.	Fertilize more often during the plant's growing season (see encyclopedia for specific recommendations).
8 Leaves turn yellow or curl and wilt.	Too much heat.	Move the plant to a cooler spot in the house (see encyclopedia for optimum night and day temperatures for specific plants). Be sure plants are not close to a radiator or hot-air outlet.
9 Yellow or brown spots appear on leaves.	Sun scorch.	Give the plant more shade, especially during summer, by filtering sunlight through blinds or curtains or moving the plant to a window that does not receive full midday or afternoon sun. (See the encyclopedia for sunlight requirements of specific plants.)
10 White or yellow spots appear on leaves, particularly on African violets and other plants with hairy foliage.	Cold water on leaves.	When watering plants, use water at room temperature or higher.
11 White crust appears on soil surface or on sides and rims of clay pots; leaves touching the rim wilt, rot and fall off.	Build-up of salts from fertilizer.	Water the plant thoroughly to dissolve the salts; after half an hour, water again generously to carry the dissolved salts off through the pot's drainage hole. Wash salts off the pot rim and sides; coat the rim with melted wax to prevent future salt build-up from harming leaves and stems.
12 Roots fill the pot completely and may reach down through the bottom hole. Plants may wilt in between waterings and bear only a few small new leaves.	Plant is too big for its pot.	Repot plant in a container one size larger *(drawings, page 51)*.

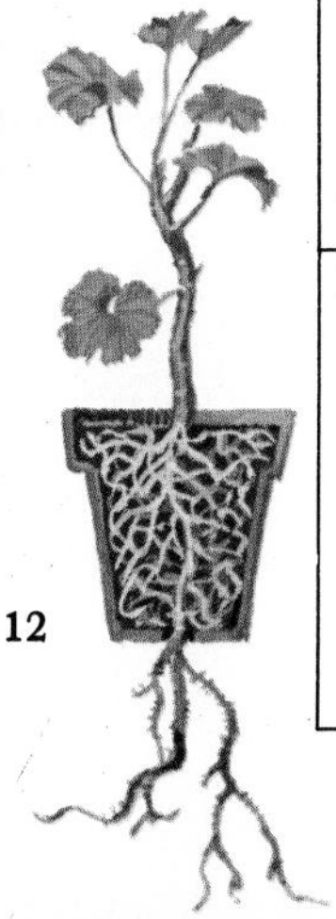

SYMPTOMS

1 Plant is stunted; flowers are malformed or streaked with darker color; leaves curl and stems are twisted and darkened. Heavily infested plants may not bloom, or if they do, buds may fail to open.

2 White, woolly spots appear on stems, at junctures of stems and leaves, and at base of buds, generally in areas hidden from bright light. Leaves develop sticky patches and entire plant looks stunted.

3 Leaves show white speckles, then slowly turn yellow. Tiny spider webs appear, first on undersides of leaves or at junctures of leaves and stems, then on stems or bridging from leaf to leaf. In severe attacks leaves turn brown and drop.

4 Leaves and stems become shiny and sticky to the touch. Leaves curl and buds may be malformed. On close examination tiny insects are visible on undersides of leaves, along stems, at the base of buds and particularly on new shoots.

5 Leaves become pale, turn yellow and drop off. Leaf surfaces are covered with a sticky substance. When plants are moved, tiny insects resembling fine white dust take flight.

6 Plants become stunted and stems and leaves are often sticky to the touch. White or brown dots appear on stems and undersides of leaves.

7 Leaves look as if their surfaces have been scraped, or may have large, ragged holes. Trails of silvery slime appear on leaves. Slimy, legless creatures can be seen during the day under pots or pot rims and among fallen leaves in the pot; at night they can be seen feeding on plants.

8 Spots of varying color and size appear on leaves and may merge to form large blotches. Leaves wither and die.

9 Stems, leaves, flowers and buds become rotten and covered with gray mold. Leaves turn brownish black.

10 Stems and roots turn mushy, dark colored and rotten; lower leaves become dark and waterlogged and collapse; top of plant may die.

CAUSE	METHODS OF CONTROL
Cyclamen mites, microscopic spiderlike pests less than $\frac{1}{100}$ inch long, suck plant juices.	Spray with dicofol. Destroy badly infested plants. Space plants so they do not touch. Wash hands well after handling infested plants to avoid transferring mites to healthy plants.
Mealy bugs, oval-bodied insects that are up to $\frac{1}{4}$ inch long and are covered with a white powdery wax, suck plant juices and excrete honeydew on which a sooty black fungus forms.	If insects are few, pick them off by hand or dab them with a cotton swab dipped in alcohol. Wash foliage with a lukewarm spray in the sink. For heavier infestations, wash the plant in tepid soapy water and rinse in clear tepid water. Severely infested plants may be sprayed with malathion.
Spider mites, yellow, brown, red or green eight-legged creatures less than $\frac{1}{50}$ inch long suck plant juices.	Direct a spray of lukewarm water on foliage to dislodge mites. In the case of severe infestations, spray with malathion or dicofol.
Aphids, pear-shaped, usually wingless insects less than $\frac{1}{8}$ inch long, suck plant juices and excrete honeydew. The insects may be green, black, yellow, brown or pink in color.	Remove individual aphids with fingers or kill them with an alcohol-dipped cotton swab. Wash by dipping the plant upside down in warm soapy water and rinse in tepid clear water; larger plants can be washed with a sponge. Spray heavily infested plants with pyrethrum, rotenone, malathion, or nicotine sulfate.
White flies, white-winged insects about $\frac{1}{30}$ inch long, lie on the undersides of leaves, where they suck plant juices and excrete a mold-forming honeydew.	Spray the undersides of leaves with a combination of either rotenone and pyrethrum or nicotine sulfate mixed with soapy water. Apply two or three times a week.
Scales, $\frac{1}{8}$-inch-long flat, oval or rounded insects with hard shells, can be seen on plants as they suck plant juices and excrete honeydew.	Scrub off scales with a toothbrush or other small brush dipped in lukewarm soapy water and rinse in lukewarm clear water. Spray with malathion or nicotine sulfate.
Slugs and snails, ranging in size from $\frac{1}{2}$ to 4 inches and in color from yellowish to black, chew holes in leaves and flowers.	Pick snails and slugs off plants at night and destroy them, or set out a saucer of beer or grape juice near the plant to attract and drown them. Get rid of hiding places by removing plant debris.
Fungus leaf spot.	Cut off and destroy infected leaves. Keep water off foliage and space plants apart for air circulation and lower humidity.
Botrytis blight, gray-mold blight.	Avoid overwatering, overfertilizing and overcrowding of plants. Keep water off leaves. Destroy infected plants or plant parts. Plants may be sprayed with zineb or ferbam.
Crown, stem and root rot.	Destroy infected plants. To avoid future infections, avoid overwatering, overfertilizing and overcrowding of plants, and keep water off foliage.

The basics of day-to-day care 4

When my aechmea or vriesia refuses to bloom, I give it an apple for company. I slice an apple, place the pieces in the pot with the plant, then put the whole thing inside a clear plastic bag and tuck the bag end underneath the pot. The apple remedy works, too. The aechmea or vriesia (or any other house plant of the bromeliad family), even if it has never flowered or given a hint it might, is stimulated to bloom several weeks or months later, depending on the variety.

This trick sounds like an old wives' tale, but it depends on a well-established chemical reaction. A cut-up apple gives off ethylene, a gas used in manufacturing plastics; the gas acts as a ripening hormone to induce blossoming. Unless you raise nothing but bromeliads—and there are people who do just that, out of affection and admiration for them—most of your house plants will never require an apple and you will never need to know more about the bloom-promoting properties of ethylene. But scientific knowledge of your house plants' needs, applied daily throughout the year, will pay generous dividends in enhanced beauty for your indoor garden, whatever you grow. While most house plants respond to the same sort of general care, each genus has a particular regimen that suits it best, and this is described under the genus entry in the encyclopedia *(Chapter 6)*.

The care of house plants is no dull chore; as I make my rounds each morning before beginning work, I find inspiration and surprise. Just the other day, a laeliocattleya orchid that I bought four years ago as a tiny seedling put out its first flowers, and they were the deep, glowing orange I had hoped for. When I acquired the laeliocattleya, its label read "yellow-orange expectancy," but with hybrid orchids grown from seed one does not know exactly what hue will emerge, for the characteristics of one or another parent may prove dominant. If this one lives up to expectations, its flowers should remain perfect for weeks. On another morning, tiny mouse-ear leaves on a gloxinia that had been resting—leafless, bloomless and to the uninitiated, apparently dead—informed me

The predecessor of today's popular Easter lily, Lilium longiflorum, is the beautiful and ancient Madonna lily, L. candidum, shown here in a pen-and-ink-and-chalk detail from the notebooks of Leonardo da Vinci.

that the plant soon would flower again. On a dwarf orange tree, the buds of blossoms began to swell even as last year's fruit was clinging to its branches.

My tour of inspection, however, has practical as well as pleasurable purpose. It is the starting point for effective care of my plants. I look for plants that need repotting—if one requires watering daily, this unusual thirst is a sign that its roots have filled its ball of soil. (I carry a watering can on my rounds, but use it only where necessary.) I turn each pot 90°, because plants always grow toward the light from the window and will become lopsided if left unturned; from outside they will look beautiful but inside only the backs of their stems will show. I pick off faded flowers and leaves. I consider whether lanky stems should be pruned, or pinched back, to induce more compact growth, and whether I should root the cut-off tips *(Chapter 5)* to produce new plants for friends. I examine tips of stems, the undersides of leaves and leaf axils—the points where leaves sprout from stems—for signs of insect infestation *(pages 62-65)*. And, feeling a bit like a fussy mother-in-law, I look for dust on the leaves, and note which plants need a rinsing.

Occasionally I add fertilizer, which ranks next to light and water in importance to the health of plants. House plants depend on regular feeding more than do outdoor plants, because water dissolves and carries off some of the nutrients in their limited soil, and their roots, confined by the walls of pots, cannot reach for more, as garden plants can. But fertilizer supplied in excess or at the wrong times can prove as harmful as incorrect watering. So understanding when and how to apply fertilizer is an important step to maintaining healthy, handsomely blooming plants.

FEEDING POTTED PLANTS First, just any kind of fertilizer will not do for your house plants. You may not be able to use indoors the fertilizers you prefer in your garden. Organic fertilizers, which are so valuable outdoors, can be used on house plants. But most of them break down and release their nutrients slowly—too slowly for ideal feeding of indoor plants, which do better when given small amounts of fertilizer regularly. Moreover, many organic fertilizers are too messy and smelly to be used indoors. So most house-plant gardeners depend on the cleaner and faster-working chemical fertilizers for the compounds of nitrogen, phosphorus and potassium that all plants require.

Almost any fertilizer specifically designed for house plants is satisfactory because it will contain all three of the elements plants need; these may be in the ratio of 5-10-5 (5 per cent nitrogen compounds, 10 per cent phosphorus compounds, 5 per cent potassium compounds), 10-10-5, 12-31-14 or other combinations. Some house-plant growers use mixtures slightly higher in nitrogen, such as 23-19-17 or 20-10-10, to make up for the fact that nitrogen is dissolved out of the soil more rapidly in a pot under constant watering than in an outdoor garden. Plants such as azaleas and gardenias need fertilizers that leave an acid residue after they have broken down; these fertilizers contain such compounds as diammonium phosphate or ammonium sulfate and are often labeled "for acid-loving plants."

In addition to varying in chemical composition, house-plant fertilizers also vary in physical characteristics. They are sold in four forms: powders, crystals or tablets that are mixed with water to make liquid fertilizer; concentrated liquid fertilizers that are diluted with water; sticks, pills or tablets that are inserted dry into the soil to dissolve slowly when plants are watered; and dry powders that are scratched into the surface of the soil.

I have used all four kinds, and they all work well. Some indoor gardeners use the dry powders, but many amateurs find this method of application a time-consuming chore. The fertilizers that are dissolved in water make their nutrients available quickly and are convenient to use; most people prefer them. Since the concentration of active ingredients varies from brand to brand, follow the instructions on the label when preparing the solution. Never feed a plant until you have determined that its soil is moist; when the soil is dry, even fertilizer that is dissolved in water may burn tender roots. Water dry soil lightly, then pour on enough of the fertilizing solution to soak completely through the soil—when some drips out the bottom of the pot, the plant has had enough. The frequency of application, however, depends on the plant (encyclopedia).

The fertilizing schedule must be modified, of course, when you use the "slow-release" sticks, pills or tablets, since they are specially compounded for spreading out the application over a long period of time. They are meant to be buried an inch or so deep in the soil, and as close to the pot walls as possible to avoid burning the plant roots. When used up, they must be replaced, and this requirement is their chief disadvantage, since it is not always easy to tell when the last bit has dissolved. They are easy to dispense, however, and especially handy if you are going away and leaving the care of your plants to someone you do not trust with the fertilizing.

Do not get the notion from what I have said that your flowering house plants should be fed fertilizer constantly. They can utilize it only when they are growing well, and they grow best only under ideal light conditions. So in northern regions, where winter suns are wan, most house plants should be fed sparingly, if at all, from November to February. A dormant plant—as my gloxinia was until it showed its tiny leaves—should not be fed at all; neither should a plant that is obviously sick, with wilting, withering or

A LEAF IN THE MAIL

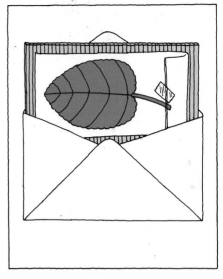

African violet fanciers often mail a leaf from a prized variety to a faraway friend so that he can raise a new plant from it (page 93). The packaging technique is simple: cut the leaf stem as long as possible so that the withered end can be trimmed back on arrival, before rooting; insert the leaf in a plastic sandwich bag, seal the bag with tape and slip it into an envelope with a sheet of corrugated cardboard as a backing to prevent its being crushed by the post office canceling machine.

drooping foliage. Neither dormant nor ailing plants can convert the fertilizers' nutrients into new growth. A newly transplanted one should not be fed for two or three weeks, to give it time to reestablish its roots and cope with the extra nourishment.

With these cautions in mind, begin regular feeding of your flowering house plants as the days lengthen and new growth starts, and continue applications on the schedule prescribed for each plant. But do not overdo the feeding. I know the temptation common to so many indoor gardeners. They pick up a bottle of liquid fertilizer and read the label that says, perhaps, "One teaspoonful to a quart of water." They think: "How could such a little be enough?" And they decide to use a tablespoon instead. If ever you are so tempted, apply a taste of fertilizer to your tongue. It will not hurt you, but it will sting, and you will reach for a glass of water. Imagine how it will burn the tender roots of your plants. In case honest error leads to an overdose, give the plants the drink of water you would demand for yourself. Set them where their pots can drain quickly and safely, and water them over and over again for an hour or two. That may save them.

The need for restraint with fertilizer was impressed on me by a successful African-violet grower, who once told me: "I read the label on the package, then use one half the amount suggested and apply it at twice the interval suggested." Perhaps he erred on the side of caution, but his plants consistently flourished, demonstrating that with fertilizers, less is better than more.

SHOWER AND SPONGE BATHS

In the routine of house-plant care, cleanliness ranks in importance right after food, drink and light. Like small boys, all plants benefit from a fortnightly bath. A good bath will get rid of most insects, insect eggs and mites, which may or may not be visible, but which will damage the plants if left undisturbed. And removing the dust that accumulates on leaves is essential for proper appearance.

Plants light enough to carry should be taken to the sink at least once every two weeks and given a tepid shower. Use the rinsing hose with which most modern kitchen sinks are fitted, and apply a firm but not overly forceful spray to both sides of the leaves and to the stems, taking care not to bruise soft new growth with too much pressure. In the case of fuzzy-leaved plants, I do not use a direct spray, which can injure the leaves; instead I turn the plant upside down, holding it lightly in its pot, and swish the leaves around in a sink of tepid water. If a plant is too large to be moved, wash it with a damp cloth or sponge. Whatever you use to wash down the plants, do the job early in the day, with water warmer than room temperature. Then set the plants to dry where there is good circulation of air and no direct sunlight. I never use anything but plain, tepid water on my plants in their fortnightly baths. It makes old leaves look young again. Specially formulated baths seem unnecessary to me, for I am not convinced that normally soft green leaves become more attractive when they are made shiny by treatment with oil or chemical preparations. Part of the joy of plants lies in the tremendous variety of their leaf textures and shades.

Regular baths wash away most insects before they can do any harm, but some pests are tenacious. The peskiest are frequently those that arrive on newly purchased plants or that move indoors in autumn on plants that have spent the summer in the open. So it is good practice to isolate such plants for a few weeks until their freedom from pests has been established.

The most common invaders are aphids and mealy bugs. Aphids are tiny, pear-shaped insects, and mealy bugs are scaly creatures that look like bits of cotton fluff. Aphids and mealy bugs both suck the juices from the tender tips of plants; aphids also can be found on the undersides of leaves and mealy bugs frequently attack at the junctures of leaves and stems. Less common than mealy bugs and aphids are red spider mites and cyclamen mites, both tiny members of the spider family. Red spider mites spin fine webs on the undersides of leaves of such plants as azaleas and min-

GIVING A HOUSE PLANT A BATH

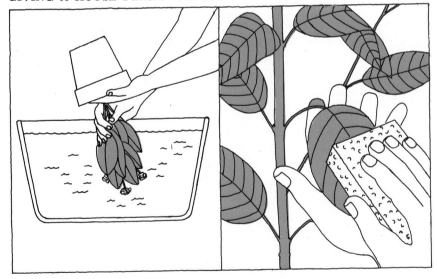

To wash dust off a small plant or one with tender, fuzzy leaves, swirl it around upside down in tepid water, holding as shown. If the dirt sticks, use mild soap (not a detergent), then rinse the plant in clear tepid water.

To bathe larger plants that are too cumbersome to carry to the sink, wipe off their leaves with a sponge dipped in tepid water; if you use soapy water to remove sticky dirt, sponge off with clear water.

iature roses, and suck their juices until the foliage becomes speckled white. Cyclamen mites assault African violets, begonias and geraniums as well as cyclamens. Too small to be visible, they suck the juices from the plant cells, deforming the plants, causing their leaves to curl and wither and preventing buds from opening.

Fortunately most of these pests can be controlled, one way or another. If aphids defy the fortnightly bath of tepid water, douse the plant's leaves and stem in a tub filled with tepid soapy water —but be sure to use old-fashioned mild soap, not a detergent. Swish the plant around, then rinse it in plain tepid water. If any aphids survive—they rarely do—spray with rotenone or pyrethrum, which are harmless to human beings and other mammals (they are toxic to fish, though, and should not be used near an aquarium).

If mealy bugs persist, touch them with a cotton swab dipped in alcohol. Only if that remedy fails should you turn to an insecticide spray. The most suitable kind for mealy bugs is malathion, which is available at garden supply centers. Since it is slightly toxic and has an obnoxious odor, use it with the windows wide open or move the potted plants outdoors before spraying.

Malathion is also effective against red spider mites. For cyclamen mites, use dicofol. This treatment will salvage plants that have not been too seriously infested, but heavily damaged plants should be destroyed.

Before using any insecticide, read the label on the package carefully. Make sure that the treatment is suitable to your plants, for some species are dangerously sensitive to certain preparations. If the chemical must be mixed with water before use, adhere strictly to the instructions for dilution. If the insecticide comes in an aerosol spray can, as many insecticides do, spray only at the distance specified on the label—usually 18 inches. The spray is squirted out of the can by a pressurized gas that emerges very cold; it may severely chill a plant that is too close to the jet.

Disease is less of a problem than insect attack. House plants seldom get sick because most plant diseases are caused by fungi, which need moisture to spread; since house-plant foliage is ordinarily dry—so long as you are careful with your watering—fungi get little opportunity to flourish. When diseases appear, the usual cause is excess moisture from overwatering or from some practice such as watering so late in the day that daylight warmth cannot dry out the plants. When the improper practices cease, so do the diseases—generally. The chart on pages 64-65 describes the symptoms of important house-plant diseases, as well as common pests, and prescribes specific treatments.

Treat your sick plants but never maintain a plant hospital on your window sill. Diseased plants or plants infested with insects

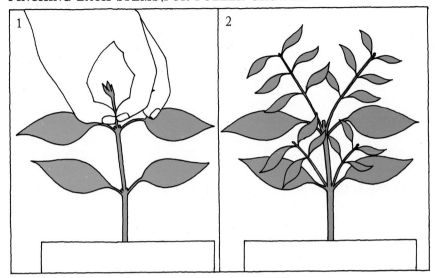

To get compact, bushy house plants with many flowers, pinch off the ends of new stems, using your thumbnail to sever the stem if needed. Pinch as close as you can to the top leaves without injuring the tiny buds below.

The energy that the tip would have put into flowering now goes to the buds, producing new branches, all of which can bear flowers. Repeat the process on the new stems, if needed, to control the plant's shape.

should be kept away from the others. And when the disease seems incurable or the pest infestation defies control, the plants should be consigned to the trash barrel, pots and all. Otherwise they may set off an epidemic in your indoor garden.

Apply the same Draconian measures to plants that simply look worn out, particularly when you notice spindly growth during your rounds of inspection in late spring. Such plants may have lost most of their lower leaves and no longer look attractive. Since it is nearly impossible to rejuvenate tired old plants, replace them with husky young ones, full of vigor and the promise of abundant blossoms. On the other hand, you should save plants like glory lilies and gloxinias, which may simply be in a period of dormancy before putting out new growth. Bulbs such as hyacinths, tulips and narcissus, that blossomed during the winter, should also be saved for setting out in the garden in the fall. And woody plants—hoya, hibiscus, calliandra, jasmine—which may look as if they are on their last legs, will gain a new lease on life in a summer outdoors.

A SUMMER IN THE GARDEN

Spring is also the time to prepare your potted plants for a season in the fresh air outside the house. Many of them benefit from a summer outdoors, either in the garden itself or on a porch or patio. But some should not go outdoors at all. I never put my African violets outside, although some gardeners find that they do well enough in a shady, protected place on a porch. Among the plants that gain the most from a few months in the fresh air are calliandras, which like full sun, camellias, which prefer shady spots, and potted citrus trees—orange, lemon and lime—which perk up splendidly on sunny patios. No plants should be transferred abruptly to direct sunlight outdoors from the limited light that they have been used to indoors. Make the shift a gradual one, first putting the plants in a relatively shady spot, then closer to the sunlight, and finally in full sun. Locations that get morning sun are preferable; the heat of the afternoon sun in summer is often too intense and can burn the leaves of some plants.

When moving plants outdoors, try to put them in a spot that is sheltered from gusty winds, which can dry out the plants and even knock the pots over. It is best to set the plants on a hard surface such as a paved terrace or wall; if they are set on the ground or on grass, they may send roots down through the pot's drainage hole into the soil. I find that the best way to take care of house plants outdoors in summer is to sink them below ground level; this shields the pots and roots from sun and wind and helps them stay cool and moist. To do this, choose a well-drained spot within easy reach of a hose. Dig a bed 6 to 8 inches deep, and as long and as wide as necessary to accommodate your plants without crowding; each should have its full share of light and air. Fill the bed with gravel or with 3 or 4 inches of gravel topped by a similar layer of moist peat moss to hold moisture; roots are not likely to grow down into a bed of gravel. Set the pots into the bed, burying them up to their rims. Do not actually set the plants in the bed until both nighttime and daytime temperatures are mild enough so that they will not be damaged by chill (minimum night temperature requirements of specific plants are indicated in the encyclopedia).

Every week or so give each pot a twist in its bed to make doubly sure that, despite the gravel, no roots are spreading out through the drainage hole. This method makes it easy to retrieve your plants at summer's end and return them to the house. Some house plants, such as begonias and impatiens, can be tapped out of their pots and set, ball of soil and all, in a hole in the garden; many gardeners do this to fill in empty spaces in their flower beds. But don't do this unless you are willing to leave the plant in the garden. By the time summer is over the roots will have spread so much that you may find it impossible to repot the plant without drastic—possibly harmful—pruning. If you decide that the risk is worth taking, for the sake of the garden's summer appearance, you can take cuttings from the plants, and start new ones for the house, in the manner described in Chapter 5.

The first few weeks in the garden are a time for house plants to renew their strength. But they will require help from you. To protect them against diseases and hostile insects, spray the plants thoroughly. Outdoors you can use an all-purpose pesticide that might be unsuitable inside the house. You can also begin foliar feeding, a very effective method of fertilizing that is too messy for indoor use. In this process, plant nutrients dissolved in water are sprayed on the leaves, which absorb them to supplement food the plants take in with their roots. Foliar nutrients should be administered at the same frequency as other fertilizers. Never use a solution stronger than that recommended on the label, for it may burn the leaves. The practice of foliar feeding has its critics among some horticulturists who doubt that certain plants absorb much nutrient through their leaves, but it is my experience that potted plants respond well to it when they have been moved outdoors; some older plants that have occupied the same large pots for a long period seem to benefit especially from foliar feeding.

You need not bring your plants indoors at the first sign of autumn. In many parts of the country, night temperatures even in October do not fall to harmful levels, and as long as Indian summer lingers, the plants may continue to flourish in the garden. But keep an eye on the outside thermometer and an ear tuned to weather

HANDLING DRAINAGE FROM HANGING PLANTS

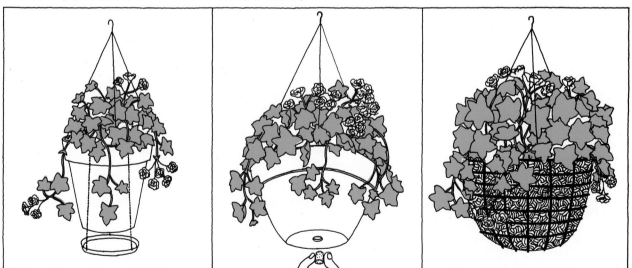

A small pie tin will catch water that drips from a hanging plant in an ordinary pot. To hang the tin, punch three holes in its rim, tie a string to each hole and to short stakes driven into the soil inside the pot rim.

To eliminate messy dripping without suspending a saucer beneath a hanging pot, plug the drainage hole with a cork. Water the plant at the sink, then let it drain thoroughly before you hang it up again.

Plants hung outdoors can be placed, unpotted, in baskets lined with sphagnum moss. To water them, take the basket down and immerse it in a sink or tub, then set it aside for a while to drain before rehanging it.

forecasts. When the temperature drops below the ideal night temperature indicated in the encyclopedia for your plants, it is time for them to come indoors. Hose them down to knock off any bugs that may be on them and thoroughly clean off the outside of the pots before bringing them in to settle down for the winter.

WHEN PLANTS REST

Whether or not they have spent the summer outdoors, all plants except annuals and some tropical plants need a period of rest. Without it they weaken and die, and one of the most important aspects of house-plant culture is recognizing when a plant is entering this period and understanding how to take care of the plant while it rests. Many a neophyte, misreading the symptoms, has tossed out a plant that would have flourished the following year. I know one indoor gardener, by no means inexperienced (he has a small greenhouse), who received an orchid cactus as a gift and kept it in the greenhouse. When it had failed to flower by the following May, he asked the donor's advice. "Throw it away," she suggested. He tossed it, pot and all, behind the garage and forgot about it. A month later he happened to look behind the garage and discovered that the plant had produced six blossoms in its abandoned state. He rescued it and put it on his terrace. At last count it had 28 blossoms and was promising more. The plant had merely needed a rest from the warmth, moisture and light of the greenhouse.

Different plants rest in different ways and at different seasons —times that were apparently fixed ages ago by the climatic changes in the regions where their ancestors originated. Some merely cease to flower but retain their green leaves. Some stop growing but give no other sign that they are resting. Some drop their leaves but retain moisture in their stems and branches, and stand like green skeletons. Some go into the extreme form of rest that horticulturists call dormancy: all vegetation aboveground dies down and the plant appears dead, although belowground it may be in a state somewhat similar to animal hibernation; in fact, it may even be growing, though it gives no sign.

The requirements of resting or dormant plants vary widely and are described, species by species, in the encyclopedia section. It is important to follow them closely—the future production of blooms, and even a plant's very survival, often depends upon the care given during its resting period. For example, all too many indoor gardeners, hearing that gloxinias are related to African violets, give them identical care. After their flowers fade, they continue to provide them with fertilizer and abundant water. Plied with food and moisture, but deprived of rest, the plants eventually die. Success with Christmas cactus, too, depends largely on the treatment given the plant during its resting season. It will show no sign of

ORCHIDS BY ACCIDENT

Orchids are often thought to be delicate plants, but their innate toughness is demonstrated by the discovery of cattleya orchids—the familiar corsage plants with the large lavender, pink or white flowers. The first cattleya to come to the attention of Western botanists arrived in England in 1818—as packing material for rare mosses and lichens shipped by boat from Brazil. A curious horticulturist, William Cattley, decided to pot some of the odd-looking roots and stems. Six years later, the first magnificent cattleyas to be grown in cultivation blossomed under his care.

needing any kind of special care, but if it is not kept quite dry, un-fertilized and at a temperature of about 55° during November and December, it may not flower when flowering time arrives.

The general guidance given above applies to virtually all house plants—even orchids. While they are often held in awe as delicate, exotic plants, they are so easy to grow that they are found in homes all over the world, from small Manhattan apartments to the mansions of Hong Kong millionaires. Most orchids even thrive outdoors in summer. I put mine outside every year in Massachusetts. Since the majority need at least partial shade, I find the best place for them is among the branches of trees. I hang them by using standard pot hangers, which clip to the pots and have hooks, like those of clothes hangers, that slip over small branches. I fertilize the plants regularly, water them with a hose, and bring them back indoors, refreshed, in fall.

While you can grow lovely orchids without the expertise of the fictional detective Nero Wolfe, your way will be easier if you understand some of the peculiarities of these plants. First of all, do not start out by trying to raise them from seeds, as Wolfe and his gardener Theodore do. A single pinch of seeds, often as fine as talcum powder, will produce thousands of plants, but even if you had

THE DISPLAY AND CARE OF ORCHIDS

To show off orchids attractively and give them the light and moisture they need, set the pots in a window in a large ceramic dish or other decorative container that will act as a humidifying tray (page 41). Water *in the bottom of the pebble-filled tray will supply the surrounding air with moisture as it evaporates (orchids do best in humidity of 60 per cent or more). Mist the foliage at least twice a day (page 40).*

room for them, tending them might tax your patience: some orchids require five to seven years to progress from germination to flowering. In any case, raising orchids from seeds is a job for experts, requiring special culturing materials, tools and skills.

If you are willing to wait several seasons for flowers, and you have had some experience in cultivating orchids, you can raise plants from seedlings. They cost little, and if you buy those that are 2 or 3 inches tall, they will thrive under the care prescribed for mature plants—but they will not bloom for two to five years. Most people want flowers right away, and they buy established plants as they would rosebushes or azaleas. Although some rare specimens have sold for as much as $10,000, the popular orchids cost no more than other good house plants. When shopping, however, inspect the plants carefully. For growing in the house, it is best not to buy bare-root divisions or plants that were collected in the jungle, for they will take too long to accommodate themselves to indoor conditions. For your first few orchids, it is best to buy plants that are already in bud; with an orchid-grower's help, select types that blossom at different times of the year.

The special care that orchids require consists mainly of attention to their specific needs for ventilation, humidity and light. Light, in particular, has a powerful influence on blooming; give the plants too much or too little and you will get few flowers or none at all. Whether or not the quantity of light is right is indicated by the color of the foliage. Generally, a light green color signals that all is well, a deep rich green means that the light is inadequate for optimum production of flowers, and a yellowish green means that there is too much light. Natural light is generally regulated by curtains. In the northern part of the country, most orchids can stand full winter sunshine from November to March; during the rest of the year a thin curtain should be drawn between them and the sun from midmorning to midafternoon. In the South, the curtain should be drawn during the hottest part of the day throughout the year.

Many orchids will also grow satisfactorily under artificial light. But for mature plants, limit the hours of artificial lighting to the season's normal period of daylight, and keep the plants in rooms that remain dark at night. The length of the daily period of darkness controls the plants' internal regulating mechanisms, and if it is too short, the plants may not flower, or may flower erratically. Young plants, however, reach maturity faster if they get 16 hours of artificial light daily.

Orchids' tastes in humidity are rather finicky. The ideal level for plants indoors in winter is 60 per cent or higher, far greater than that usually maintained in a heated house. You can install a room humidifier, one of the standard appliances sold by department stores, but it is simpler to increase humidity in a limited region around the plants. An atomizer or misting device that sprays a fine mist over the plants will accomplish the purpose, but only if used several times a day. You will have less routine work if you keep the plants in humidifying trays. Set the pots in plastic or metal trays that have been filled to a depth of an inch or more with perlite, pebbles, charcoal, marble chips or other material and ½ inch to an inch of water. The pots should rest on this material without sinking into the water level; if it proves too soft to support the plants' weight, put half a brick beneath each pot before filling in the tray with the pebbles or perlite.

Although orchids prefer fairly high humidity, they are paradoxically averse to excess water. Overwatering is particularly harmful to the group of orchids that does not grow in the earth, the epiphytes, which cling to the bark of trees or perch in their crotches. They are accustomed to alternating periods of moisture and dryness about their roots, and the *Cattleya* genus of epiphytes—the plants most orchid fanciers begin with—can survive for long periods without water. Orchids that grow on the ground in soil—the terrestrial orchids—demand that the medium they live in be kept slightly moist but not wet. The signs of excess moisture are little brown spots on flowers, brown watery spots on the foliage, and blackened stems. Treat these conditions by withholding water and humidity and moving the plant to a spot where air circulates more freely and dries the plants between waterings. But you are unlikely to encounter such problems if you simply water your orchids sparingly early in the day, and keep them properly potted in a porous mixture *(page 60)* and well ventilated.

When orchids are growing rather than resting, every third or fourth watering should be accompanied by a feeding. Orchids grown in fir bark should be given a high-nitrogen fertilizer such as 20-10-10 or 30-10-10, because bacteria breaking down the bark absorb part of any nitrogen given the plants.

With such care, most orchids blossom regularly—some for two weeks, some for nearly two months. Blossoms may be as small as $\frac{1}{32}$ of an inch across or as large as 12 inches across. Some bloom continuously, others only once a year.

If orchids, for all their delicate beauty, turn out to be easy to grow once you know how, the same cannot be said for all house plants. Some are indeed delicate and require continual, skilled attention. If your time is limited, choose among the undemanding plants. There are many of them, in all shapes and sizes, that are equal in beauty to their more difficult shelfmates. It is far better to have a healthy, blooming geranium or begonia than a once gorgeous but now neglected gardenia.

HOW THE PASSIONFLOWER GOT ITS NAME

During the Sixteenth Century, the Catholic missionaries who discovered the passionflower vine (page 137) blooming in the jungles of South America used it to teach the story of the Passion of Jesus Christ. Its 10 outer petals, they instructed local Indians, represented the 10 apostles present at the Crucifixion; the rays of the inner corona were the Crown of Thorns; the pollen-bearing anthers were Christ's wounds; and the three pollen-receiving stigmas were the nails used to fix His body to the Cross. The missionaries even likened the vine's coiling tendrils to the cords and whips that bound and scourged the Lord, and the lobed leaves to the hands of His tormentors.

The experts share their secrets

The name its members gave the Indianapolis Friendly Cactus and Succulent Society—one of the country's more than 14,000 gardening organizations—is an indication of the genial camaraderie among the enthusiasts who grow house plants. They meet to exchange information on potting and lighting, propagation techniques and fertilizers; they arrange lectures and publish newsletters (which may feature cake recipes along with technical discourses on hybridization); they swap cuttings and seeds, and set up displays at county fairs. The larger national organizations, such as the African Violet Society of America and the American Gloxinia and Gesneriad Society, publish scholarly periodicals and arrange the flower shows at which the best plants are judged for excellence.

The winners of blue ribbons in these contests are the high scorers on a rating scheme worked out by the societies. Oddly enough, flowers may not be the most important consideration when flowering house plants are judged. African violets can win no more than 50 points (of a possible 100) for their blossoms, gloxinias no more than 40. Judges pay the greatest attention to such characteristics as vigor, health and shape. Also important is the leaf pattern and condition, a housekeeping evaluation that can penalize a plant for sun-browned leaves, spent flowers or having outgrown its pot. And in judging a begonia, even the label is an important factor; correct identification is one indication of a grower's attention to detail. (Before Gene and Nettie Daniels entered their prize-winning Alto Scharff Ziesenhenne in competition, they took the plant to Rudolf Ziesenhenne himself—the botanist who bred it originally—to make sure it was correctly labeled.)

While competition may be intense, the victorious growers take pride in sharing with others the special techniques that brought blue ribbons and silver cups to their plants. On the following pages three champion indoor gardeners display prize-winning examples of their specialties—African violets, begonias and gloxinias—and disclose the sometimes unconventional procedures that brought them triumphs.

A mass of blossoms and symmetrical foliage won Emory Leland a ribbon for this Master Blue African violet.

Engineering violets

Six years after he first horned in on his wife's hobby, Seattle architectural engineer Emory Leland had more than 300 African violet plants under cultivation in his basement. Besides winning more than 100 blue ribbons and many silver cups, bowls and platters in local competitions, he had become a national judge for the African Violet Society of America.

Leland claims he grows violets to forget business worries, but he does so with the precision of a professional engineer. Since sunlight is unreliable in Seattle's cool northerly climate, the plants are raised under fluorescent lamps, special growth-inducing types paired with standard ones to provide 10 to 15 watts of lamp power per square foot of growing area. The lights are turned on for 12 hours at night, when the house is cool, keeping the temperature at about 75°, compared with 65° during the day.

Leland also turns on a cool-vapor electric humidifier, when necessary, to maintain relative humidity between 40 and 50 per cent. He feeds his plants lightly, never more than once a week, and rotates several standard fertilizers because he feels no single one ensures a balanced diet. And when it is time for watering, Leland sprinkles his plants with thermometer-tested 80° to 90° water, always when the room is getting warmer, not cooler. The return for such attention to detail can be seen in the pictures here.

Emory Leland uses a battery-testing bulb to water his prize-winning African violets, growing on basement shelves under fluorescent lamps.

The flat, wheel-shaped crown, symmetrical leaf pattern and neat appearance of Leland's Tommie Lou plant are show-winning points.

Leland regulates his plants' shapes by moving them closer to or farther from the light and by turning them so that they grow symmetrically.

The many large and softly tinted double blooms of this example of the Tommie Lou variety rate a high score with judges of African violets.

To encourage abundant and outsized flowers like these, Leland changes fertilizer when he is preparing plants for exhibition, feeding them a little less nitrogen and a little more phosphorus and potash than usual.

Luck with begonias

Photographer Gene Daniels and his wife Nettie of Camarillo, California, caught the begonia bug at a state fair. Dazzled by a display of plants in flower, they joined the American Begonia Society on the spot and later bought a drab plantlet at a club meeting. This Alto Scharff Ziesenhenne, to use its proper name, grew into the magnificent specimen shown on the opposite page; its prize-winning details appear at left and below.

The Danielses' success seems due half to beginner's luck and half to advice found in a 12-year-old article they ran across. They left the plant in its original 3-inch pot for nearly a year; it thrived, although fast-growing begonias are supposed to be transferred to larger pots after about six months to prevent crowding of their roots. In spite of warnings that ugly leaf spots often result from watering the leaves, the Danielses sprayed the hairy leaves heavily to remove dust. Against most experts' advice, they fertilized frequently; and when new growth burgeoned in response to the rich diet, they snapped off new tips to achieve a symmetrical shape.

Gene and Nettie Daniels' readiness to modify rules and follow their instincts was justified—in less than five years their home was filled with 250-odd varieties of begonias and a baker's dozen blue ribbons—the first won by the plant they grew from their initial purchase.

The delicate flowers of the Danielses' prize-winning begonia (opposite) exhibit a desirable creamy inner texture and hairy red outer surface.

The fine hair that covers this type of begonia leaf blurs and softens the contrast between the reddish underside and the green-colored top.

Hairs create a thin silver edge around the green top surface, outlining the shapely leaf form sought by growers of this variety.

The Danielses inspect a begonia in the room they built when their begonia collection outgrew their house—the walls are worn-out fluorescent tubes.

This prize-winning begonia rates 97 points (of an unattainable 100) for such characteristics as symmetry, color, perfect leaves and blossoms.

Mothering gloxinias

Mrs. Iris August of Bay Shore, New York, was started on her rise to eminence among gloxinia fanciers when she refused to accept the well-meant advice of a florist. She had received a gloxinia in full bloom as an anniversary gift, and when it stopped flowering, she sought expert guidance. The florist said to throw it away and get a new one, explaining that if it were allowed to rest for a while in a dark closet, it might grow new leaves, but would not necessarily blossom again. But Mrs. August stubbornly (she says) decided to wait out the plant's dormant period. Her plant, properly lighted, fed and watered, soon produced 12 blossoms.

Heartened by this victory, Mrs. August then tackled a more challenging horticultural task: creating new hybrids by crossbreeding gloxinias and propagating the seeds. Once again she achieved quick success, winning a gold bowl at an international flower show for the plant she named August Snow. Within the next three years she took 37 blue ribbons and won permanent custody of the Annual Sweepstakes Trophy of the American Gloxinia and Gesneriad Society.

Mrs. August's plants grow under fluorescent lights that are timed to burn 15 hours a day in winter, 16 in summer, in the basement of her Long Island home. The temperature is kept between 70° and 75° during the day and a bit cooler at night, and the humidity is usually maintained above 60 per cent, using two room dehumidifiers in summer and a furnace humidifier in winter. As her gloxinias come into bloom, she moves them upstairs, and scarcely a room throughout the August home lacks living ornaments.

Seen from above in the picture at top, Mrs. Iris August's new hybrid gloxinia, Kenny A, shows near-perfect symmetry and healthy appearance.

Kenny A deserves high scores for erect posture and the proportions between its flowers and foliage, seen in profile view in the lower picture.

d early could
acks for snails

Spring Time: 'Spring Bouquet' laurustinus, compact clusters of small
white flowers, is densely foliated from
the ground up. The leathery, forest
green leaves are about 2 inches long.

ome with plastic lids to create
use-like environment with
se. However, seedlin
or in a real gree
ated to the o
ought be
tting

...ality is cancer tr[...]
to helping my
[...]nt on me and t[...]
Hospital.

[...]best doctors. Just call 1-888-[...]

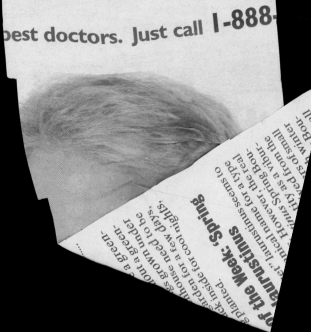

of the Week: 'Spring

plained, turns into for a type of laurustinus seems to be the real [...] technical name never flower. Spring Bou- House's a vibur- nity kept from all rived from winter lor Bou[...]

green- [...]t a green [...]out under own to be groups need days. house a few days. [...]den for cool nigh[...] [...]ck inside for

Mrs. Iris August beams in triumph at her first flower show as her gloxinia, August Snow, wins two awards: a blue ribbon and a gold bowl.

Deep red 2½-inch petals with wavy lighter edges distinguish Kenny A, crossbred from two champion gloxinias Mrs. August developed.

Growing new plants from old ones 5

In one way, indoor gardeners often resemble those old-fashioned Latin Americans whose code of hospitality requires them to offer you any of their possessions that you admire. ("You really like my cravat, señor? Please, you must take it. I insist.") If you praise an indoor gardener's plant, the chances are that he will press on you a leaf, a segment of stem or even a bit of root so that you may grow a plant like his. I would not be surprised if that pleasant custom went back to the oldest Latins of them all, the Romans. For Pliny the Elder (23-79 A.D.) wrote in his *Natural History* about the ways in which plants can reproduce themselves without going through the process of producing seed, and he refers familiarly to "slips" and "cuttings" and "layering"—which are among the subjects of this chapter, and all of which have the same purpose: to make roots grow where no roots grew before.

When plants reproduce themselves by seed, as most of them do, they are behaving sexually, uniting male and female. But almost all of them can reproduce asexually as well. Bulb plants such as tulips produce not only seeds but little bulbs, each a potential plant of its own, surrounding the mother bulb the way chicks surround a hen. Many types of plants send out long shoots called runners that spread along the ground and take root to start independent life as they go. A single leaf cut from an African violet soon becomes the parent of one or more identical plants. The methods that plants have developed for asexual increase—or vegetative reproduction, as botanists call it—are manifold, and gardeners not only have been able to adapt them, but to devise a few of their own. (Pliny attributes the first ventures in this field to "mere accident," which, he says, "taught us to break off branches from trees and plant them because stakes driven into the earth had taken root.") Even the bits of a leaf can grow into plants. All these methods work because many parts of every plant contain cells capable of reproducing the whole plant. In practice, a method of vegetative reproduction that succeeds with one kind of plant may not succeed

A window greenhouse in New York City is well equipped for starting plants (in flats on floor) and displaying mature ones. The roof opens to adjust warmth and humidity; a timer and electric eye control lights.

with another. The rex begonia, for example, will grow from bits of leaf but not from root cuttings; gardenias and impatiens, among others, reproduce themselves from sections of stem, but not from leaf cuttings; and Martha Washington geraniums can be multiplied from sliced-off chunks of root.

But with seeds so plentiful and so cheap, the neophyte gardener may well wonder, why bother? The compelling answer is that only by asexual or vegetative reproduction can you be sure that you will obtain a young plant just like its parent in leaf and blossom characteristics, if not in exact shape and size. In fact, I should not even use the word parent, for the young plant is really a continuation of the plant from which it came, a duplicate rather than an offspring. They are such exact copies because they contain only the inherited characteristics of one progenitor. Seeds, contrarily, may not breed true, as horticulturists say. This means that a young plant grown from seed may or may not closely resemble its parents. The fertilized seed contains inheritance factors from both parents, and the result is likely to be a mixture.

Many house plants are the result of crossbreeding because crossbreeding, by deliberately mixing inheritance, can enhance the beauty and vigor of plants and produce new varieties as well. But most indoor gardeners prefer the certain results of vegetative reproduction. It has several other important advantages as well. Not the least of these is the fact that the new plants will reach maturity and begin to produce flowers much more rapidly than those started from seed. When young, they are much less vulnerable to disease and injury than young seedlings. And seeds, no matter how sparingly you spread them, yield far more seedlings than the indoor gardener is likely to be able to accommodate.

TAKING STEM CUTTINGS

Of the methods of vegetative reproduction illustrated on these pages, stem cutting is probably the simplest and most frequently successful. It works well with geraniums, gardenias, angel wing begonias and the many other plants that develop firm stems. The best time to take a stem cutting is during a plant's period of active growth, usually spring and summer, unless the encyclopedia (*Chapter 6*) specifies otherwise. In looking for a likely piece to cut, choose the upper part of a stem of the current year's growth, but a section that is fairly mature; if it is light green and succulent, it is too young and may rot before new roots develop, and if it is brownish and tough, it is too old and will lack the vigor to sprout roots easily. If possible, avoid making the cutting on a stem that has flowers or flower buds; such a cutting will root but usually will not produce as good a plant as a nonblossoming shoot. If you do use a flowering stem, remove the buds or flowers before rooting. The length of the

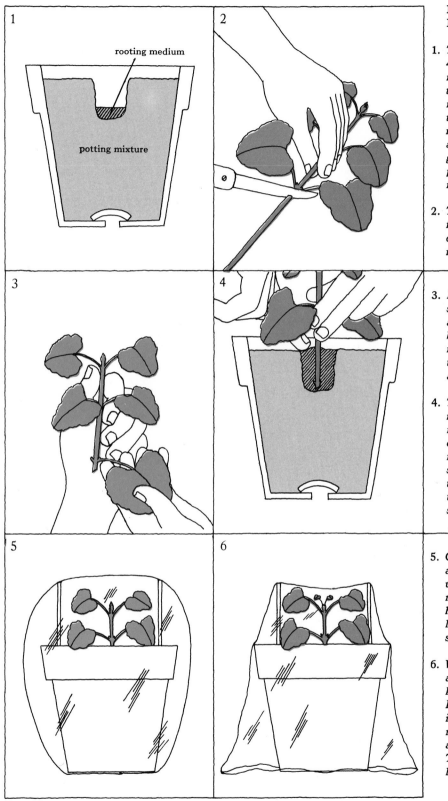

PROPAGATING PLANTS FROM STEM CUTTINGS

1. *To root a stem cutting, first fill a 4- to 5-inch pot with moist potting mixture and scoop out a hole in the center 1 inch across and 1½ inches deep. Fill the hole one third full of a moist mix of peat moss and coarse sand, or sand alone. As new roots form and grow they will spread out into the potting mix to seek nutrients, making transplanting unnecessary.*

2. *Take a cutting up to 6 inches long from the top of a stem, slicing diagonally with a sharp knife or razor blade just below a leaf joint.*

3. *Hold the cutting gently as you strip off the lower leaves and also remove any flowers or flower buds. Moisten the cut end, dip it in rooting powder to stimulate the growth of new roots and shake off any excess powder.*

4. *The cut end is inserted in the rooting medium in the hole, which is then filled to the top with more of the same mixture and tamped firm with the forefinger. Make sure that the stem is in the center, that it remains upright and that the lowest leaves do not touch the soil surface, or they may rot.*

5. *Cover the plant and the pot with a clear plastic food bag propped up on stakes. This holds in moisture and keeps the humidity high. Set the plant in a well-lighted location but not in direct sun, which could burn the leaves.*

6. *When new growth has sprouted and become established, you will know that roots have formed. Before removing the bag, loosen it for two or three days so the new plant will not be shocked by a sudden change in conditions. Then place it in a suitable location and give it normal care.*

THE WALKING IRIS

Neomarica (page 134), a relative of the common iris, spreads across the ground by "walking"; its long stalks repeatedly droop over, take root and grow up again. Given the chance indoors, it will do the same from one pot to another. As its flowers fade, baby plants develop in their place atop each stalk. When the little plants grow large enough, they weigh down the stalk, which bends in a graceful arc until its tip touches down. If the baby plants make contact with moist soil, they will take root, and a new walking iris will rise to begin the odd ambulatory process all over again.

cutting will vary from plant to plant but it usually will be 3 to 6 inches. The exact length of the cutting is determined by the fact that it should contain at least two but not more than six nodes, or joints, where leaves have sprouted; if the leaves have fallen off, nodes manifest themselves by a slight thickening of the stem, like the knuckles on fingers. The best place to cut is about ⅛ inch beneath the lower node. Use a sharp knife or a razor blade, not scissors, which squeeze and often injure the plant cells. It is usually easiest to cut diagonally. Strip off the lowest leaves but retain the upper ones: the cutting will need a few leaves to manufacture food while roots are being established, but it must not have so many that the rootless cutting cannot supply them with enough water. (If you retain too many, you soon will know, for the leaves will wilt; you may be able to save the cutting by stripping off more leaves.)

The simplest way to make the cutting sprout roots is to pop it into a translucent jar of tepid water and put it in a shaded spot, but this system may have drawbacks. Many hardy foliage plants such as English ivy and philodendron will root that way, but flowering plants tend to form weak, brittle roots in water, and I recommend that you use something more solid to initiate a strong root system in the new plants. There are a number of rooting techniques, and normally even-tempered gardeners argue with the vehemence of medieval theologians about which is the best. For most of the methods—whether you are rooting a geranium stem or a begonia leaf—you will need much the same supplies:

○ Rooting hormone, a chemical that stimulates and accelerates root formation. It is obtainable at florists' shops and garden centers, generally in easy-to-use powder form.

○ A potting mixture, prepared to suit the needs of the plant you are rooting *(encyclopedia, Chapter 6).*

○ Enough 4- or 5-inch clay or plastic pots to accommodate each of the cuttings individually.

○ Enough clear plastic food bags from the supermarket to make a miniature greenhouse over each pot.

○ Rooting medium, such as coarse sand, half-and-half coarse sand and peat moss, shredded sphagnum moss, vermiculite (the agricultural type of expanded mica) or perlite.

Coarse sand (but of course not the salty ocean-beach variety) is often the cheapest and most effective medium; it drains well and permits air to get down where the roots are to form. The half-and-half mixture of coarse sand and peat moss retains moisture better than pure sand does, and may be used where extra moisture will speed root formation, as in the case of gardenias and azaleas. Perlite, vermiculite and shredded sphagnum moss also hold water well while permitting air to enter; you might want to try all

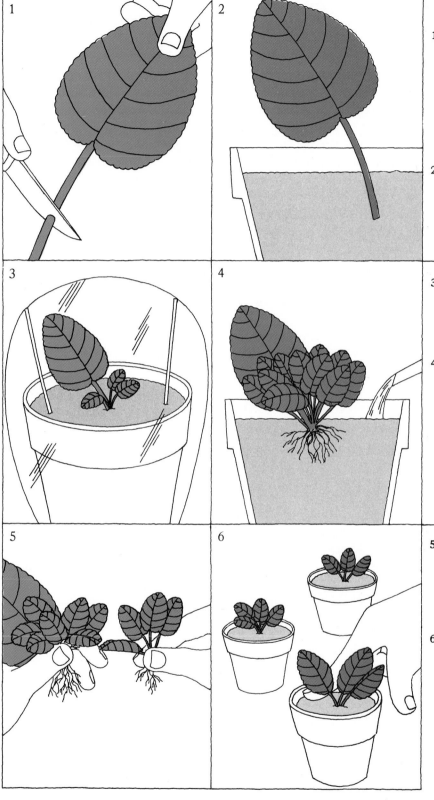

STARTING NEW PLANTS FROM LEAF CUTTINGS

1. *African violets and gloxinias, like other gesneriads without central stalks, are normally propagated from leaf cuttings. Select a medium-sized healthy leaf. Hold the tip with one hand, and with the other hand slice through the stem with a sharp knife about 2 inches below the base of the leaf.*

2. *Insert the stem of the leaf into a pot filled with half sand, half peat moss, perlite or vermiculite. Make sure the stem stands at an angle so that it will not shade the new plants to come at the base.*

3. *Cover the pot with a clear plastic bag, propping it up with pencils, plant markers or stakes. In two to three weeks small shoots should appear at the base of the leaf.*

4. *When the young plants have grown to the point where their leaves are about a third of the size of the parent leaf, loosen the bag for two or three days to allow the new plants to become accustomed to room conditions. Then remove the bag and water so the soil is moist but not soggy. About half an hour later, knock out the pot's contents (drawings, page 52).*

5. *After pulling the clump of shoots free of the parent leaf and shaking off loose soil, separate the individual plants, pulling them apart carefully so as not to injure the fragile new roots.*

6. *Place each of the new plants in an individual pot 2½ to 3 inches in diameter. Gently firm the potting mixture with your fingers to within ½ inch of the pot rim as illustrated on page 51. Soak the plant until water comes out the bottom drainage hole. When the roots finally fill the small pots, transfer the plants to larger ones.*

three to see which works best for you. If you use sphagnum moss, be sure to soak it first in very hot water to make it absorbent; in cold water, it is likely to float and remain impermeable.

ROOTING THE CUTTINGS   Like most lifelong gardeners, I have a favorite way to root a stem cutting. Step-by-step instructions are shown in the sequence of drawings on page 91. The reason I like this method is that it is not necessary to transplant the cutting after it has taken root and become an independent plant. The cutting goes into a little bit of rooting medium that is poured into a cup-shaped hole poked in a potful of potting mixture. After the roots sprout and grow through the rooting medium, they can keep right on growing into the potting mixture that fills the rest of the pot; unlike the rooting medium, this contains nutrients that the new plant now must have. The plant develops completely from a cutting into a flowering specimen right where it is, without any need for repotting.

For successful rooting, take pains with watering and with the use of the hormone powder. Shake a small quantity of rooting powder onto a piece of paper. Dip the cutting's lower end in water, let it drip until it is only barely moist and then dip it into the powder, some of which will stick to it. Then shake the cutting to remove any surplus powder and insert the cut end in the rooting medium.

PROPAGATING BEGONIAS BY VEIN CUTTINGS

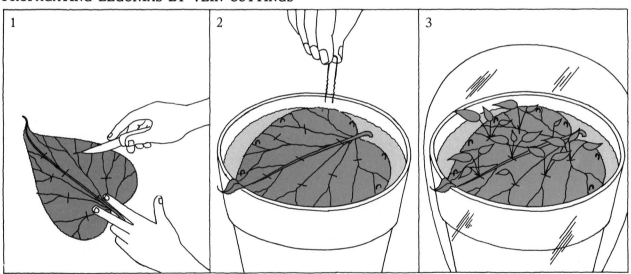

To start a number of rex begonias from a single leaf, cut the leaf from the plant, turn it upside down so that you will be able to see the veins more easily and then make six or seven cuts through the larger veins.

Lay the leaf right side up on moist sand in a pot. Poke the stem into the sand so that moisture can continue to enter the leaf. Keep the cuts in contact with the sand by securing the leaf with hairpins at the edges.

Cover the pot with a plastic bag. In two to three weeks new plants should appear at the slits. When they are 2 inches high, loosen the bag; remove it after two or three days and transfer each plant to its own pot.

Fill in the rest of the cup-shaped hole with more rooting medium and tamp it down so that the cutting stands upright.

After you have watered the pot lightly and placed it in its clear plastic bag, set it in a well-lighted spot out of direct sunshine —a window sill behind a sheer curtain will be just right. Do not water it again unless the inside of the plastic bag looks dry; fine droplets on the bag indicate there is about the right amount of moisture, but if the droplets form large drops that run down the sides, open the bag and drain the excess water out; leave the bottom of the bag slightly loose for a while to make sure excess moisture does not build up again. Then be patient. Rooting takes at least two weeks for most plants, and it may take several months depending on the species, the health of the plant and the time of year you make the cutting. I know of a stubborn 11-year-old girl who waited ten months for an azalea cutting to root. She won—it finally did.

Once the cutting has rooted—you can tell because it will send out new growth—loosen the bag to give the new plant a chance to become acclimated to the conditions of the room. Two or three days later, remove it. The new plant can then be treated like any others of its kind, and allowed to keep on growing where it was born, so to speak, until it gets too big for the pot. This system has one disadvantage—which never bothers me much because I usu-

INCREASING BEGONIAS BY LEAF SECTIONS

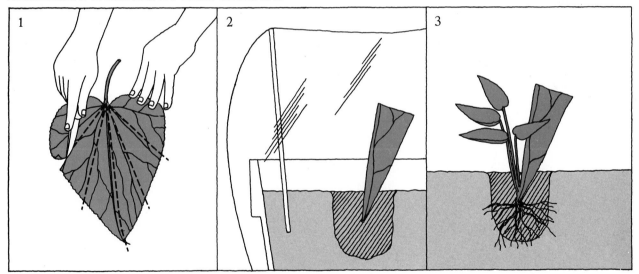

To propagate rex begonias without having to transplant new shoots, turn a leaf upside down and cut the leaf into elongated triangles, each including a main vein and a segment of the stem at the base of the leaf.

Stand each leaf section, point down, in a pot prepared as for stem cuttings (page 91). Cover the pot tightly with a clear plastic bag propped up by stakes; loosen the bag if droplets run down the sides.

In two to three weeks, shoots should appear from the base of the leaf. When they become 2 or 3 inches tall, loosen the bag to let the new plant adjust to room conditions for two or three days. Then remove the bag.

ally start only a few cuttings at a time: you can put only one cutting in a pot. In the conventional method, which uses rooting medium alone, you can put several cuttings in one pot. But then you have to transfer them to separate pots when they have rooted.

STARTING LEAF CUTTINGS   Many house plants, such as African violets and gloxinias, lack stems suitable for cuttings, but they can be rooted from leaf cuttings, for which there are two techniques. The method best suited to African violets and gloxinias involves snipping off a leaf and its petiole, or stem, close to its base with a sharp knife or razor blade. The rooting procedure *(drawings, page 93)* differs from that prescribed for stem cuttings only in three aspects. The leaf stem should be set in the rooting medium at an angle rather than straight up in the manner used for stem cuttings. Then the leaf will not shade the new plants. When the roots have formed, new petioles and leaves will shoot up at the base of the parent stem, and you have to leave room for them. Also, several new plants usually appear, and these are divided by being pulled apart and then planted each in its own pot. Finally, in leaf cuttings, you do not need to use rooting powder.

Rex begonias do not even need a leaf stem from which to send out new roots. They will root from the leaf alone, if you cut the leaf's major veins—the thicker of the lines branching from the stem—and pin the leaf, with hairpins, vein side down on the rooting medium *(drawings, page 94)*. Roots and new plants will start wherever you cut the veins. This works because rex begonias apparently have very vigorous regenerative cells in their veins. They are so vigorous, in fact, that you can even cut a single leaf into wedges and root each wedge separately *(drawings, page 95)*. But each wedge must have at least one major vein in it as well as a piece of the leaf stem—otherwise roots are not likely to form.

NEW PLANTS BY DIVISION   Many plants, notably African violets, develop what horticulturists call multiple crowns; that is, they send up a number of stems from the surface of the soil in clumps or clusters. Although they are joined at the base, like Siamese twins, they are in effect separate plants and dividing them is an easy method of multiplication. When the plant has formed such clumps, knock the whole plant out of its pot; the best time to do this is while plants are dormant, or if they have no dormant period, either before or after the flowering period. Separate the crowns or stems by hand where there are natural divisions that come apart easily; if no natural divisions are obvious, cut them apart with a knife and forestall infection by dusting the cuts with a fungicide powder. Make sure each division has its own set of leaves and roots. Plant each division in a separate pot filled with potting mixture—no rooting medium or hormone is necessary. Just make sure that the stem is planted at the same height in relation to the soil surface as it was before. Water lightly once, then water sparingly until the new plants have become well established.

RUNNERS AND OFFSETS

Strawberry geraniums, episcias and some other plants propagate themselves by sending out runners, trailing stems that creep along the ground and put out roots beneath each cluster of leaves as they go. The easiest way to capitalize on this characteristic in the case of indoor plants is to guide a runner to an adjacent flowerpot filled with potting mixture. Wherever the runner begins to develop leaves, just pin it to the soil with a hairpin: it will root without help from hormone or rooting medium. But do not sever the runner from its parent until the new plant is growing vigorously.

Instead of runners, many bromeliads develop offsets, or shoots, around their bases. You can create a new plant from such a shoot after it has formed roots of its own—poke in the soil mixture to find out. Then simply sever an offset with a sharp knife and set it in its own pot. No hormone treatment is necessary.

NEW PLANTS FROM LAYERING

For plants that have long, flexible branches—jasmines and daphnes, for example—an easy method of vegetative reproduction is soil layering. In this method a branch is notched about halfway

PROPAGATING PLANTS FROM RUNNERS

Plants that develop runners, such as strawberry geraniums, normally multiply by creeping out along the ground, rooting as they go—as the longest runner from the potted plant shown above is attempting to do.

Leaving the runner attached to the parent plant, place it in a separate pot containing potting mixture. Fasten the young plant down with a hairpin behind the leaves growing from the node where roots will form.

When new leaves have appeared in abundance and have begun to fill the pot, the plant has established its own root system; it is no longer dependent on the parent plant and the runner can now be severed.

through on its underside, 4 to 8 inches from its tip. The notch is dusted with rooting powder and buried about half an inch deep in potting mixture—rooting medium is unnecessary—in a pot adjacent to the parent plant. The buried portion is held down with a hairpin or clothespin and the end of the branch is left exposed. When new growth at the tip or around the notch indicates that roots have formed at the notch, the new plant can be severed from its parent. Some plants—calliandras, for example—have inflexible branches and for them soil layering is impracticable, but air layering (*drawings, below*) achieves the same result.

STARTING WITH SEEDS

Vegetative reproduction is the quickest and easiest way of getting new flowering plants, but do not overlook seed propagation if you want lots of plants, and are willing to wait. The essentials for seed

PROPAGATING PLANTS BY AIR LAYERING

1. *A woody plant such as a hibiscus or a camellia can be propagated by a method that is called air layering. First make four or five slits about an inch long around a stem 4 inches from the tip, cutting only through the bark, not into the wood (inset). Dust each of the slits with rooting powder.*

2. *Wrap a clear plastic bag around the stem below the slits and stuff it with moistened sphagnum moss. The bag, of medium-weight food wrap, should be tied with raffia fiber or with cotton string.*

3. *Tie the bag firmly at the top, then wind more raffia or string around the rest of the moss ball to give it support. In a few weeks you should be able to see small roots that have grown out from the slits and are spreading into the moss.*

4. *After about eight weeks, when the moss is filled with roots, the plastic can be removed and the new plant cut free. Sever the stem from the parent just below the moss and pot the new plant, moss and all, in the potting mixture recommended for the parent (see the encyclopedia, Chapter 6).*

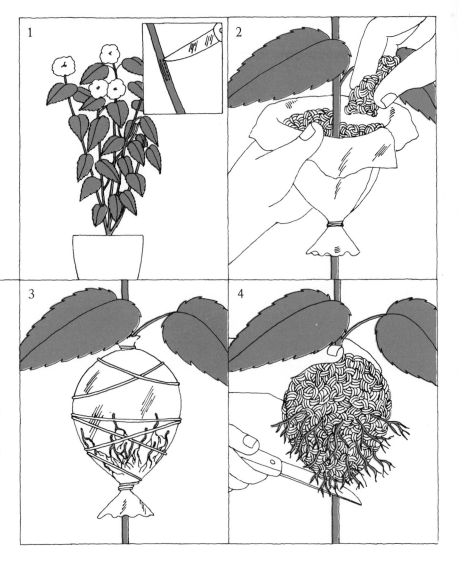

germination are moisture, fresh air and the proper temperature, which for most plants is between 65° and 70°. You will need, besides seeds, milled sphagnum moss, potting mixture, 4-inch pots, and clear plastic bags. Fill each pot with potting mixture and firm the mix with the heel of your hand so that its surface is ½ to ¾ inch below the pot's rim. Then sow the seeds on the surface of the soil. Scatter the seeds sparingly to avoid crowding the future seedlings; each tiny plant must have light, air and soil of its own to thrive and to avoid the common fungus disease known as "damping off," which can kill young seedlings overnight. Unless the seeds are extremely fine, like those of gloxinias and begonias, cover them with a thin layer of dampened milled sphagnum moss, then sprinkle water on the surface with a fine spray, or let the pot stand in a tray of water until the surface appears moist. (Remember to soak sphagnum moss with hot water before you cover seeds with it.) If you are planting very fine seeds, first cover the soil with a ¼-inch layer of moistened sphagnum moss. Then spread a pinch of the seeds sparingly atop the layer of moss—they will slip in to the proper depth. Do not water from the top—you would wash the seeds too deeply into the moss. Instead, let the pot stand in a tray of water until the surface is moist.

The next step is to slip the pot into a clear plastic bag and place it in a well-lighted place out of direct sun. As soon as the seedlings have germinated, take off the plastic bag. Plants that like sun (*encyclopedia*) can be moved into direct sunlight in a few days; others should stay behind a sheer curtain. Do not be tempted to transplant the seedlings as soon as you see what looks like a pair of leaves. Those first deceptive bits of green are not true foliage, but what are called seed leaves. When the first real leaves have appeared—and they will be unmistakably typical of the parent plant —you can transplant each seedling to its own pot.

A GLASS-JAR GREENHOUSE

It is all quite simple, really. But if you want to try something a little different, do as I sometimes do, and substitute a jar for the plastic bag and the pot. I use a square wide-mouthed jar because it will not roll. After cleaning it, I lay it on its side and put in a layer of about ¾ inch of moist potting mixture. I spread the mixture and tamp it lightly with a long spatula, then scatter the seeds sparingly with a long-handled spoon. Then I mist the interior with an atomizer, put the jar's cover on loosely, and set my miniature greenhouse on a window sill behind a sheer curtain until the seedlings are large enough to transplant. The long-handled spoon will get them out. If you keep several jars of seedlings in various stages of growth, you can have an unusual display right in your living room, and you can always delight a visitor with a gift of a young plant.

An encyclopedia of flowering house plants

What colors do African violets come in? Does your living room window provide enough sun for a pot of azaleas? How do you propagate fuchsias? Which species of orchids are most easily grown? These questions, and many others like them, are answered in the following encyclopedic chapter, which lists the characteristics and needs of 145 genera of outstanding flowering house plants.

The entries specify the natural-light requirements of each plant and note those plants especially suited to growing by artificial light. Each entry also includes the preferred ranges of temperature, with emphasis on night temperatures, which are critical if the plant is to get rest for flowering and general health. The need for coolness at night often determines where plants can be located; camellias, daphnes and hyacinths, for example, should have night temperatures of 40° to 50° and thus should be placed in a room that gets little or no heat. But plants are adaptable; if their environment falls short of the ideal, they probably will thrive, though they may grow less vigorously or blossom less spectacularly.

Most flowering house plants respond to standardized growing procedures. Unless a special potting mixture is indicated, use one consisting of 1 part packaged potting soil, 1 part coarse peat moss and 1 part sharp sand or perlite; add 3 to 5 ounces of ground limestone per bushel except where indicated otherwise. Unless a special fertilizer is recommended, use any standard complete fertilizer —that is, a mixture of nitrogen, phosphorus and potassium compounds—specifically designed and labeled for house plants.

All the plants are listed alphabetically by their Latin botanical names, which are recognized throughout the world. In the case of the white Italian bellflower, *Campanula isophylla alba,* for example, the genus name, *Campanula,* is followed by the species name, *isophylla;* the third name, *alba,* indicates the white-flowered variety. Common names are cross-referenced to their Latin equivalents. For quick reference a chart with the characteristics and requirements of the illustrated plants appears on pages 152-154.

A sampling of the year-round color that can be enjoyed indoors is provided by artist Allianora Rosse in a grouping of 24 of the flowering house plants described and illustrated in the following encyclopedia.

FLOWERING MAPLE
Abutilon megapotamicum variegatum

CHENILLE PLANT
Acalypha hispida

MAGIC FLOWER
Achimenes 'Charm'

A

ABUTILON

A. hybridum, A. megapotamicum variegatum, A. striatum thompsonii (all called flowering maple)

Flowering maples, which have maplelike leaves 2 to 3 inches long, bear drooping bell-like flowers about 2 inches across that bloom year round. *A. megapotamicum variegatum* has red-and-yellow blossoms with large, dark brown pollen-bearing anthers; old plants trail as long as 5 feet and are suited to hanging baskets. Bushy varieties, which are generally pruned to stay about 2 feet tall, include *A. striatum thompsonii*, with orange-salmon flowers, and *A. hybridum*, with white, yellow, salmon or purple blooms.

HOW TO GROW. Give flowering maples at least four hours of direct sunlight a day. Night temperatures of 50° to 55° and day temperatures of 68° to 72° are ideal. Keep soil moist and fertilize once a month. Propagate in spring from stem cuttings of new growth or from seeds.

ACALYPHA

A. godseffiana, A. hispida (chenille plant),
A. wilkesiana (copperleaf, beefsteak plant)

The chenille plant is notable for its 8- to 20-inch plumes of fuzzy red flowers, which seem ready-made for drapery fringes; a variety, *A. hispida alba*, bears pinkish white flowers. Both bloom profusely in fall and winter and will blossom the year round under optimum conditions. They have coarse, 3- to 5-inch dark green leaves. The other two species are noted more for their striking foliage than for their flowers, which appear sparsely and only in winter. The 3- to 4-inch-long leaves of *A. wilkesiana* have tones of red, copper and pink; *A. godseffiana* has 2- to 3-inch-long dark green leaves edged with white. All acalyphas are upright, bushy plants that are usually pruned to 2 or 3 feet.

HOW TO GROW. Acalyphas flourish in direct sunlight but will also do well in a bright room without direct sun. Ideal temperatures are 60° to 65° at night and 70° or higher during the day. Keep soil moist and fertilize monthly for continuous bloom. To rejuvenate old plants, prune severely in early spring, leaving only 8 to 12 inches of growth. Propagate from stem cuttings of new growth in summer.

ACHANIA See *Malvaviscus*

ACHIMENES

A. hybrids
(all called magic flower, nut orchid, widow's-tear)

Aglow with masses of satiny flowers 1 to 2½ inches across, achimenes offer a brilliant floral display from spring to fall. Relatives of the African violet, these bushy gesneriads ultimately grow 8 to 12 inches tall; their spreading branches are lined with glistening, often hairy leaves 1½ to 3 inches long. Available colors include pastel blue, deep pink, pure yellow (with silvery foliage), deep red with yellow throats, deep purple and bright rose pink. All are attractive in hanging containers.

HOW TO GROW. Achimenes do best in bright indirect or curtain-filtered sunlight and can be grown in 14 to 16 hours of artificial light a day. Night temperatures of 65° to 70° and day temperatures of 75° or higher are ideal. Plant in a mixture of 2 parts peat moss to 1 part packaged potting soil and 1 part sharp sand or perlite. Keep the mix moist and fertilize monthly during the blooming season. After flowering, let plants die to the ground. Store dormant rhizomes at 60° over winter in plastic bags with dry peat moss, vermiculite or perlite. Propagate during dormancy by dividing the tiny rhizomes that appear on roots or leaf stems, or plant seeds or stem cuttings in spring.

ADAM'S-APPLE See *Ervatamia*

AECHMEA
A. caudata, A. chantinii, A. fasciata (urn plant), *A.* 'Foster's Favorite'

Aechmeas are bromeliads with central floral spikes up to 2 feet tall and 8- to 10-inch-long spiny-edged leaves that form water-holding cups at their bases. *A. caudata* has clusters of beadlike yellow flowers; the leaves of the variety *A. caudata variegata* are striped lengthwise in white. *A. chantinii* has 1½-inch red bracts tipped with yellow, and brownish-green leaves with silver stripes. *A. fasciata* bears pink 1½-inch bracts dotted with tiny blue flowers; its light green leaves have silver bands. A fine hybrid, Foster's Favorite, has wine-red leaves, pendant spikes of dark blue ½-inch flowers and small pear-shaped red berries.

HOW TO GROW. Aechmeas do best in bright indirect or curtain-filtered sunlight, night temperatures of 60° to 65° and day temperatures of 70° or higher. Pot in equal parts of coarse sand and peat moss. Keep the mix moist and fertilize monthly. Keep the cup at the base of the leaves filled with water. Propagate from shoots that appear at the base of the plant after it flowers.

AESCHYNANTHUS, also called TRICHOSPORUM
A. hybrids; *A. parvifolius*, also called *A. lobbianus* (lipstick plant); *A. pulcher* (lipstick plant); *A. speciosus* (all called basketvine)

Basketvines, so named because they are best displayed in hanging containers, are gesneriads with gracefully trailing stems 2 to 3 feet long, tipped with 2- to 4-inch tubular flowers. *A. parvifolius* has waxy, yellow-throated scarlet flowers with deep purple, leaflike outer petals (calyces); the flowers of *A. pulcher* have green calyces. Both bloom in spring, producing buds that resemble lipsticks. *A. speciosus* bears waxy, scarlet-tipped orange flowers in winter and spring. An excellent hybrid, Black Pagoda, provides waxy, brown-specked yellow and green flowers continuously through the year; it has mottled green-and-red foliage.

HOW TO GROW. Basketvines do best in at least four hours of direct sunlight a day in winter and bright indirect or curtain-filtered sunlight the rest of the year. Night temperatures of 65° to 70° and day temperatures of 75° or higher are ideal. Pot in a mixture of 2 parts peat moss to 1 part packaged potting soil and 1 part sharp sand or perlite. Keep the mix moist and fertilize monthly. After the plants flower, cut the stems back to a height of about 6 inches to produce new growth. Propagate from stem cuttings, preferably in spring.

AFRICAN VIOLET See *Saintpaulia*

AGAPANTHUS
A. africanus, also called *A. umbellatus; A.* hybrids; *A. praecox orientalis*, also called *A. orientalis* (all called agapanthus, blue African lily, lily of the Nile)

Agapanthuses are prized for their 1- to 2-foot-long straplike leaves and great clusters of 1- to 4-inch lilylike flowers, which bloom in summer. *A. africanus* bears blue flowers (as many as 30 to a cluster) and grows 18 to 24 inches tall. Among the hybrids, two excellent ones are Peter Pan, with blue flowers atop stalks 12 to 18 inches high, and Dwarf White, with white blooms on 18- to 24-inch stalks. *A. praecox orientalis* is much larger, growing 4 to 5 feet tall and has 100 or more blue or white flowers in a cluster.

HOW TO GROW. Give agapanthuses at least four hours of direct sunlight a day but protect them from direct midday sun in summer. They do best in temperatures of 50° to

URN PLANT
Aechmea fasciata

LIPSTICK PLANT
Aeschynanthus parvifolius

AGAPANTHUS
Agapanthus 'Peter Pan'

55° at night and 68° to 72° during the day. Keep the soil moist and fertilize every two weeks during the growing season; apply less water and no fertilizer the rest of the year. Propagate in February or March by dividing the fleshy roots, or sow seeds in spring. Agapanthuses bloom more profusely if their roots fill the pots.

AGATHAEA See *Felicia*

ALLAMANDA
A. cathartica, A. neriifolia

Allamandas, handsome vines that grow 2 to 4 feet tall, bear fragrant 3- to 5-inch flowers in spring and summer. *A. cathartica* has yellow blossoms; *A. neriifolia* has yellow flowers streaked with orange.

HOW TO GROW. Allamandas do best in at least four hours of direct sunlight a day, night temperatures of 60° to 65° and day temperatures of 70° or higher. Keep the soil moist and fertilize every two weeks from April through September; apply less water and no fertilizer the rest of the year. Propagate from stem cuttings in spring.

ALLOPHYTON See *Tetranema*
ALYSSUM See *Lobularia*
AMARCRINUM See *Crinodonna*
AMARYLLIS See *Hippeastrum*
AMARYLLIS FORMOSISSIMA See *Sprekelia*

ANANAS
A. comosus variegatus, A. nanus (both called pineapple)

A. nanus, the most common pineapple plant grown indoors, has arching, 12- to 15-inch grayish green leaves surrounding a 15-inch spike of red buds resembling a pincushion; the buds open into purple flowers, which are followed by a 2-inch-high, fragrant, edible pineapple. A larger variety of these bromeliads, *A. comosus variegatus,* has green, cream and pink striped leaves that form rosettes 2 feet or more across. Violet flowers atop a 2- to 4-foot spike are followed by a full-sized fruit.

HOW TO GROW. Pineapples do best in at least four hours of direct sunlight a day, night temperatures of 60° to 65° and day temperatures of 70° or higher. Pot in a mixture of 2 parts peat moss to 1 part packaged potting soil and 1 part sharp sand or perlite; do not add lime. Keep moist and fertilize monthly. Propagate from shoots that appear at the base of the plant after it flowers, or plant the rosette of leaves from the top of the fruit.

ANGRAECUM
A. distichum, also called *Mystacidium distichum*

This charming miniature orchid, which grows only 3 to 5 inches tall, may bear 100 or more sweetly fragrant, milky white ¼-inch blossoms, set closely together on loosely spreading 6-inch stems (*photograph, page 55*). The flowers bloom profusely in fall and intermittently through the rest of the year. Thick ¼-inch leaves are folded tightly and evenly on the stems like braids.

HOW TO GROW. *A. distichum* does best in bright indirect sunlight, night temperatures of 55° to 70° and day temperatures of 68° or higher. It grows especially well on a slab of tree fern but will also thrive in a mixture of 2 parts fir bark or shredded tree-fern fiber and 1 part coarse peat moss. Place the pot on a humidifying tray (*page 77*) and keep the potting medium slightly damp at all times. Fertilize monthly with a 20-10-10 or similar high-nitrogen formula diluted ¼ teaspoon per quart of water.

ANGRAECUM FALCATUM See *Neofinetia*

ALLAMANDA
Allamanda cathartica williamsii

PINEAPPLE
Ananas comosus variegatus

ANTHURIUM
A. andreanum (tailflower),
A. scherzerianum (flamingo flower, pigtail plant)

Visitors to the tropics are captivated by the strange pet-allike leaves, or bracts, of anthuriums. The bracts, orange red, pink or white, and glossy as patent leather, bear yellow taillike structures called spadices, on which are crowded the plant's minuscule true flowers. *A. andreanum* has bracts 4 to 6 inches wide atop upright stems 2 to 3 feet tall. *A. scherzerianum,* seldom over 12 inches tall, has nearly oval 2- to 3-inch-long bracts that bear curly spadices. Both species bloom continuously; single bracts last up to a month.

HOW TO GROW. Anthuriums do best in bright indirect or curtain-filtered sunlight, night temperatures of 60° to 65° and day temperatures of 68° or higher. Pot in equal parts of fir bark and coarse sphagnum moss. Set the pot in a humidifying tray *(page 41)*. Keep moist and fertilize every two weeks. As high crowns and aerial roots develop, cover the crowns with moist sphagnum moss. Propagate from small root-bearing side shoots that appear on the stems.

APHELANDRA
A. aurantiaca, A. squarrosa

Favorites in Victorian conservatories, aphelandras, with gaudy flower clusters 4 to 8 inches high, are popular again. Leading varieties are the yellow *A. squarrosa louisae* and the *A. squarrosa* hybrids Brockfeld, Dania and Fritz Prinsler; the scarlet *A. aurantiaca* and the orange-scarlet *A. aurantiaca roezlii.* All blossom for about six weeks in fall, occasionally at other seasons. They are normally pruned to stay 12 to 18 inches tall.

HOW TO GROW. Aphelandras do best in bright indirect or curtain-filtered sunlight, night temperatures of 60° to 65°, day temperatures of 70° or higher. Pot in 2 parts peat moss, 1 part packaged potting soil and 1 part sharp sand or perlite. Place the pot on a humidifying tray *(page 41)*. Keep moist from March through October; give less water the rest of the year. Fertilize every two weeks during flowering. In March cut back half of the previous season's growth and repot. Propagate from stem cuttings in spring.

APOSTLE PLANT See *Neomarica*

ARDISIA
A. crispa, also called *A. crenulata; A. japonica*

Massive clusters of pea-sized red berries give ardisias special appeal at Christmas, when the fruit is mature. The berries often cling to plants for a year, even after the next season's tiny, fragrant, white or red flowers appear in mid-winter or early spring. *A. crispa* may grow 3 feet tall, *A. japonica* 2 feet. After the plants reach 18 to 24 inches, they lose their lower leaves and appear treelike.

HOW TO GROW. Ardisias do best in bright indirect or curtain-filtered sunlight, night temperatures of 50° to 55° and day temperatures of 68° to 72°. Keep soil moist and fertilize every two weeks. To keep the plants bushy, cut them down to 2 inches in early spring; keep the soil quite dry until new shoots appear, then remove all but the three strongest shoots. Repot in fresh soil. Propagate in spring from seeds, stem cuttings or air layers *(page 98)*.

ASTER ROTUNDIFOLIUS See *Felicia*

AZALEA
Many hybrids commonly known as azaleas

Azaleas bear masses of red, pink, white or multicolored 1- to 4-inch blossoms for two to four weeks in late winter or early spring. Plants grow from 6 inches to 2 feet tall.

FLAMINGO FLOWER
Anthurium scherzerianum

APHELANDRA
Aphelandra squarrosa louisae

ARDISIA
Ardisia crispa

AZALEA
Azalea 'Albert-Elizabeth'

WAX BEGONIA
Begonia semperflorens 'Lucy Locket'

HOW TO GROW. Azaleas thrive in at least four hours of direct or very bright indirect sunlight a day, with night temperatures of 40° to 55° and day temperatures of 68° or lower. Pot in a mixture of 2 parts peat moss to 1 part packaged potting soil and 1 part sharp sand or perlite; do not add lime. Keep the potting medium moist. Fertilize with azalea (acid-type) fertilizer every two weeks from the time the flowers fade in spring until new buds form during the late summer; do not fertilize in fall, winter or while plants are flowering. If the leaves lose their rich green color, moisten the soil monthly with a solution of 1 ounce iron sulfate to 2 gallons of water, or iron chelate mixed and applied according to the instructions on the label. Propagate from stem cuttings of new growth.

B

BASKETVINE See *Aeschynanthus*
BEEFSTEAK PLANT See *Acalypha*

BEGONIA
B. rex (rex begonia), *B. semperflorens* (wax begonia), *B. elatior* hybrid (Rieger begonia)

Begonias make up the largest genus of plants suitable for indoor culture. The most popular species, the wax begonia, has satiny flowers that measure less than an inch across. They come in white, salmon pink or rose red, with oval, waxy green or reddish leaves as large as 4 inches. Wax begonias bloom profusely and continuously, growing 6 to 14 inches tall. Rieger begonias, recently introduced from Europe, have bright blossoms with great clusters of 2- to 3-inch red, pink, rose, yellow or orange flowers that bloom for months at a time. Rex begonias bear 1- to 2-inch pink or white flowers usually in the spring, but they are prized most for their large, often hairy leaves, which are shaped like elephant-ears and come in striking shades of green, red, bronze, silver or rose.

HOW TO GROW. Wax and Rieger begonias require at least four hours of direct sunlight a day from November through March, but should be given bright indirect or curtain-filtered light the rest of the year; rex begonias need to be protected from direct sunlight at all times. All three do best in night temperatures of 50° to 60°, day temperatures of 68° to 72°. Pot in a highly organic soil mixture (up to 1 part peat moss to 1 part packaged potting soil). During the growing season, let wax begonias dry slightly between thorough waterings but let the others remain barely damp; withhold moisture from the Rieger begonias when the plants are dormant. Fertilize every two weeks during the growing season. Wax begonias can be grown from seeds or propagated from stem cuttings any time; Rieger begonias can be reproduced from cuttings of young stems taken before flowers appear; rex begonias can be grown from stem or leaf cuttings or by division in summer or fall.

BEGONIA, STRAWBERRY See *Saxifraga*
BELLFLOWER See *Campanula*

BELOPERONE
B. comosa, B. guttata (both called shrimp plant)

The shrimp plant is named for the appearance of its hanging 3- to 4-inch-long formations of petallike bracts from which the tiny white true flowers protrude. The bracts come in yellow, yellow and red, or solid red, depending on the variety. The oval hairy leaves, often as long as the bracts, are pea green, and in the case of *B. comosa* are sometimes bordered in brick red. Both species bloom through the year. Pinch off the tips of stems to keep plants at a height of 12 to 18 inches.

HOW TO GROW. Shrimp plants do best in at least four hours of direct sunlight a day, night temperatures of 50° to 55° and day temperatures of 68° to 72°. Allow soil to become slightly dry between waterings. Fertilize every two weeks. Propagate from pinched-off tips.

BILLBERGIA

B. 'Fantasia,' B. norrida tigrina, B. leptopoda (permanent wave plant), *B. nutans* (Queen's tears), *B. pyramidalis*

Billbergias are bromeliads that bear petallike bracts and tubular flowers on stalks 1 to 2 feet long, each stalk surrounded by straplike leaves that form a water-holding cup. Fantasia produces white-marbled leaves and rose-colored bracts with blue-tipped rose flowers in summer; *B. horrida tigrina* has reddish brown leaves with narrow silver bars and rose-colored bracts with violet-tipped green flowers in late winter; *B. leptopoda* has curly-tipped cream-mottled leaves and rosy red bracts with green-tipped blue flowers in early spring; *B. nutans* has gray-green leaves and rose-colored bracts with blue-edged green flowers in winter; *B. pyramidalis* has gray-barred green leaves and scarlet bracts with blue-tipped crimson flowers in winter.

HOW TO GROW. Billbergias do best in at least four hours of direct sunlight a day, but should be given indirect or curtain-filtered sunlight at midday in summer. Night temperatures of 60° to 65°, day temperatures of 70° or higher are ideal. Use a lime-free mixture of equal parts coarse sand and peat moss. Keep moist; fertilize every two weeks. Keep the cup at the base of the leaves full of water. Propagate from shoots that appear at the base after flowering.

BIRD-OF-PARADISE FLOWER See *Strelitzia*
BLACK-EYED-SUSAN VINE See *Thunbergia*

BOUGAINVILLEA

Bougainvilleas are fast-spreading tropical vines noted for their spectacular clusters of papery 1-inch petallike bracts, which range in color from bright purple through shades of red and pink to copper, yellow and white. A brilliant red variety, Barbara Karst—as well as other varieties, if given ample sun and high temperatures—will blossom almost continuously, but under less than optimum conditions most varieties bloom from early spring to late summer and rest in fall and early winter.

HOW TO GROW. Bougainvilleas do best in at least four hours of direct sunlight a day, night temperatures of 60° to 65° and day temperatures of 70° or higher. Allow the soil to become moderately dry between thorough waterings and fertilize every two weeks during the growing season; omit fertilizer and reduce water while the plants are resting. Repot in very early spring, but do not disturb the roots. Bougainvilleas can be pruned to bush form or trained to a trellis. Propagate from stem cuttings in spring.

BRASSAVOLA

B. nodosa (lady-of-the-night orchid)

Delightfully fragrant from early evening until the middle of the night, *B. nodosa* blooms year round, bearing long-lasting 3- to 4-inch blossoms in white, yellow or pale green, with white flaring lips *(photograph, page 55)*; as many as 50 flowers may be in bloom simultaneously. Plants, which have pencil-shaped leaves, rarely grow taller than a foot.

HOW TO GROW. *B. nodosa* does best in bright indirect sunlight, night temperatures of 55° to 70° and day temperatures of 68° or higher. It can be grown in a mixture of 2 parts fir bark or shredded tree-fern fiber and 1 part coarse peat moss, or simply on a slab of tree fern. Place the pot on a humidifying tray *(page 77)* and let the potting me-

SHRIMP PLANT
Beloperone guttata 'Yellow Queen'

BILLBERGIA
Billbergia 'Fantasia'

BOUGAINVILLEA
Bougainvillea 'Barbara Karst'

107

BROWALLIA
Browallia speciosa major

YESTERDAY, TODAY AND TOMORROW
Brunfelsia calycina

POCKETBOOK FLOWER
Calceolaria herbeohybrida 'Multiflora Nana'

dium become moderately dry between thorough waterings. Fertilize monthly with a 20-10-10 or similar high-nitrogen formula diluted ¼ teaspoon per quart of water.

BRASSIA
B. caudata (spider orchid)

Spider orchids are aptly named for the appearance of their flowers; the fragrant, waxy, long-lasting blooms of *B. caudata (photograph, page 57)* have 2½-inch greenish yellow petals with brown spots and leaflike outer petals or sepals that grow 5 to 8 inches long. Flower spikes 15 inches or more in length bear up to 12 flowers each, usually in fall and early winter. The arching leaves, 8 to 10 inches long, are green with reddish brown spots.

HOW TO GROW. *B. caudata* does best in at least four hours of direct sunlight a day, night temperatures of 65° to 70° and day temperatures of 75° or higher. Pot in a mixture of 2 parts fir bark or shredded tree-fern fiber and 1 part coarse peat moss, or mount on a slab of tree fern. Place the pot on a humidifying tray *(page 77)*. Keep moist; fertilize monthly with a 20-10-10 or similar high-nitrogen formula diluted ¼ teaspoon per quart of water.

BROWALLIA
B. hybrids, B. speciosa major, B. viscosa compacta

Spreading, trailing plants with thin stems that grow up to 3 feet long, browallias bear masses of satiny 1- to 2-inch trumpet-shaped blossoms all year. The hybrid Blue Bells Improved, and a variety of *B. viscosa compacta* called Sapphire are blue flowered; *B. speciosa major* bears blue or white flowers; the hybrid Silver Bells has white flowers.

HOW TO GROW. Browallias need at least four hours of direct sunlight a day from November through February but should have morning sun only and no direct rays the rest of the year. They do best in night temperatures of 55° to 60° and day temperatures of 68° to 72°. Pot in a mixture of 2 parts peat moss to 1 part packaged potting soil and 1 part sharp sand or perlite. Keep moist; fertilize every two weeks, monthly in winter. Propagate from seeds in June or July, or from stem cuttings in August.

BROWALLIA, ORANGE See *Streptosolen*
BROWALLIA JAMESONII See *Streptosolen*

BRUNFELSIA
B. calycina
(yesterday, today and tomorrow; chameleon plant)

This species is named for the changing colors of its sweetly scented, 2-inch flowers, which are dark purple with white eyes the first day they appear, become lavender on the second day and by the third day have turned to white. Under ideal conditions they bloom abundantly all year but generally they rest for a few weeks in late spring.

HOW TO GROW. Brunfelsias do best in at least four hours of direct sunlight a day from November through February, with indirect or curtain-filtered sunlight the rest of the year. Night temperatures of 50° to 55° and day temperatures of 68° to 72° are ideal. Keep soil moist and fertilize every two weeks while the plants are actively growing; use less water and no fertilizer when they are resting. To keep plants compact and bushy, pinch off the ends of the stems periodically; these tips may be rooted in spring.

BURLINGTONIA See *Rodriguezia*
BUTTERCUP, BERMUDA See *Oxalis*

C

CACTUS, CHRISTMAS See *Schlumbergera*

CACTUS, EASTER See *Schlumbergera*
CACTUS, ORCHID See *Epiphyllum*
CACTUS, QUEEN-OF-THE-NIGHT See *Epiphyllum*

CALCEOLARIA

C. herbeohybrida, also called *C. multiflora; C. integrifolia,* also called *C. rugosa* (both called pocketbook flower, slipperwort)

Calceolarias have large leaves up to 6 inches long and saclike two-lipped blossoms up to 2 inches across. The flowers, which bloom profusely in spring, come in red, pink, maroon, bronze or yellow, usually with brown or purple markings. Many strains of *C. herbeohybrida* are available commercially, ranging from 6 to 12 inches in height. *C. integrifolia,* a shrubby type, grows 12 to 24 inches tall and blooms from spring to fall. Calceolarias are difficult to bring to flowering size and are generally bought from florists at blooming time, then discarded when flowering stops.

HOW TO GROW. Calceolarias do best in bright indirect or curtain-filtered sunlight, night temperatures of 40° to 45° and day temperatures of 55° to 60°. Avoid wetting the crowns of thick foliage at soil level; keep the soil barely moist so that it dries by nightfall. Do not fertilize when plants are blossoming. Propagate from seeds in September to flower in March. *C. integrifolia* can also be propagated from stem cuttings in fall.

CALLA LILY See *Zantedeschia*

CALLIANDRA

C. haematocephala, also called *Inga pulcherrima* (red powder puff); *C. inequilatera* (pink powder puff); *C. tweedii* (powder puff, Trinidad flame bush)

Powder puffs are well named, for their 2- to 3-inch flower heads are fluffy with hundreds of delicate, bright red or watermelon-pink stamens. The plants blossom for many weeks during the winter and spring from the time they are about 12 inches tall; their foliage, bronzy when new, is attractive year round. They grow into bushy mounds and are usually kept 2 to 3 feet tall by trimming.

HOW TO GROW. Powder puffs do best in at least four hours of direct sunlight a day, with night temperatures of 60° to 65° and day temperatures of 70° or higher. Keep the soil barely moist. Fertilize monthly from March through September. To shape plants or restrict growth, prune in late spring or early summer, after flowering has ended. Propagate from cuttings of newly grown stems in spring or by air layering any time *(page 98).*

CAMELLIA

C. japonica (common camellia), *C. reticulata* (netvein camellia), *C. sasanqua* (sasanqua camellia)

Camellias are renowned for the perfection of their white, pink, red or multicolored flowers, up to 5 inches across. They bloom profusely for four to six weeks—*C. sasanqua* usually in October and November, *C. japonica* and *C. reticulata* from mid-September to mid-April, depending upon the variety. The plants have oval, dark green leaves up to 4 inches long, and are usually pruned back to keep their height at about 2½ to 3 feet.

HOW TO GROW. Camellias do best in bright indirect or curtain-filtered sunlight, night temperatures of 40° to 45° and daytime temperatures of 68° or lower. Pot in a mixture composed of 2 parts peat moss, 1 part packaged potting soil and 1 part sharp sand or perlite; do not add lime. Keep the potting medium well moistened at all times and feed with a camellia-azalea-rhododendron (acid-type) fertilizer or a dusting of cottonseed meal in early spring, late

PINK POWDER PUFF
Calliandra inequilatera

COMMON CAMELLIA
Camellia japonica 'Debutante'

109

WHITE ITALIAN BELLFLOWER
Campanula isophylla alba

ORNAMENTAL PEPPER
Capsicum annuum conoides

NATAL PLUM
Carissa grandiflora nana compacta

spring and midsummer. To produce large blossoms, snap off all but one bud in each cluster. To restrict plant size, prune after all flowering has stopped. Propagate from stem cuttings in June.

CAMPANULA
C. elatines (Elatine bellflower), *C. fragilis* (fragile bell-flower), *C. isophylla* (Italian bellflower)

Bellflowers bear an abundance of 1- to 1½-inch flowers from midsummer until late fall, purplish in *C. elatines,* purplish blue with white centers in *C. fragilis,* pale blue in *C. isophylla mayii* and white in *C. isophylla alba.* All have trailing 6- to 12-inch stems that make them ideal for hanging containers.

HOW TO GROW. Bellflowers do best in at least four hours of direct sunlight a day, except in midsummer, when they should be given bright indirect or curtain-filtered sunlight. Night temperatures of 50° to 55° and day temperatures of 68° to 72° are ideal. Plant in a potting mixture composed of 2 parts peat moss to 1 part packaged potting soil and 1 part sharp sand or perlite. Keep the mixture evenly moist and fertilize monthly during the growing season, usually March through November; leave the mixture slightly dry, without any fertilizer, during the rest of the year. Propagate from stem cuttings in spring.

CAPE COWSLIP See *Lachenalia*

CAPSICUM
C. annuum (ornamental pepper)

This species is notable not for its tiny white flowers, but for its masses of colorful, pungent fruit. The 2- to 3-inch-long peppers, a form of chili pepper, appear in summer and fall and change colors as they ripen—green, white, yellow, red or purple fruits sometimes appearing simultaneously on a single plant. The plants, which begin to bear fruit when they are six to eight months old, grow about a foot high.

HOW TO GROW. Ornamental pepper plants do best in at least four hours of direct sunlight a day, night temperatures of 60° to 65° and day temperatures of 70° or higher. Keep the soil moist but do not fertilize. Plants are treated as annuals and should be discarded when no longer attractive; propagate from seeds in early spring.

CARDINAL FLOWER See *Rechsteineria*

CARISSA
C. grandiflora (Natal plum)

The charm of the Natal plum lies in its rich green, closely set 1-inch-long oval leaves and fragrant flowers, 1½ to 2 inches across, which are followed by 1½- to 2-inch scarlet fruits that look like plums but taste like cranberries. The flowers are apt to bloom at any time of the year, often when ripe fruit is still clinging to the branches. Bushy, spreading dwarf varieties such as Boxwood Beauty or *C. grandiflora nana* rarely grow over 18 to 24 inches tall, and they can be kept even smaller by pruning.

HOW TO GROW. Natal plums do best in at least four hours of direct sunlight a day, night temperatures of 50° to 65° and day temperatures of 68° or higher. Keep moist; fertilize every three or four months. The dwarf varieties may be propagated from stem cuttings at any time.

CATTLEYA
C. gaskelliana, C. labiata, C. mossiae (Easter orchid), *C. trianae* (Christmas orchid)

The most familiar of all orchids, commonly used in corsages, cattleyas are easy-to-grow house plants whose showy

5- to 7-inch flowers appear atop 12- to 18-inch stalks. *C. labiata* (*photograph, page 55*) bears two to seven ruffle-lipped blossoms in fall; the flowers vary from dark mauve and rose to pure white or white with a rosy lip, often with yellow throats. *C. trianae* produces light pink to deep lavender flowers, singly or in clusters of up to five, between November and February. *C. mossiae* bears two to five rosy lavender flowers on each stalk in spring. *C. gaskelliana*, a fragrant, slightly shorter species, bears 10- to 14-inch spikes of up to five medium to dark lavender flowers in summer.

HOW TO GROW. Cattleyas do best in at least four hours of direct sunlight a day but should be shielded from hot sun during midday. They flourish in night temperatures of 55° to 65° and day temperatures of 68° or higher. Pot in a mixture of 2 parts fir bark or shredded tree-fern fiber and 1 part coarse peat moss. Place the pot on a humidifying tray (*page 77*) and let the potting medium become moderately dry between thorough waterings. Fertilize monthly with a 20-10-10 or similar high-nitrogen formula diluted ¼ teaspoon per quart of water.

CESTRUM
C. diurnum (day-blooming jasmine), *C. nocturnum* (night-blooming jasmine), *C. parqui* (willow-leaved jasmine)

Like other plants called jasmines, cestrums are extremely fragrant. Their white to greenish yellow blossoms, about 1 inch long, bloom in clusters intermittently all year, followed usually by black berries. *C. diurnum*, fragrant by day, has glossy 3- to 4-inch-long leaves. *C. nocturnum* is fragrant at night; the berries are white, the thin oval leaves may grow up to 8 inches long. *C. parqui*, also fragrant at night, has willowlike leaves 2 to 5 inches long. All species are gangling but can be kept under 2 feet tall by periodically pinching off the stem tips.

HOW TO GROW. Cestrums do best in at least four hours of direct sunlight a day, night temperatures of 60° to 65° and day temperatures of 70° or higher. Keep the soil moist; fertilize every three to four months. To encourage branching, prune old growth after flowers fade. Propagate by stem cuttings at any time.

CHAMELEON PLANT See *Brunfelsia*
CHENILLE PLANT See *Acalypha*
CHERRY, BARBADOS See *Malpighia*
CHERRY, CLEVELAND See *Solanum*
CHERRY, JERUSALEM See *Solanum*
CHERRY PIE See *Heliotropium*
CHINCHERINCHEE See *Ornithogalum*

CHIRITA
C. lavandulacea, C. sinensis

The most common of these gesneriads, *C. lavandulacea*, bears flowers about 1¼ inches across, with flaring lavender lobes and white throats, from late summer through most of the following year but lasts only a year. The soft, hairy leaves may be up to 8 inches long, and plants grow 12 to 24 inches tall. *C. sinensis*, a tuberous-rooted summer-flowering species bearing clusters of tiny lavender flowers, grows only 6 inches tall and forms a rosette of elliptical, dark green, hairy leaves blotched with silver.

HOW TO GROW. Chiritas do best in at least four hours of direct sunlight a day in winter, abundant but indirect light at other times. *C. sinensis* can also be grown under 14 to 16 hours a day of artificial light. Night temperatures of 65° to 70° and day temperatures of 75° or higher are ideal. Keep moist; place the pot on a humidifying tray (*page 41*). Fertilize monthly during the growing season. Propagate from stem cuttings at any time.

NIGHT-BLOOMING JASMINE
Cestrum nocturnum

CHIRITA
Chirita lavandulacea

TOP: MARGUERITE
Chrysanthemum frutescens   BOTTOM: FLORISTS' CHRYSANTHEMUM
Chrysanthemum morifolium 'Princess Anne'

OTAHEITE ORANGE
Citrus taitensis

CHRYSANTHEMUM
C. frutescens (marguerite, Boston or Paris daisy); *C. morifolium,* also called *C. hortorum* (florists' chrysanthemum)

Marguerites produce great numbers of daisylike white, yellow or pink flowers, 2 to 3 inches across, that bloom intermittently throughout the year; their gray-green, lacy leaves are 3 to 6 inches long. Plants start to blossom when 6 inches tall and can be kept to less than 18 inches by pinching off the tips of stems. Florists' chrysanthemums, on the other hand, blossom for only two or three weeks and are prized for their quantities of white, golden yellow, bronze, maroon, pink or lavender flowers, which come in many shapes and sizes.

HOW TO GROW. Marguerites need at least four hours of direct sunlight a day. They do best in night temperatures of 40° to 55° and day temperatures of 68° or lower. Keep the soil moist; fertilize every two weeks. Propagate any time from stem cuttings. Treat florists' chrysanthemums the same as marguerites, but keep them out of direct sun when flowering. They may be planted in the garden when the flowers fade; if they survive they will revert to their normal fall flowering. Propagate by stem cuttings or division in early spring.

CIGAR PLANT See *Cuphea*
CINERARIA See *Senecio*

CITRUS
C. limonia (lemon); *C. mitis* (calamondin or Panama orange); *C. reticulata,* also called *C. nobilis deliciosa* (tangerine, Temple orange or Satsuma orange); *C. sinensis* (sweet or common orange); *C. taitensis,* also called *C. otaitense* (Otaheite orange)

The fragrant inch-sized blossoms of citrus plants bloom intermittently throughout the year, but most profusely in spring and fall; the fruit follows the flowers and often stays on the plants for many months. Most plants started from cuttings begin to flower and fruit in their first year and may be kept under 4 feet in height indefinitely by pinching off the tips of stems. Among the best varieties for indoor gardeners are *C. limonia meyeri,* whose fruits are somewhat less acid than ordinary lemons; *C. limonia ponderosa,* which bears quantities of edible lemons that may be up to 5 inches in length and as much as 2½ pounds in weight; *C. mitis,* which generally grows less than 2 feet high indoors and produces tart oranges an inch or less in diameter; *C. reticulata,* whose varieties produce tangerines, Temple oranges and Satsuma oranges; *C. sinensis,* which bears full-sized oranges that make delicious eating; and *C. taitensis,* which produces a heavy crop of tart oranges, each only an inch or so in diameter.

HOW TO GROW. Citrus plants need at least four hours of direct sunlight a day, night temperatures of 50° to 55° and day temperatures of 68° to 72°. Let the soil dry slightly between waterings. Fertilize in very early spring, early summer and late summer. To control size, pinch off new growth any time. Propagate from stem cuttings taken between midsummer and late fall.

CLERODENDRON See *Clerodendrum*

CLERODENDRUM, also called CLERODENDRON
C. fallax, also called *C. speciosissimum; C. fragrans pleniflorum; C. thomsonae* (glory bower)

Clerodendrums are large plants well suited to big pots and tubs, but they may be kept at a height of 2 to 3 feet by pinching off the tips of stems. All species bear large clusters of 1- to 2-inch flowers. *C. fallax* blooms in summer, bearing bright red blossoms. *C. fragrans pleniflorum,* with hyacinth-scented blush-white blossoms, blooms intermittently through the year. *C. thomsonae* trails beautifully from hanging baskets. It bears snow-white flowers, balloon-like at the base, with flaring scarlet petals; the flowers bloom in spring and summer, sometimes into winter if given enough warmth.

HOW TO GROW. Clerodendrums do best in bright indirect or curtain-filtered sunlight, night temperatures of 60° to 65° and day temperatures of 70° or higher. Keep the potting mixture well moistened while the plants are growing, and on the dry side while they are resting. Fertilize every two weeks during the growing season only. To produce more flowers, which are borne only on new growth, prune the plants after they have stopped blooming. Propagate from stem cuttings in spring.

GLORY BOWER
Clerodendrum thomsonae

CLIVIA
C. cyrtanthiflora, C. miniata (both called Kafir lily)

Kafir lilies, bulb plants that bloom in winter, bear clusters of 12 to 20 brilliantly colored lilylike flowers, up to 3 inches across, atop 12- to 15-inch stalks that rise from waxy, dark green, straplike leaves 18 to 24 inches long. *C. miniata* bears orange to scarlet blossoms with yellow throats; *C. cyrtanthiflora* has salmon-pink flowers.

HOW TO GROW. Kafir lilies do best in bright indirect or curtain-filtered sunlight, night temperatures of 50° to 55° and day temperatures of 68° to 72°. From midwinter until late summer, let the soil become slightly dry between thorough waterings and fertilize every month or two with a standard house-plant fertilizer. In the fall let the plants rest without fertilizer and with only enough moisture to keep them from wilting. Propagate in late spring from the small bulbs that develop around the large ones. Since Kafir lilies bloom more abundantly if their roots are not disturbed, repot them only when the plants become extremely overcrowded (about every three or four years).

KAFIR LILY
Clivia miniata

COFFEA
C. arabica (Arabian coffee)

At the bases of their 4- to 6-inch-long, glossy green leaves, Arabian coffee plants bear clusters of sweetly scented, ¾-inch white flowers intermittently throughout the year; these mature into pulpy, glistening red, ½-inch berries. Within each berry are two seeds, the "beans" from which coffee is made. Plants, which do not begin to blossom or bear fruit until they are three or four years old, grow upright to a height of 4 feet or more unless the tips of stems are pinched off.

HOW TO GROW. The Arabian coffee plant does best in curtain-filtered sunlight, night temperatures of 60° to 65° and day temperatures of 70° or higher. Keep the soil evenly moist; fertilize every two weeks from March to October, monthly the rest of the year. Try to avoid touching the leaves, which are thin and tender. Propagate from seeds at any time or from cuttings of upright-growing tips. Do not attempt to propagate from cuttings of side branches, since they generally develop into poorly shaped plants.

COLUMNEA
C. affinis, C. gloriosa, C. linearis, C. hybrids

Ablaze with tubular 2- to 4-inch flowers through the year, columneas are tropical trailing plants from Central and South America that make stunning displays in hanging containers. The leaves of these gesneriads, set in pairs and often hairy, grow 1 to 5 inches long, and stems reach 4 feet if their tips are not pinched off. *C. affinis* has yellow

ARABIAN COFFEE
Coffea arabica

COLUMNEA
Columnea 'Yellow Dragon'

CRINODONNA
Crinodonna corsii

CRINUM
Crinum 'Ellen Bosanquet'

flowers covered with orange hairs; *C. gloriosa,* red blossoms with yellow throats; *C. linearis,* rosy pink flowers with white hairs. Three excellent hybrids are Anna C. (dark crimson flowers), Early Bird (orange red with yellow bases) and Yellow Dragon (bright yellow). The blossoms are frequently followed by ½-inch white oval fruit.

HOW TO GROW. Columneas do best in bright indirect or curtain-filtered sunlight, but they also grow well in 14 to 16 hours of artificial light a day. Night temperatures of 65° to 70° and day temperatures over 75° are ideal. (Columnea species should be given night temperatures of 50° to 60° in winter to assure full flowering.) Plant in a mixture of 2 parts peat moss to 1 part packaged potting soil and 1 part sharp sand or perlite; keep the mix moist and fertilize monthly. To encourage new branches, prune the plants after a period of flowering. Propagate in summer from stem cuttings, root divisions or seeds.

COPPERLEAF See *Acalypha*
CORAL PLANT See *Russelia*

CRINODONNA
C. corsii, also called *Amarcrinum howardii*

Crinodonnas bear great clusters of fragrant pink flowers, some as large as 4 inches in diameter, in late summer and early fall. The blossoms appear atop 3-foot-high stalks that are surrounded by dark green straplike leaves 1½ to 3 inches wide and up to 2 feet long.

HOW TO GROW. Crinodonnas do best in at least four hours of direct sunlight a day, with night temperatures of 50° to 55° and day temperatures of 68° to 72°. Keep soil moist and fertilize monthly during the growing season; reduce moisture and do not feed while plants are dormant over the winter. Plant 3- to 4-inch bulbs, one bulb to a 6- to 8-inch pot, as soon as they are available in late summer or early fall; leave the top third of the bulb out of the soil. Crinodonnas bloom best when their roots are undisturbed, so repot only after three or four years. Propagate from the small bulbs that develop alongside larger ones.

CRINUM
C. bulbispermum, C. hybrids, *C. moorei* (all called crinum, Bengal lily, milk-and-wine lily)

Crinums are majestic bulb plants whose massive, fragrant clusters of 3- to 6-inch lilylike flowers bloom atop 2- to 3-foot stalks in late summer and fall; arching out from the base of the stalks are straplike leaves 2 to 4 feet long. *C. bulbispermum* bears rosy red blossoms with white inside; the hybrid Ellen Bosanquet has wine-red flowers; the Cecil Houdyshel hybrid, light pink blooms; *C. moorei* bears blush-pink flowers.

HOW TO GROW. Crinums do best in at least four hours of direct sunlight a day (curtain-filtered sunlight during the hottest part of the summer), night temperatures of 50° to 55° and day temperatures of 68° to 72°. Keep the soil moist and fertilize monthly during the growing season (April through September). Let the soil become slightly dry and do not fertilize when the plants are resting. Propagate in early spring from the small bulbs that develop beside larger ones.

CROCUS
Many species and hybrids known as crocus

Harbingers of spring, the many species and hybrids of crocuses make fine midwinter pot plants, growing 4 to 5 inches high and sending up 2-inch cup-shaped blossoms just as the slender, grasslike leaves begin to emerge from the corms, or thickened underground stems. Among the particularly attractive types available are Pickwick (with blossoms striped pale and deep lilac), Jeanne d'Arc (white), Little Dorrit (amethyst blue), Remembrance (purple) and E. P. Bowles (buttercup yellow).

HOW TO GROW. Crocuses do best in at least four hours of direct sunlight a day, night temperatures of 40° to 45° and day temperatures of 68° or lower. Keep the soil well moistened as long as the foliage is green; do not fertilize at any time. Crocuses are often bought as fully blossoming plants from florists or nurseries in the midwinter months, but they may also be started from large-sized dormant corms; plant the corms in pots in October and keep them in a cold frame until mid-January or later, at which time they may be brought indoors.

CROSSANDRA
C. infundibuliformis (firecracker flower), also called *C. undulaefolia*

House plants with pastel, salmon-orange flowers that bloom year round are rare—a fact that makes crossandras interesting selections for indoor gardens. Overlapping blossoms appear above dark green leaves, 2 to 3 inches long. The plants begin to bloom seven to nine months after they are started from seed, and grow about a foot tall.

HOW TO GROW. Crossandras do best in at least four hours of direct sunlight a day except during the hottest part of the year, when they should be protected by a sheer curtain or blind. Night temperatures of 60° to 65° and day temperatures of 70° or higher are ideal. Plant in a mixture of 2 parts peat moss to 1 part packaged potting soil and 1 part sharp sand or perlite; keep the potting medium well moistened at all times and fertilize every two weeks year round. Propagate from seeds in spring or from stem cuttings made at any time of the year.

CRYPTANTHUS
C. bivittatus, also called *C. rosea picta; C. fosteriana; C.* 'It'; *C. zonatus zebrinus* (all called earth star)

The bromeliads known as earth stars derive their name from the starlike spread of their flat, oddly marked leaves, which surround clusters of tiny flowers. The plants listed here bear white blossoms in summer and differ mainly in foliage. *C. bivittatus* has bronze-green leaves with lengthwise white stripes; *C. fosteriana* has chocolate-brown leaves with zebralike gray stripes; the hybrid It, dull green with orange-pink and cream stripes; and *C. zonatus zebrinus,* reddish brown leaves with zigzag silvery bands. All of them spread about a foot or more except *C. bivittatus,* which grows only 4 to 6 inches across.

HOW TO GROW. Earth stars do best in bright indirect or curtain-filtered sunlight, night temperatures of 60° to 65° and day temperatures of 70° or higher. Plant in a mixture of 2 parts peat moss to 1 part packaged potting soil and 1 part sharp sand or perlite; do not add lime. Allow the mixture to dry slightly between waterings and fertilize monthly from midspring through early fall. Propagate from shoots that appear at the base of the plant between the leaves.

CUPHEA
C. hyssopifolia (elfin herb), *C. ignea,* also called *C. platycentra* (cigar plant), *C. miniata* 'Firefly'

Cupheas are low bushy plants that grow 6 to 10 inches high and bloom abundantly all year round. A favorite for generations has been the cigar plant, which gets its name from its ¾-inch-long, cigar-shaped scarlet flowers, complete with ashlike tips; varieties of the plant are available in lavender, pink, rose, purple and white. Two other types produce tiny bell-like flowers—elfin herb with lavender

CROCUS
Crocus 'Pickwick'

FIRECRACKER FLOWER
Crossandra infundibuliformis

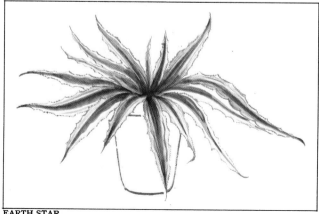

EARTH STAR
Cryptanthus 'It'

blooms, and Firefly with bright red blooms. All have inch-long green leaves that turn red at the edges in the sun and are oval in shape, except for the elfin herb, which has needlelike leaves.

HOW TO GROW. Cupheas do best in at least four hours of direct sunlight a day, night temperatures of 50° to 55° and day temperatures of 68° to 72°. Keep the soil moist; fertilize every two weeks. Propagate any time from stem cuttings or seeds. Cupheas started from seeds begin to flower when they are about four or five months old.

CYCLAMEN
C. persicum, C. 'Puck'

Among the loveliest of house plants, cyclamens bear 2- to 3-inch flowers whose petals sweep up like the wings of butterflies. The flowers bloom in shades of pink, red and white above thick dark green leaves that often have silvery markings. Plants blossom profusely from midautumn until midspring and grow about a foot tall. The hybrid known as Puck grows only 6 inches tall; its rose-pink flowers bloom much of the year.

HOW TO GROW. Cyclamens do best in bright indirect or curtain-filtered sunlight, night temperatures of 40° to 55° and day temperatures of 65° or lower. Plant in a mixture of 2 parts peat moss to 1 part packaged potting soil and 1 part sharp sand or perlite. Keep the mixture moist; fertilize every two weeks. Repot when necessary after the plant stops flowering, placing the beetlike root at least half out of the fresh potting mixture. Plants may be propagated from seeds in early spring. Puck reaches blooming size in four to six months, but *C. persicum* strains require 15 to 18 months to bloom so most gardeners purchase these plants from florists when they are already in flower.

CYMBIDIUM
C. hybrid miniatures

Miniature cymbidium orchids rarely grow more than 12 inches high but bear spikes of up to 30 flowers, 2 to 3 inches across, that range in color from mahogany, bronze and maroon to green, yellow, pink and white. The blossoms open from fall to spring, depending upon the variety, and often last for two to three months. The one shown in the photograph on page 55 is Minuet, a pinkish brown cymbidium introduced in 1931 as the first hybrid miniature.

HOW TO GROW. Miniature cymbidiums do best in at least four hours of direct sunlight a day but should be protected from hot midday sun to keep the leaves from turning brown. Night temperatures of 50° to 60° and day temperatures of 68° or higher are ideal. Plant in equal parts of fir bark, redwood-bark fiber and coarse peat moss. Place the pot on a humidifying tray *(page 77)*. Keep the mixture wet and fertilize monthly with a 20-10-10 or similar high-nitrogen formula diluted ¼ teaspoon per quart of water.

CYPRIPEDIUM See *Paphiopedilum*

D
DAFFODIL See *Narcissus*
DAISY, BLUE See *Felicia*
DAISY, BOSTON See *Chrysanthemum*
DAISY, KINGFISHER See *Felicia*
DAISY, PARIS See *Chrysanthemum*

DAPHNE
D. odora, also called *D. indica, D. sinensis*
(winter daphne)

D. odora lives up to its botanical name with a notable sweet fragrance. Clusters of ½-inch-wide pink to reddish

CIGAR PLANT
Cuphea ignea

CYCLAMEN
Cyclamen persicum giganteum

purple flowers bloom indoors from November until March. The 2- to 3-inch-long leaves are a shiny, leathery green and are edged with creamy yellow in the variety *D. odora marginata*. Plants are usually kept to a height of 1 to 2 feet by pruning them back.

HOW TO GROW. Winter daphne does best in bright indirect or curtain-filtered sunlight, night temperatures of 40° to 45° and day temperatures of 68° or lower. Keep the soil barely damp. A single feeding of slow-acting azalea-rhododendron-camellia (acid-type) fertilizer or cottonseed meal in early spring is sufficient for the year. Propagate in summer from stem cuttings or by air layering (*page 98*).

DENDROBIUM
D. loddigesii

Of the hundreds of orchids in the *Dendrobium* genus, one of the best for indoor culture is *D. loddigesii,* whose 1½- to 2-inch, fragrant long-lasting flowers bloom in late winter or early spring. The blossoms, lilac pink with oversized orange-centered lips, appear singly all along the trailing stems above 3-inch leaves (*photograph, page 57*).

HOW TO GROW. *D. loddigesii* does best in bright indirect or curtain-filtered sunlight, with night temperatures of 50° to 60° and day temperatures of 60° to 70°. It can be grown on a slab of tree fern or in a mixture of 2 parts fir bark or shredded tree-fern fiber and 1 part coarse peat moss. Keep the potting medium well moistened during the growing season and place the pot on a humidifying tray (*page 77*). Fertilize monthly from spring through midfall with a 20-10-10 or similar high-nitrogen formula diluted ¼ teaspoon per quart of water. In late fall and winter, withhold fertilizer and provide only enough water to keep the plant from shriveling.

DIPLADENIA
D. amoena; D. boliviensis; D. sanderi rosea; D. splendens, also known as *Mandevillea splendens*

These handsome vines bear masses of silky 2½- to 3-inch flowers, much like those of morning glories, among glossy 1- to 2-inch leaves. *D. amoena,* with rose-pink flowers, and *D. boliviensis,* with white flowers, usually blossom from March through September; *D. sanderi rosea,* with salmon-pink flowers, blooms continuously through the year. *D. splendens* bears pinkish white flowers up to 4 inches across in summer. Plants begin to flower when they are less than 1 foot in height, and may easily be kept below 3 feet in height by pinching off the tips of the stems.

HOW TO GROW. Dipladenias do best in bright indirect or curtain-filtered sunlight, night temperatures of 60° to 65° and day temperatures of 70° or higher. Allow soil to become slightly dry between thorough waterings; fertilize every two weeks except when the plants are resting. Propagate by stem cuttings in early spring.

DOUBLE-DECKER PLANT See *Rechsteineria*

DYCKIA
D. brevifolia, also called *D. sulphurea;*
D. fosteriana 'Silver Queen'

In summer these bromeliads bear 15 to 20 waxy flowers, each ½ to 1 inch long, on a slender, 1- to 2-foot branching stalk that rises above stiff rosettes of arching leaves. *D. brevifolia* has bright orange, tubular flowers above dark green leaves; the variety called Silver Queen has orange-red flowers set above scalloped, silvery gray leaves.

HOW TO GROW. Dyckias do best in full sun or very light shade, night temperatures of 50° to 55° and day temperatures of 68° to 72°. Pot in a mixture composed of 2 parts

WINTER DAPHNE
Daphne odora

DIPLADENIA
Dipladenia amoena

117

DYCKIA
Dyckia fosteriana 'Silver Queen'

ORCHID CACTUS
Epiphyllum hermosissimus

EPISCIA
Episcia 'Ember Lace'

peat moss, 1 part packaged potting soil and 1 part sharp sand or perlite; do not add lime. Allow the potting medium to become moderately dry between thorough waterings; fertilize every two weeks. Propagate from the new shoots that appear at the base of the plants.

E

EARTH STAR See *Cryptanthus*
EDELWEISS, BRAZILIAN See *Rechsteineria*
EGYPTIAN STAR CLUSTER See *Pentas*
ELFIN HERB See *Cuphea*

EPIDENDRUM
E. cochleatum (clamshell orchid)

This orchid is noted for the purplish black and green, clamshell-shaped lip and slender, 2½- to 3½-inch yellowish green petals of its flowers, which hang gracefully upside down in clusters of three to 10 from the top of 8- to 10-inch flower spikes *(photograph, page 58)*. The faintly fragrant flowers may appear at any time of the year, some plants blooming almost continuously.

HOW TO GROW. *E. cochleatum* does best in bright indirect sunlight, night temperatures of 50° to 65° and day temperatures of 68° or higher. It can be grown on a slab of tree fern or potted in a mixture composed of 2 parts fir bark or shredded tree-fern fiber and 1 part coarse peat moss. Place the pot on a humidifying tray *(page 77)* and keep the potting medium abundantly moistened. Fertilize monthly with a 20-10-10 or similar high-nitrogen formula diluted ¼ teaspoon per quart of water.

EPIPHYLLUM
E. ackermannii, also called *Nopalxochia ackermannii; E. oxypetalum,* also called *Phyllocactus latifrons* (queen of the night); *E.* hybrids (all called orchid cactus)

Without spines or leaves but ornamented by richly colored flowers, the orchid cactus is one of the most spectacular flowering plants in cultivation. Blossoms, which are often fragrant, appear directly from soft, waxy stems that consist of flattened or ribbed sections loosely joined together. Although orchid cacti usually bloom in the spring, a number of hybrids, such as *E. hermosissimus,* are winter flowering. There are also day- and night-flowering types. Plants range from 12-inch window-sill specimens to giants 5 to 6 feet tall, and flowers vary in size from 2½ to 10 inches across. In addition to the hybrids, of which there are thousands, two good house-plant species are *E. ackermannii,* whose many 4- to 6-inch scarlet flowers open mainly in the daytime, and *E. oxypetalum,* sometimes called "queen of the night" because its waxy, white, 4- to 6-inch flowers open in the evening.

HOW TO GROW. Orchid cacti do best in bright indirect or curtain-filtered sunlight, night temperatures of 50° to 55° and day temperatures of 68° to 72°. (Higher night temperatures in winter cause stems rather than flower buds to grow.) Pot in a mixture of 2 parts peat moss to 1 part packaged potting soil and 1 part sharp sand or perlite. Keep the mix moist and fertilize every two weeks from April to August with a low-nitrogen house-plant fertilizer such as 5-10-10; keep fairly dry and omit fertilizer the rest of the year. Propagate from stem cuttings in summer.

EPISCIA
E. dianthiflora, E. hybrids, *E. lilacina, E. punctata* (all called episcia, flame violet)

Episcias, gesneriads well suited to hanging containers, have handsome 2- to 3-inch leaves and dainty ½- to 1½-inch flowers that bloom continuously from early spring to early fall. *E. dianthiflora* bears downy green leaves and white flowers, *E. lilacina* has dark bronze leaves and lavender flowers, *E. punctata* has green leaves and purple-spotted white blossoms. Various hybrids have white, pink, yellow or red flowers.

HOW TO GROW. Episcias do best in bright indirect or curtain-filtered sunlight and will also grow well in 14 to 16 hours of artificial light a day. Night temperatures of 65° to 70° and day temperatures of 75° or higher are ideal. Pot in a mixture of 2 parts peat moss and 1 part packaged potting soil and 1 part sharp sand or perlite. Keep the potting medium moist at all times and place the pot on a humidifying tray *(page 41)*. Fertilize once a month during the growing season. Pinch off the tips of the stems to encourage branching. For fresh growth, cut back the plants when they have stopped blooming. Propagate from runners *(page 97)* or from stem cuttings at any time.

ERANTHEMUM
E. nervosum, also called *E. pulchellum, Justicia nervosa, Daedalacanthus nervosus; E. wattii* (both called eranthemum, blue sage)

Spikes of handsome flowers about an inch across appear among the slender 3-inch green leaves of eranthemums throughout the winter and early spring. *E. nervosum* bears blue flowers and grows 18 to 24 inches tall; *E. wattii* produces purple flowers and grows less than a foot high.

HOW TO GROW. Eranthemums do best in at least four hours of direct sunlight a day in winter and light shade in summer. Night temperatures of 60° to 65° and day temperatures of 70° or higher are ideal. Keep the soil moist and fertilize every two weeks during the growing season; reduce water and omit fertilizer in late spring and early summer. Prune to about 5 inches above the base after this resting period and pinch off the tips of stems during the summer to encourage branching and bushy growth. Propagate from stem cuttings of new growth.

ERVATAMIA
E. divaricata, also called *E. coronaria, Tabernaemontana divaricata, Nerium coronarium* (butterfly gardenia, crape jasmine, fleur d'amour, Adam's-apple, Nero's-crown)

With their glossy, dark green 3- to 4-inch leaves and exquisitely fragrant 2-inch-wide white flowers, which bloom throughout the summer and intermittently the rest of the year, butterfly gardenias—especially the many-petaled variety, *E. divaricata plena*—might easily be mistaken for true gardenias, except that their flowers are smaller and have frilly petals. Plants may grow to a height of 2 feet or more if not pruned.

HOW TO GROW. Butterfly gardenias do best in at least four hours of direct sunlight a day, night temperatures of 65° to 70° and day temperatures of 75° or higher. Keep the soil moist at all times; fertilize every two weeks from April to September, monthly during the rest of the year. Before new growth starts in early spring, prune back plants to keep them at the desired height, and repot them in fresh potting mixture in larger containers if needed. Propagate from stem cuttings of new growth in spring.

EUCHARIS
E. grandiflora, also called *E. amazonica* (Amazon lily)

The fragrant, snowy white flowers of the Amazon lily are a familiar sight in bridal bouquets. Clusters of three to six flowers, each about 2 inches across, appear two or three times a year on stalks 18 to 24 inches tall, which are set among shiny 8-inch-long leaves.

HOW TO GROW. Amazon lilies do best in bright indirect

BLUE SAGE
Eranthemum nervosum

BUTTERFLY GARDENIA
Ervatamia divaricata plena

AMAZON LILY
Eucharis grandiflora

POINSETTIA
Euphorbia pulcherrima 'Eckespoint C-1'

ARABIAN VIOLET
Exacum affine 'Midget'

or curtain-filtered sunlight, night temperatures of 65° to 70° and day temperatures of 75° or higher. Plant in a mixture composed of 2 parts peat moss, 1 part packaged potting soil and 1 part sharp sand or perlite. Keep the potting medium very moist and fertilize during the growing season; at other times keep the plants in light shade, water them less frequently and do not fertilize. Propagate by separating the small bulbs that develop beside larger ones.

EUPHORBIA

E. pulcherrima (poinsettia); *E. fulgens,* also called *E. jacquinaeflora* (scarlet plume)

Poinsettias, whose bright red petallike bracts appear in late fall, have long been esteemed as Christmas plants. The true flowers are tiny greenish yellow nubs in the centers of the bracts, which may be white or pink as well as red. Most florists' plants are 1 to 2 feet tall, but 3- to 4-foot plants are not uncommon. The bracts—some as much as a foot across—may stay colorful for three months or more. A lesser-known relative is the scarlet plume, so named because its 2-foot arching stems with narrow willowlike leaves are studded with waxy, orange-scarlet flowers, ½ inch in diameter, in winter.

HOW TO GROW. Both species do best in at least four hours of direct sunlight a day in a draft-free location. Night temperatures of 50° to 65° and day temperatures of 68° or higher are ideal. Soil should be allowed to dry slightly between thorough waterings. Cut back plants in late spring after flowering and repot in fresh potting soil. Cuttings from the tips of new growth can be rooted in summer. Fertilize every two weeks in spring and summer; do not fertilize the rest of the year. Flowers will develop only on plants that have had an alternation of a light period and at least 14 hours of uninterrupted darkness each day for approximately 40 days. To ensure flowers for Christmas, place plants in a closet or in a dark corner of a basement or storage room, from late afternoon till morning from the latter part of September through October.

EXACUM

E. affine (Arabian violet)

Masses of fragrant ½-inch blue flowers with prominent yellow pollen-bearing stamens appear among the shiny ½- to 1-inch heart-shaped leaves of the Arabian violet. This charming 6- to 8-inch-high plant, unlike the more familiar African violet, blooms profusely for only four months or so and should then be discarded. *E. affine atrocaeruleum* has dark lavender flowers; Blithe Spirit bears white blossoms; Midget produces blue flowers.

HOW TO GROW. Arabian violets do best in bright indirect or curtain-filtered sunlight, with night temperatures of 60° to 65° and day temperatures of 70° or higher. Pot in a mixture of 2 parts peat moss to 1 part packaged potting soil and 1 part sharp sand or perlite. Keep the potting medium moist at all times and fertilize every two weeks. Sow the dustlike seeds, which germinate readily, in spring for flowering plants during fall and winter.

F

FELICIA

F. amelloides, also called *F. capensis, Agathaea coelestis, Aster rotundifolius* (blue daisy or blue marguerite); *F. bergeriana* (kingfisher daisy)

These sky-blue, yellow-centered daisies, which bloom almost continuously year round, make unusual additions to house-plant collections. The flowers grow on wiry stems above pebbly textured, ½-inch oval leaves. *F. amelloides,* which can be kept about 12 inches tall by pinching out leg-

gy stems, has 1- to 1½-inch blossoms; the variety called
Santa Anita has flowers 2½ to 3 inches across. The di-
minutive *F. bergeriana,* an annual, bears ½- to ¾-inch
flowers on dainty 6-inch plants. Flowers of both species
open only in sunshine.

HOW TO GROW. Felicias do best in at least four hours of
direct sunlight a day, night temperatures of 50° to 55° and
day temperatures of 68° to 72°. Keep soil damp and fertilize every two weeks. Both species can be propagated
from seeds (sown in midsummer, they produce fine flowering plants by late fall). *F. amelloides* can, and its named
varieties must, be grown from stem cuttings in spring.

FIRECRACKER VINE See *Manettia*
FLAME BUSH, TRINIDAD See *Calliandra*
FLAME VINE, MEXICAN See *Senecio*
FLAME-OF-THE-WOODS See *Ixora*
FLAMING SWORD See *Vriesia*
FLAMINGO FLOWER See *Anthurium*
FLEUR D'AMOUR See *Ervatamia*
FLOWER OF THE WEST WIND See *Zephyranthes*
FLOWERING MAPLE See *Abutilon*

FORTUNELLA

F. hindsii (dwarf kumquat, Hong Kong wild kumquat), *F.
margarita* (Nagami kumquat, oval kumquat)

Both these species of kumquats bear small fragrant white
flowers in spring, followed by highly decorative fruit in fall.
F. margarita, generally kept to about 2 feet high indoors,
has shiny dark green leaves about 1½ inches long; its
1½-inch golden-orange fruit remains on the plant from
October to January or later and may be made into pre-
serves. *F. hindsii,* which grows about a foot high, bears decorative cherry-sized scarlet-orange fruit.

HOW TO GROW. Kumquats do best in at least four hours
of direct sunlight a day, night temperatures of 50° to 55°
and day temperatures of 68° to 72°. Allow the soil to dry
slightly between thorough waterings. Fertilize three times
a year, in very early spring, early summer and late summer.
Propagate from stem cuttings in late spring, or from seeds
sown at any time.

FOUNTAIN PLANT See *Russelia*
FOXGLOVE, MEXICAN See *Tetranema*

FUCHSIA

F. hybrids, *F. triphylla* (honeysuckle fuchsia)
(all called fuchsia, lady's-eardrop)

Fuchsias are well known for their delicate hoopskirt-
shaped 1½- to 3-inch flowers, which are set among crisp
oval leaves on 1- to 3-foot stems. Although most fuchsias
bloom in spring and summer, many blossom throughout
the year. Among them are the hybrids Abundance (a trailing plant with light pink double flowers), Cascade (trailing, with pink and red single blooms), Mrs. Victor Reiter
(trailing, with crimson and white single flowers) and Pink
Cloud (upright and arching, with pink single flowers). The
so-called honeysuckle fuchsia, *F. triphylla,* which grows
about 18 inches high, bears clusters of 1-inch tubular flowers throughout the year; the variety Gartenmeister Bon-
stedt has salmon-orange flowers among reddish leaves, and
Swanley Yellow, despite its name, has orange blossoms.

HOW TO GROW. Fuchsias do best in at least four hours of
direct sunlight a day, but should be protected from midday
sun in summer. Night temperatures of 50° to 55° and day
temperatures of 68° to 72° are ideal. Keep the soil moist
when plants are flowering and fertilize every two weeks;
fertilize monthly and keep the soil slightly drier for those

BLUE MARGUERITE
Felicia amelloides

NAGAMI KUMQUAT
Fortunella margarita

FUCHSIA
Fuchsia 'Pink Cloud'

plants that rest in fall and winter. Prune summer-flowering plants to about 6 inches from the soil level when plants are resting in midfall to early winter. Propagate named varieties from stem cuttings of new growth.

G

GARDENIA
G. jasminoides, also called *G. grandiflora*
(gardenia, Cape jasmine)

The goal of many a gardener is to grow a richly fragrant gardenia in the house. Of the many varieties in cultivation, *G. jasminoides veitchii* is the one most often grown indoors; its waxy, snow-white flowers, about 3 inches across, normally appear in winter and spring among shiny, dark green 4- to 6-inch leaves on bushes 1 to 3 feet tall. Varieties that bear the larger (up to 5 inch) flowers familiar in corsages—among them Belmont, Mystery, Hadley and McLellan 23—are also sometimes grown in pots.

HOW TO GROW. Gardenias do best in at least four hours of direct sunlight a day. Most will blossom continuously if they have night temperatures of 60° to 65°, but will not set new flower buds if night temperatures go above 65°. Day temperatures of 68° to 72° are ideal. Pot in 2 parts peat moss to 1 part packaged potting soil and 1 part sharp sand or perlite; do not add lime. Keep the mix moist and well drained. Fertilize monthly. Bud drop, common among plants newly brought indoors from a greenhouse, can be reduced by syringing buds with tepid water and by setting plants on a humidifying tray *(page 41)*. Propagate any time from stem cuttings of new growth, making sure to cover the pot with a clear plastic bag to conserve moisture.

GARDENIA, BUTTERFLY See *Ervatamia*
GARLIC, SOCIETY See *Tulbaghia*

GAZANIA
G. longiscapa hybrids (gazania, treasure flower)

The daisylike gazania, most varieties of which are hybrids of *G. longiscapa,* bears long-lasting 3- to 4-inch dark-centered flowers in yellow, gold, cream, yellow orange, pink or bronze red. The blossoms open only in sunshine, closing at night and on cloudy days. The plants, which bloom year round, grow 6 to 12 inches tall with the blossoms arching over clumps of slender, irregularly lobed leaves that are dark green above and felty white underneath.

HOW TO GROW. Gazanias do best in at least four hours of direct sunlight a day, night temperatures of 50° to 55° and day temperatures of 68° to 72°. Soil should be allowed to become nearly dry between thorough waterings. Fertilize monthly throughout the year. Propagate from seeds in spring or by division of old plants at any time.

GELSEMIUM
G. sempervirens (Carolina jasmine)

Clouds of fragrant yellow 1-inch flowers adorn this vine in winter and early spring, appearing among gleaming 1½- to 3-inch willowlike leaves. Plants can be allowed to trail from hanging containers or trained to small trellises up to 4 feet high, through which the slender canes of the vine should be interwoven.

HOW TO GROW. Carolina jasmine does best in full sun or very light shade, night temperatures of 50° to 55° and day temperatures of 68° to 72°. Keep soil moist and fertilize monthly except when plants are resting in the fall. Plants may be propagated easily by air layering *(page 98)*, from stem cuttings taken in spring from established new growth, or from seeds in spring. Prune after flowering in spring to keep plants to the desired size.

GARDENIA
Gardenia jasminoides veitchii

GAZANIA
Gazania 'Sunshine Hybrids'

GERANIUM See *Pelargonium*
GERANIUM, JUNGLE See *Ixora*
GERANIUM, STRAWBERRY See *Saxifraga*

GLORIOSA
G. rothschildiana, G. superba
(both called glory lily, climbing lily)

This graceful, tuberous-rooted ornamental vine, which bears impressive 3- to 4-inch lilylike flowers, climbs to a height of 3 or 4 feet, clinging to supports by means of tendrils at the tips of its lancelike leaves. *G. rothschildiana* has scarlet and yellow flowers, *G. superba* deep orange and red flowers. Because glory lilies go through alternate periods of growth and dormancy, they can be brought into blossom at any season if they are planted at different times of the year. Most gardeners plant them in April to flower in midsummer, the normal blooming season (late summer to fall for *G. superba*).

HOW TO GROW. Glory lilies do best in at least four hours of direct sunlight a day, night temperatures of 65° to 70° and day temperatures of 75° or higher. Keep the soil moist and fertilize every two weeks until the flowers fade; withhold moisture and food during the dormant season, normally October through January. Propagate by dividing tubers in the spring.

GLORY BOWER See *Clerodendrum*

GLOXINERA
G. hybrids

Many interesting variations exist among these tuberous-rooted gesneriads, products of the crossbreeding of gloxinias and rechsteinerias. Some have glossy heart-shaped foliage; others have furry oval leaves. Some flower continuously, but most bloom in late spring and summer; others may be grown to flower at various times of the year, according to when they are planted. The taller varieties, 6 to 10 inches high with 2- to 3-inch flowers, include Alfred K, with flaring tubular salmon-pink flowers; Rosebells, with slipper-shaped rose flowers; and Velvet Charm, with vivid pink tubular flowers. Miniature gloxineras, ranging from 3 to 6 inches in height, with ½- to 1-inch flowers, include Doll Baby, with lavender-blue, yellow-throated slipper-shaped blossoms; Krishna, with bright pink tubular flowers; and Ramadeva, with bright pink tubular flowers that bloom year round.

HOW TO GROW. Gloxineras do best in bright indirect or curtain-filtered sunlight and can be grown in 14 to 16 hours of artificial light a day. Night temperatures of 65° to 70° and day temperatures of 75° or higher are ideal. Pot in a mixture of 2 parts peat moss to 1 part packaged potting soil and 1 part sharp sand or perlite. Keep the mix moist and fertilize monthly during the growing season. After flowering, omit fertilizer and keep the mix on the dry side until the foliage withers. Tubers can either be allowed to rest where they are or stored out of the way in closed plastic bags filled with barely damp peat moss or vermiculite. When they sprout, usually in two to four months, they should be repotted in fresh potting mixture. Some miniatures do not resprout easily and are grown annually from seeds, blossoming in three to four months. Propagate continuously blooming plants from leaf cuttings—from stem cuttings of upright plants—or from seeds any time.

GLOXINIA See *Sinningia*
GOLDFISH PLANT See *Hypocyrta*
GRANADILLA See *Passiflora*
GRECIAN VASE PLANT See *Quesnelia*

CAROLINA JASMINE
Gelsemium sempervirens

GLORY LILY
Gloriosa rothschildiana

GLOXINERA
Gloxinera 'Rosebells'

123

GUZMANIA
Guzmania monostachya

BLOOD LILY
Haemanthus multiflorus

COMMON HELIOTROPE
Heliotropium arborescens

GUZMANIA
G. lingulata; G. monostachya, also called *G. tricolor*

Guzmanias have long been favored by bromeliad fanciers because their spikes of bright petallike bracts stay colorful for months. The smooth-edged, glossy leaves, which form a water-holding rosette, are often colorful too, with delicate brown, purple or maroon lines running lengthwise. *G. lingulata cardinalis* has red bracts with yellowish white flowers rising from a rosette 18 inches or more across formed by slender purplish green leaves. *G. lingulata minor* bears scarlet, yellow or orange bracts, with yellowish white flowers, above 8- to 12-inch rosettes formed by straplike leathery leaves with purple markings. *G. monostachya* has 12- to 18-inch rosettes composed of bayonetlike yellow-green leaves around a stout stem bearing salmon-red bracts set with white flowers.

HOW TO GROW. Guzmanias do best in bright indirect or curtain-filtered sunlight, but can take direct sun in winter. Night temperatures of 60° to 65° and day temperatures of 70° or higher are ideal. Pot in a mixture of 2 parts peat moss to 1 part packaged potting soil and 1 part sharp sand or perlite; do not add lime. Keep moist; fertilize monthly. Keep water in the cup formed by the leaf rosette. Propagate from shoots that appear at base of plants.

H

HAEMANTHUS
H. coccineus, H. hybridus, H. katherinae, H. multiflorus (all called blood lily)

Blood lilies, so called because of the color of their globular flower clusters, make spectacular pot plants. Each flower cluster, 6 to 12 inches across, is composed of many ¾- to 2-inch tubular blossoms—each with six protruding pollen-bearing stamens that are usually yellow—and is set on an upright stem 8 to 20 inches high. Plants bear two or more huge leaves up to 18 inches long and 6 inches wide. *H. coccineus* produces coral-red flowers in fall; *H. katherinae* (pink) and the hybrids Andromeda (salmon pink) and King Albert (scarlet) bloom in late spring or early summer; *H. multiflorus* bears red flowers in summer.

HOW TO GROW. Blood lilies do best in at least four hours of direct sunlight a day, night temperatures of 50° to 55° and day temperatures of 68° to 72°. Keep moist and fertilize monthly during the growing season; keep nearly dry and omit fertilizer during late fall and winter. Propagate while the plants are resting by removing the small bulbs that develop beside the larger ones. Plant one bulb to a pot, setting the tip just above the soil. The pot should be 2 inches larger in diameter than the bulb. Plants flower more profusely if repotted only every three to five years. Each spring wash out part of the old soil with a hose without disturbing roots and replace with fresh soil.

HAERIA See *Schizocentron*
HELIOTROPE See *Heliotropium*

HELIOTROPIUM
H. arborescens, also called *H. peruvianum* (common heliotrope, cherry pie); *H.* hybrids (all called heliotrope)

The delightful fragrance of heliotropes is so pervasive that a single cluster will perfume a whole room. Many modern varieties are hybrids of the vanilla-scented *H. arborescens,* which bears large clusters of minute, soft-textured purple flowerlets year round. The hybrids come in shades of lavender, purple, blue and white and produce clusters of flowers 3 to 6 inches across. Heliotropes can be grown as bushy plants 6 to 12 inches or more tall, or they can be trained to single stems 3 to 4 feet tall.

HOW TO GROW. Heliotropes do best in at least four hours of direct sunlight a day, night temperatures of 50° to 55° and day temperatures of 68° to 72°. Keep moist; fertilize every two weeks. Propagate from seeds or stem cuttings any time. Some gardeners let plants rest in fall, pruning them to keep the desired height and to force branching and abundant flowers in late winter and spring.

HETEROCENTRON See *Schizocentron*

HIBISCUS
H. rosa-sinensis (Chinese hibiscus, rose of China),
H. schizopetalus (fringed hibiscus)

The fragile beauty of hibiscus flowers, which bloom year round, belies the ease with which these plants are grown and their remarkable longevity of 25 years or more. The papery blossoms of the Chinese hibiscus grow up to 5 inches across and range from snowy white through cream to yellow, salmon, orange and scarlet. A notable variety, *H. rosa-sinensis cooperi*, has 2½-inch scarlet flowers and narrow, 2-inch leaves marked with olive green, pink, crimson and white. The fringed hibiscus has pendulous 2½-inch orange-red flowers with lacy-edged petals. Plants can be kept under 3 feet tall by pruning.

HOW TO GROW. Hibiscuses do best in at least four hours of direct sun a day, night temperatures of 60° to 65°, day temperatures of 70° or higher. Keep moist; fertilize monthly. Propagate from stem cuttings of new growth.

HIPPEASTRUM
H. hybrids (amaryllis)

Known to most gardeners as amaryllis, *Hippeastrum* hybrids have smooth-textured lilylike flowers, sometimes 8 to 10 inches across. They bloom in winter or spring in clusters of three or four blossoms atop 1- to 2-foot stems just as the dark green strap-shaped leaves arise from the bulbs. Most bulbs send up a second flower stalk when the first one begins to fade. Seed-grown bulbs are sold by color; superior varieties that have been propagated vegetatively are sold by name. Among the latter are Appleblossom (blush pink), Beautiful Lady (salmon orange), Fire Dance (bright red), Scarlet Admiral (deep scarlet) and White Giant (snowy white).

HOW TO GROW. Amaryllises do best in at least four hours of direct sunlight a day, night temperatures of 60° to 65° and day temperatures of 70° or higher. Keep plants cool and out of direct sun while in bloom. Plant one bulb to a pot, allowing 2 inches of space between bulb and pot. Water well once, then wait for the stalk to appear before watering again. Keep moist and fertilize monthly until leaves turn yellow in late summer, then reduce water and omit fertilizer until about a month before flowers are desired. Before plants start new growth, wash away some of the old soil and replace with fresh soil. Repot every three to four years. Propagate from small bulbs that develop beside the large ones. Plants propagated from seeds require three to four years to reach flowering size.

HOLLY, MINIATURE See *Malpighia*
HOLLY, SINGAPORE See *Malpighia*

HOYA
H. australis; H. bella, also called *H. paxtonii; H. carnosa; H. cinnamomifolia; H. coronaria*, also called *H. grandiflora; H. purpurea-fusca* (all called waxplant)

Vines with 2- to 4-inch leaves, waxplants take their name from their long-lasting clusters of ½- to 1-inch star-shaped flowers, which are sweetly fragrant and so shiny

CHINESE HIBISCUS
Hibiscus rosa-sinensis

AMARYLLIS
Hippeastrum 'Fire Dance'

WAXPLANT
Hoya carnosa

HYACINTH
Hyacinthus 'King of the Blues'

COMMON BIGLEAF HYDRANGEA
Hydrangea macrophylla

GOLDFISH PLANT
Hypocyrta nummularia

they appear to be made of wax. Recommended species are *H. australis,* whose red-centered blush-white flowers appear in fall; *H. bella,* a bushy plant that bears white flowers with rosy violet centers in summer; *H. carnosa,* which bears pinkish white flowers with red centers in summer and has foliage that is sometimes edged with pink and cream; *H. cinnamomifolia,* which bears yellowish green flowers with purple-red centers in the summer; *H. coronaria,* whose summer-blooming yellow flowers have five red dots at the base of each blossom; and *H. purpureafusca,* whose fall-blooming brownish red flowers have white hairs in a purple center. The latter is also known as Silver Pink because of the silvery pink blotches on its leaves.

HOW TO GROW. Waxplants do best in at least four hours of direct sunlight a day but can also be grown in bright indirect or curtain-filtered sunlight. Night temperatures of 60° to 65° and day temperatures of 70° or higher are ideal. Water freely during flowering, but allow the soil to become almost dry between waterings when the plants are resting. Fertilize every two months in spring and summer. Train the vines on a 2- to 4-foot trellis. Do not remove the leafless spurs or stubs, on which new flowers appear every year. New plants may be started at any time by air layering (*page 98*) or from stem cuttings.

HYACINTH See *Hyacinthus*
HYACINTH, GRAPE See *Muscari*

HYACINTHUS
H. orientalis (large-flowered hyacinth),
H. orientalis albulus (French Roman hyacinth)

Hyacinths, which bear their waxy, trumpet-shaped flowers in clusters 6 to 10 inches high, bring winter-weary indoor gardeners one of the first sweet scents of spring. The most popular are the large-flowered varieties of *H. orientalis,* which include Amsterdam (salmon pink), Bismarck (pale blue), City of Haarlem (primrose yellow), L'Innocence (white), King of the Blues (indigo blue) and Pink Pearl (deep pink). French Roman hyacinths, *H. orientalis albulus,* bear blue, pink, or white flowers. Fairy hyacinths, a crossing of large-flowered hyacinths with French Roman hyacinths, produce several flower clusters from each bulb.

HOW TO GROW. Hyacinths do best in at least four hours of direct sunlight a day, except during flowering, when they need partial shade. Night temperatures of 40° to 45° and day temperatures of 68° or lower are ideal. Keep soil very moist while plants are growing, then dry after foliage matures. Save soil-grown bulbs for planting outdoors. Plants are usually bought in bud and bloom from December through April. Do not try to propagate hyacinth bulbs.

HYDRANGEA
H. macrophylla, also called *H. hortensis*
(common bigleaf hydrangea, house hydrangea)

One of the unforgettable joys of spring is the sight of hydrangeas, whose enormous clusters of soft-textured flowers come in pink, red, lavender, blue and purple as well as white. Each cluster, which may be 8 to 10 inches in diameter, is composed of a mass of 1- to 1½-inch flowers set among shiny, oval 2- to 6-inch dark green leaves. Hydrangeas purchased in bloom are usually 18 to 24 inches tall and bloom for six weeks or more with proper care.

HOW TO GROW. Hydrangeas do best in bright indirect or curtain-filtered sunlight, night temperatures of 55° to 60° and day temperatures of 68° to 72°. Keep the soil very wet; do not fertilize. Since it is extremely difficult to carry this species over from year to year indoors, discard the plants after flowering, or, if winter temperatures do not fall below 0°, replant it outdoors to blossom each summer. Give it rich, moist soil in full sun or light shade.

HYPOCYRTA

H. nummularia, also called *Alloplectus nummularia; H. strigillosa,* also called *Nemanthus strigillosus; H. wettsteinii,* also called *Nemanthus wettsteinii* (goldfish plant)

The plump, bright 1-inch flowers of these gesneriads look like puffy tropical fish, complete with tiny mouths, hanging on stems that grow 1 to 2 feet long. *H. nummularia* has orange-red flowers ringed with purple near the opening of the pouchy lobes, and ¾- to 2½-inch oval leaves. It blossoms intermittently throughout the year, profusely in summer, fall and winter. *H. strigillosa* bears orange-red flowers in winter and spring among lancelike velvety, dark green leaves. *H. wettsteinii,* which may bloom almost continuously, but chiefly in summer and fall, bears flowers with red and yellow pouches and ¾-inch oval glossy leaves. All are well suited for growing in hanging containers.

HOW TO GROW. Hypocyrtas do best in bright indirect or curtain-filtered sunlight and can be grown in 14 to 16 hours of artificial light a day. Night temperatures of 65° to 70° and day temperatures of 75° or higher are ideal. Pot in a mixture of 2 parts peat moss to 1 part packaged potting soil and 1 part sharp sand or perlite. Keep moist; fertilize monthly. Propagate from stem cuttings or seeds any time.

I

IMPATIENS

I. wallerana, also called *I. holstii, I. sultani* (patient Lucy)

Patient Lucy, beloved for its ability to bloom year round in dim light even for neophyte gardeners, is a name that suits this charming species far better than the genus name *Impatiens,* which refers to the manner in which the plants' seed pods explode when ripe, catapulting seeds in all directions. A favorite for generations, it grows 6 inches to about a foot tall, bearing soft, flat flowers 1 to 2 inches across in pink, red, orange, purple, gold, white or red and white. The shiny 1- to 2-inch leaves may be green, maroon or a variegated green and white.

HOW TO GROW. Patient Lucy does equally well in bright indirect or curtain-filtered sunlight, in shade or in 14 to 16 hours of artificial light a day. Night temperatures of 60° to 65° and day temperatures of 70° or higher are ideal. Pot in 2 parts peat moss to 1 part packaged potting soil and 1 part sharp sand or perlite. Keep moist; fertilize every two weeks. Propagate any time from stem cuttings or seeds.

INGA See *Calliandra*

IPOMOEA, also called PHARBITIS

I. purpurea, I. tricolor (both called morning glory)

These decorative vines with their trumpet-shaped 2½- to 8-inch flowers and 2- to 3-inch heart-shaped leaves make handsome additions to indoor gardens in winter. *I. purpurea* and *I. tricolor* bear blossoms up to 4 inches across in blue, purple, scarlet, pink, white or multicolors.

HOW TO GROW. Morning glories do best in at least four hours of direct sunlight a day, night temperatures of 60° to 65° and day temperatures of 70° or higher. Keep the soil barely moist and feed monthly with a half-strength fertilizer beginning when the plants are 4 inches tall. Propagate from seeds in midsummer for flowers in winter. Scratch the seeds with a knife or sandpaper to aid water absorption and plant six to eight seeds to a 10-inch flowerpot. When the seedlings are 2 inches high, thin them out, leaving the three strongest plants. Give these a light trellis or thin stakes to twine on. Discard plants after flowering.

PATIENT LUCY
Impatiens 'Scarlet Baby'

MORNING GLORY
Ipomoea 'Early Call'

FLAME-OF-THE-WOODS
Ixora coccinea

JACOBINIA
Jacobinia suberecta

JASMINE
Jasminum polyanthum

IRIS, WALKING See *Neomarica*
IVY, GERMAN See *Senecio*
IVY, PARLOR See *Senecio*

IXORA

I. coccinea, I. hybrids, *I. javanica*
(all called ixora, flame-of-the-woods, jungle geranium)

Ixoras are compact plants that bloom primarily in summer and intermittently the rest of the year with proper care, in colors ranging from bright red through orange, yellow, pink and white. The species most often cultivated is *I. coccinea,* whose four-petaled red flowers, 1 inch across, grow in clusters 4 to 6 inches or more in diameter; the leaves, bronze toned when new, mature to a dark, shiny green. *I. javanica* bears slightly larger salmon-red flowers. Many hybrid varieties are also suitable for house culture. Plants can easily be kept below 2 feet by pruning.

HOW TO GROW. Ixoras do best in at least four hours of direct sunlight a day, night temperatures of 60° to 65° and day temperatures of 70° or higher. Pot in a mixture of 2 parts peat moss to 1 part packaged potting soil and 1 part sharp sand or perlite; do not add lime. Keep moist; fertilize every two weeks in spring and summer, monthly the rest of the year. Propagate from stem cuttings in spring.

J

JACOBINIA

J. carnea, also called *Justicia magnifica* (king's-crown, Brazilian plume); *J. pauciflora,* also called *Libonia floribunda; J. suberecta; J. umbrosa*

These tropical plants bear slender two-lipped flowers, often in pomponlike spikes at the ends of the branches. *J. carnea* has fluffy 3- to 6-inch spikes of rosy pink 2-inch-long flowers, which bloom among coarse 4- to 8-inch oval leaves in late summer; plants reach a height of 1 to 3 feet. *J. umbrosa* is similar except that its flowers are yellow. *J. suberecta* grows about 1 foot tall and in spring produces orange-scarlet flowers about an inch long in clusters above velvety 2½-inch leaves. *J. pauciflora,* also about a foot tall, is a winter-blooming species that bears many solitary 1-inch-long tubular scarlet flowers with yellow tips among ¾-inch leaves.

HOW TO GROW. Jacobinias do best in at least four hours of direct sunlight a day in winter and bright indirect or curtain-filtered sunlight the rest of the year. Night temperatures of 60° to 65° and day temperatures of 70° or higher are ideal. Keep soil moist and place the pot on a humidifying tray *(page 41).* Fertilize every two weeks during the growing season. Since old plants are apt to be straggly, they should be cut back and repotted after flowering to force new growth; or new plants can be propagated from stem cuttings each spring.

JASMINE See *Jasminum*
JASMINE, CAPE See *Gardenia*
JASMINE, CAROLINA See *Gelsemium*
JASMINE, CRAPE See *Ervatamia*
JASMINE, MADAGASCAR See *Stephanotis*
JASMINE, STAR See *Trachelospermum*

JASMINUM

J. gracile magnificum, also called *J. simplicifolium* (royal jasmine, angelwing jasmine); *J. humile revolutum* (Italian jasmine); *J. mesneyi,* also called *J. primulinum* (primrose jasmine); *J. officinale grandiflorum,* also called *J. officinale affine, J. grandiflorum* (poet's jasmine, Spanish jasmine); *J. parkeri; J. polyanthum; J. sambac* (Arabian jasmine)

Sweet fragrance is the hallmark of most jasmines. *J. gracile magnificum* bears clusters of star-shaped 1-inch white flowers in winter and has 2-inch waxy, oval leaves. *J. humile revolutum* has clusters of 1-inch lemon-yellow flowers among feathery leaves from June to September. *J. mesneyi* bears round 2-inch yellow flowers in spring. From June to October *J. officinale grandiflorum* bears clusters of star-shaped, ⅞-inch white flowers. *J. parkeri*, only 8 to 12 inches tall, has star-shaped ¼- to ½-inch yellow flowers in summer. *J. polyanthum* produces springtime clusters of star-shaped, ¾-inch white-and-rose flowers. *J. sambac*, which blooms from early spring to late fall, bears clusters of rosette-shaped, 1-inch flowers that are gardenia white at first and gradually turn purple as they fade. One variety, Maid of Orleans, has semidouble flowers; another, Grand Duke of Tuscany, has double flowers.

HOW TO GROW. Jasmines thrive in at least four hours of direct sunlight a day. *J. humile revolutum* does best in night temperatures of 40° to 45° and day temperatures of 68° or lower; *J. sambac* and its varieties in night temperatures of 60° to 65° and day temperatures of 72° or higher; the other jasmines flourish in night temperatures of 50° to 55° and day temperatures of 68° to 72°. Keep soil moist at all times and fertilize every two weeks except when plants are resting. Propagate any time from stem cuttings. Prune all species except *J. parkeri* after the blooming period to keep plants under 3 feet tall. The height of jasmine plants can also be controlled by weaving their branches through a low trellis.

JUSTICIA See *Jacobinia*

K

KALANCHOE
K. blossfeldiana, K. 'Jingle Bells'

Colorful, winter-blooming house plants whose flowers last for many weeks, *K. blossfeldiana* varieties grow 8 to 12 inches high with an equal spread and bear masses of ¼- to ½-inch four-petaled red or yellow blossoms that may nearly cover the waxy, thick, 1- to 2-inch leaves. Excellent red varieties include Tetra Vulcan, Scarlet Gnome, Tom Thumb and Brilliant Star; a bright yellow variety is Yellow Tom Thumb, and a strain with various-colored flowers is Hummel's Hybrids. A trailing type, Jingle Bells, bears ¾-inch bell-shaped, pendulous coral flowers.

HOW TO GROW. Kalanchoes do best in at least four hours of direct sunlight a day, night temperatures of 50° to 60° and day temperatures of 68° to 72°. Allow the soil to become nearly dry between thorough waterings and fertilize every two weeks until the plants come into flower. Propagate from stem cuttings in early fall, or, for finer plants, sow seeds any time from January to July (the later the sowing, the smaller the plants will be when they begin to blossom). To ensure blooms for the Christmas season, give plants at least 14 hours a day of uninterrupted darkness from about September 1 through early October.

KING'S-CROWN See *Jacobinia*

KOHLERIA
K. amabilis, K. bogotensis, K. eriantha,
K. hybrids, K. lindeniana

Kohlerias are easily cultivated 8- to 30-inch plants with conspicuous hairy leaves and tubular five-petaled flowers that occur in a variety of colors, often spotted with contrasting hues. Some of these gesneriads grow upright, but most have trailing stems that make them suitable for hanging containers. *K. amabilis* bears abundant 2-inch rose-pink

KALANCHOE
Kalanchoe blossfeldiana 'Tetra Vulcan'

KOHLERIA
Kohleria amabilis

CAPE COWSLIP
Lachenalia pendula

flowers with red dots from late winter through spring and summer; *K. bogotensis* (1-inch-long red-spotted yellow flowers) and *K. eriantha* (1-inch red-orange flowers with red spots) bloom in winter and spring; *K. lindeniana* has ½-inch fragrant lavender and white flowers with yellow throats in late fall and spring. Hybrids that bloom almost continuously include Carnival (red flowers spotted yellow); Longwood (red flowers, red-spotted white lobes); and Rongo (magenta flowers spotted deep pink).

HOW TO GROW. Kohlerias do best in bright indirect or curtain-filtered sunlight, and also grow well in 14 to 16 hours of artificial light a day. Night temperatures of 65° to 70° and day temperatures of 75° or higher are ideal. Pot in 2 parts peat moss to 1 part packaged potting soil and 1 part sharp sand or perlite. Keep moist and fertilize monthly while the plants are growing. The species listed above go into a semidormant period between blooming periods and can be cut back to encourage fresh growth while resting; keep the plants on the dry side and do not fertilize during this time. Propagate from stem cuttings of new growth, making sure to cover the pot with a clear plastic bag to conserve moisture.

KUMQUAT See *Fortunella*

L

LACHENALIA

L. aurea, also called *L. aloides aurea; L. pendula,* also called *L. bulbifera; L. tricolor,* also called *L. aloides* (all called Cape cowslips, leopard lilies)

Cape cowslips are easy-to-grow bulb plants, 9 to 12 inches tall, that bear spikes of waxy, inch-long flowers in winter and early spring. The 6- to 8-inch leaves are often purple spotted. Outstanding species are *L. aurea* (yellow flowers), *L. pendula* (multicolored coral, yellow and purple); and *L. tricolor* (green banded with red and yellow).

HOW TO GROW. Cape cowslips do best in at least four hours of direct sunlight a day, night temperatures of 40° to 45° and day temperatures of 68° or lower. Keep the soil moist and fertilize monthly during the growing season. Propagate by separating new bulbs from the old ones.

LADY'S-EARDROP See *Fuchsia*

LAELIA

L. flava, L. lundii regnellii

One of the finest orchids for growing indoors is *L. flava,* whose golden-yellow 2- to 2½-inch blossoms are borne in clusters of four to 10 on wiry, 18-inch spikes *(photograph, page 56)*. The long-lasting flowers bloom in midwinter. *L. lundii regnellii* rarely grows more than 4 to 5 inches tall, bearing one or two pale pink flowers 1 to 1½ inches across, with ruffled lips delicately veined in red.

HOW TO GROW. Laelias do best in at least four hours of direct sunlight a day, but should be shielded with a light curtain or blinds during the hottest part of the day. Night temperatures of 55° to 65° and day temperatures of 68° or higher are ideal. Pot in a mixture of 2 parts fir bark or shredded tree-fern fiber and 1 part coarse peat moss. Place the pot on a humidifying tray *(page 77)* and let the potting medium become moderately dry between thorough waterings. Fertilize monthly with a 20-10-10 or similar high-nitrogen formula diluted ¼ teaspoon per quart of water.

LAELIOCATTLEYA

Hybrids derived from *L. cattleya* and *L. laelia*

Laeliocattleyas, which bloom at various times of the year, are among the most colorful orchids suitable for ir

TOP: COMMON LANTANA
Lantana camara

BOTTOM: TRAILING LANTANA
Lantana sellowiana

door culture. Most of the varieties being bred today are large-flowering but compact plants that produce clusters of long-lasting 3- to 4-inch blossoms in shades of greenish yellow, golden yellow, orange and pink, often with vivid rose-to-purple lips. One superb yellow variety is El Cerrito (*photograph, page 57*).

HOW TO GROW. Laeliocattleyas do best in bright indirect or curtain-filtered sunlight, night temperatures of 55° to 65° and day temperatures of 68° or higher. Plant in a mixture of 2 parts fir bark or shredded tree-fern fiber and 1 part coarse peat moss. Place the pot on a humidifying tray (*page 77*) and let the potting medium become moderately dry between thorough waterings. Fertilize monthly with a 20-10-10 or similar high-nitrogen formula diluted ¼ teaspoon per quart of water.

LANTANA
L. camara (common lantana); *L.* hybrids;
L. sellowiana, also called *L. montevidensis* and
L. delicatissima (trailing lantana)

Lantanas bear abundant 1-inch clusters of tiny fragrant flowers, mainly in spring and summer and intermittently in fall and winter, among pungent, inch-long, rough green leaves. The blossoms of common and hybrid lantanas come in white, yellow, pink, red, orange and bicolored combinations. They can be kept 8 to 12 inches tall by pinching back stem tips or can be trained to grow in a tree shape with great heads of foliage and flowers above a single stem 2 to 3 feet tall. Trailing lantanas, which have rosy lilac flowers, grow up to 4 feet long and bloom most heavily in summer; they are especially graceful in hanging baskets.

HOW TO GROW. Lantanas do best in at least four hours of direct sunlight a day, night temperatures of 55° to 60° and day temperatures of 68° or higher. Allow the soil to dry slightly between thorough waterings. Fertilize every two weeks. Propagate from stem cuttings at any time.

LEMON See *Citrus*
LIBONIA See *Jacobinia*

LILIUM
L. longiflorum (Easter lily)

Easter lilies, famed for their snowy flowers and sweet fragrance, are grown by the millions each year, timed to open their blossoms for the Easter season. The flowers, 6 to 8 inches long with a 4- to 5-inch spread, bloom for about a week; the leaves are up to 6 inches long. Among the most popular because of their comparatively low stature are such varieties as Croft, which grows about 2 feet tall; Ace, 1 to 2 feet; and Estate, about 3 feet.

HOW TO GROW. Easter lilies do best in bright indirect or curtain-filtered sunlight when in flower, night temperatures of 40° to 50° and day temperatures of 68° or lower. Keep the soil moist while the plants are in blossom but do not fertilize. After the flowers fade, set the plants in the sun and water until the foliage matures. The culture of Easter lily bulbs indoors is difficult for the average house-plant gardener, and the resulting plants will rarely be as satisfactory as professionally grown plants bought from florists. You can plant the bulbs in a sunny garden, however, and they will almost surely blossom for many years.

LILY See *Lilium*
LILY, AMAZON See *Eucharis*
LILY, AZTEC See *Sprekelia*
LILY, BENGAL See *Crinum*
LILY, BLOOD See *Haemanthus*
LILY, BLUE AFRICAN See *Agapanthus*

EASTER LILY
Lilium longiflorum 'Croft'

DOUBLE SWEET ALYSSUM
Lobularia maritima flore pleno

HOLLY MALPIGHIA
Malpighia coccigera

LILY, CALLA See *Zantedeschia*
LILY, CLIMBING See *Gloriosa*
LILY, JACOBEAN See *Sprekelia*
LILY, KAFIR See *Clivia*
LILY, LEOPARD See *Lachenalia*
LILY, MILK-AND-WINE See *Crinum*
LILY, ST.-JAMES'S See *Sprekelia*
LILY, SCARBOROUGH See *Vallota*
LILY, ZEPHYR See *Zephyranthes*
LILY OF THE NILE See *Agapanthus*
LIPSTICK PLANT See *Aeschynanthus*

LOBULARIA
L. maritima, also called *Alyssum maritima*
(sweet alyssum)

Sweet alyssums are delightful little plants, 3 to 10 inches tall, with clusters of tiny, honey-fragrant, white, pink or deep lavender flowers. Most are treated as annuals and are discarded when plants get straggly. The exception is an especially fine trailing variety, *L. maritima flore pleno,* which has white, many-petaled double flowers; it blooms throughout the year and lasts for years.

HOW TO GROW. Sweet alyssum does best in at least four hours of direct sunlight a day, night temperatures of 50° to 55° and day temperatures of 68° to 72°. Keep the soil slightly moist; fertilize monthly. Propagate single-flowered varieties from seeds in late summer for winter bloom. The double-flowering type does not grow from seeds; propagate it from stem cuttings at any time.

M
MAGIC FLOWER See *Achimenes*

MALPIGHIA
M. coccigera (holly malpighia, Singapore holly, miniature holly), *M. glabra* (Barbados cherry)

Holly malpighia, an attractive, easy-to-grow plant with spiny-edged, hollylike leaves, begins to produce ½-inch pink flowers with fringed petals when it is only 3 to 4 inches tall. The flowers bloom profusely in summer, and are followed by ½-inch red fruit. Plants grow slowly to a height of about a foot and are often used as Japanese miniature bonsai plants. The Barbados cherry grows 3 feet or more tall and in summer produces a scattering of ¾-inch rose-red flowers, followed by cherry-sized red fruit.

HOW TO GROW. Both species do best in direct sunlight or very light shade, night temperatures of 55° to 60° and day temperatures of 68° to 72°. Allow the soil to become slightly dry between thorough waterings; fertilize twice a year, in early spring and early summer. Propagate in spring or summer from stem cuttings or seeds.

MALVAVISCUS
M. arboreus penduliflorus, also called *M. grandiflorus, Achania malvaviscus* (Turk's-cap, waxmallow, Scotch purse)

An upright, bushy species with 2- to 3-inch-long, heart-shaped leaves, this shrub produces 1½- to 2½-inch red blossoms from the time it is about 10 inches tall. The flowers bloom year round, but they never fully open, which accounts for one of the plant's common names, Scotch purse. Indoors, plants are generally pruned back to a height of about 2 feet. White- and pink-flowered varieties exist, but are not widely available.

HOW TO GROW. Turk's-cap does best in at least four hours of direct sunlight a day, night temperatures of 60° to 65° and day temperatures of 70° or higher. Keep the soil moist at all times and fertilize every two weeks. Old plants may be cut back to a height of 6 to 12 inches and re-potted in fresh potting mixture in early spring. Propagate from stem cuttings at any time.

MANDEVILLEA See *Dipladenia*

MANETTIA
M. inflata, also called *M. bicolor* (firecracker vine)

The firecracker vine takes its name from its hairy, 3/4-inch-long, tubular scarlet flowers tipped with yellow that bloom continuously throughout the year. Slender oval leaves, about 2 inches long, seem almost to smother the plant's threadlike, twining stems, which may be trained on a 2- to 4-foot-high trellis.

HOW TO GROW. Firecracker vines do best in very light shade, night temperatures of 55° to 60° and day temperatures of 68° to 72°. Keep the soil moist at all times and fertilize every two weeks. Propagate from stem cuttings at any time of year.

MARGUERITE See *Chrysanthemum*
MARGUERITE, BLUE See *Felicia*

MAXILLARIA
M. tenuifolia

One of the easiest-to-grow orchids, this plant bears long-lasting coconut-scented blossoms, only about 1½ inches across, that are dark red with yellow speckles (*photograph, page 58*). They bloom in summer, appearing singly on low stems above grasslike leaves. Plants normally grow to a height of 10 to 12 inches.

HOW TO GROW. *M. tenuifolia* does best in bright indirect or curtain-filtered sunlight, night temperatures of 55° to 70° and day temperatures of 68° or higher. Plant on a slab of tree fern or in a mixture of 2 parts fir bark or shredded tree-fern fiber and 1 part coarse peat moss. Place the pot on a humidifying tray (*page 77*) and keep the potting medium moist at all times. Fertilize monthly with a 20-10-10 or similar high-nitrogen formula diluted ¼ teaspoon per quart of water.

MORNING GLORY See *Ipomoea*
MOTHER-OF-THOUSANDS See *Saxifraga*

MUSCARI
M. armeniacum, M. azureum, M. botryoides,
M. tubergenianum (all called grape hyacinth)

Grape hyacinths are bulb plants that bear deliciously fragrant 6- to 8-inch spikes of tiny bell-shaped blossoms in midwinter or early spring. Four species—*M. armeniacum* (and its excellent variety, Heavenly Blue), *M. azureum,* *M. tubergenianum* and *M. botryoides*—have deep blue flowers; the variety *M. botryoides album* has white blooms. Plants grow 9 to 12 inches tall and have slender, grasslike, blue-green leaves 6 to 8 inches long.

HOW TO GROW. Grape hyacinths do best in at least four hours of direct sunlight a day, night temperatures of 40° to 45° and day temperatures of 68° or lower. Plants are often purchased at florists when already blooming in midwinter, but may also be grown from bulbs planted in pots in early fall for winter flowering. In both cases, keep the soil moist until the foliage withers; do not fertilize. During the spring and summer dormancy, let the bulbs remain dry; you can then start growth in the pots again or plant them outdoors in the garden the following fall. Propagate from the small bulbs that develop next to the larger ones.

MYSTACIDIUM See *Angraecum*

TURK'S-CAP
Malvaviscus arboreus penduliflorus

FIRECRACKER VINE
Manettia inflata

GRAPE HYACINTH
Muscari armeniacum

133

TOP: DAFFODIL
Narcissus 'King Alfred'

BOTTOM: NARCISSUS
Narcissus 'Soleil d'Or'

APOSTLE PLANT
Neomarica gracilis

N

NAEGELIA See *Smithiantha*

NARCISSUS

N. hybrids (large trumpet-flowered types are called daffodils, tazetta types are called narcissuses)

Two kinds of narcissus are of special interest as house plants: the large trumpet-flowered varieties, whose blossoms are often 4 inches or more across and rise above lancelike, gray-green leaves 10 to 12 inches long; and the tazetta varieties, which bear four to eight fragrant, 1- to 2-inch trumpet-shaped flowers on each stem. Both kinds are usually brought into flower in winter and spring; individual blossoms often remain colorful for seven to 10 days. Large-flowered hybrids are King Alfred (golden yellow flowers), Celebrity (white flowers with soft yellow trumpets), and Mount Hood (white flowers). Among the tazettas are hardy types like Geranium, whose white flowers have orange-scarlet centers, and Cheerfulness, a creamy yellow double variety. Fragrant, tender tazettas include the Paperwhite (white flowers), Soleil d'Or (yellow with orange cups), and Chinese Sacred Lily (white with golden yellow cups).

HOW TO GROW. Narcissuses do best in bright indirect or curtain-filtered sunlight when blooming, night temperatures of 40° to 45° and day temperatures of 68° or lower. Tender tazettas will grow well in night temperatures of 55° to 60°. Trumpet and hardy tazetta varieties are generally bought in bud and bloom during winter and spring. Tender tazettas, usually sold as dry bulbs, should be set in any material that supports them, such as pebbles, pearl chips, sand, peat moss or bulb fiber; plant them shallowly, so that only the bases are anchored. Keep the growing medium wet; do not fertilize. Set the bulbs in a cool dark place until new growth is about 4 inches tall, then bring them out to bloom. Discard tender tazettas after flowering. Hardy narcissus bulbs can be saved for garden planting. Propagation of narcissuses is usually left to professional growers.

NASTURTIUM See *Tropaeolum*
NATAL PLUM See *Carissa*

NEOFINETIA

N. falcata, also called *Angraecum falcatum*

This summer-flowering miniature orchid, which grows only 3 to 6 inches tall, bears spikes of five to seven long-spurred, 1-inch white blossoms (*photograph, page 57*). The flowers are especially fragrant at night.

HOW TO GROW. *N. falcata* does best in bright indirect or curtain-filtered sunlight, night temperatures of 55° to 65° and day temperatures of 68° or higher. Plant on a slab of tree fern or in 2 parts fir bark or shredded tree-fern fiber and 1 part coarse peat moss. Place the pot on a humidifying tray (*page 77*) and keep the potting medium moist. Fertilize monthly from spring through midfall with a 20-10-10 or similar high-nitrogen formula diluted ¼ teaspoon per quart of water. Do not feed in late fall and winter; water only enough to keep the plant from shriveling.

NEOMARICA

N. caerulea, N. gracilis, N. northiana
(all called Apostle plant, twelve Apostles, walking iris)

An irislike plant that grows 12 to 18 inches tall, *N. gracilis* bears sword-shaped leaves and fragrant flowers whose three outer petals are white, with yellow and brown markings at the base, and whose three inner petals are blue. Each 2-inch flower lasts a day, but plants bloom for long periods in midwinter. *N. caerulea* grows 2 to 3 feet tall; its 2- to 4-inch flowers have sky-blue outer petals, paler blue inner petals marked yellow and brown; *N. northiana* has white outer petals, violet-tipped inner petals.

HOW TO GROW. Apostle plants do best in bright indirect or curtain-filtered sunlight, night temperatures of 50° to 55° and day temperatures of 68° to 72°. Keep the soil wet; fertilize monthly. To propagate, use new plants at the tops of flower stems as you would runners *(page 97)*.

NERIUM CORONARIUM See *Ervatamia*
NERO'S-CROWN See *Ervatamia*

NICOTIANA

N. alata grandiflora, also called *N. affinis* (flowering tobacco)

Dwarf varieties of flowering tobacco—usually grown outdoors as summer annuals—also make delightful winter house plants. They grow 8 to 10 inches tall and their trumpet-shaped flowers, each about 2 inches across, range from white and pink to scarlet and include such unusual shades as lime green, chartreuse, wine red, and chocolate brown. The flowers, especially fragrant in the evening, rise above soft, hairy oval leaves 4 to 6 inches long.

HOW TO GROW. Flowering tobacco plants do best in at least four hours of direct sunlight a day, night temperatures of 50° to 60° and day temperatures of 68° to 72°. Keep the soil moist and fertilize every two weeks. Start plants from seeds in midsummer for midwinter flowering indoors, or dig plants from the garden in fall and cut them back to 6 to 8 inches before potting; they will branch freely and blossom in midwinter. Discard after flowering.

NIDULARIUM

N. fulgens, N. innocentii striatum, N. regelioides

Nidularium, a Latin word meaning "little bird nest," describes the way the flowers of this bromeliad are borne deep within the nestlike centers of rosette-shaped leaf clusters that measure from 18 to 24 inches across. Weeks before the flowers appear, which may be at any time of year, the centers of the rosettes become brightly colored, usually red. The flowers remain colorful for months. *N. fulgens* bears violet blooms among bright red, green-tipped petallike bracts, and pale green spiny-edged leaves with dark green spots; *N. innocentii striatum* has white flowers and broad, ivory-striped, spiny-edged leaves; *N. regelioides* bears orange-red flowers among smooth-edged, shiny light green leaves with dark green blotches.

HOW TO GROW. Nidulariums do best in bright indirect or curtain-filtered sunlight, night temperatures of 60° to 65° and day temperatures of 70° or higher. Pot in 2 parts peat moss, 1 part packaged potting soil and 1 part sharp sand or perlite; do not add lime. Keep moist; keep water in the cup formed by the leaf rosette and feed monthly with a quarter-strength house-plant fertilizer. Propagate from new shoots that appear at the base of plants after flowering.

O

ODONTOGLOSSUM

O. pulchellum (lily-of-the-valley orchid)

The nearly foot-high flower spikes of this orchid bear five to 10 waxy 1½-inch flowers *(photograph, page 58)*. The blossoms, white with yellow lips, bloom in winter and early spring, lasting as long as six or seven weeks, and have a strong lily-of-the-valley fragrance.

HOW TO GROW. *O. pulchellum* does best in at least four hours of direct sunlight a day, but should be shielded from sun at midday. Night temperatures of 55° to 65° and day temperatures of 68° or higher are ideal. Plant in 2 parts fir bark or shredded tree-fern fiber and 1 part coarse peat

FLOWERING TOBACCO
Nicotiana alata grandiflora

NIDULARIUM
Nidularium regelioides

135

FALSE SEA ONION
Ornithogalum caudatum

SWEET OLIVE
Osmanthus fragrans

OXALIS
Oxalis purpurea 'Grand Duchess'

moss. Place the pot on a humidifying tray *(page 77); let* the mixture dry moderately between thorough waterings. Fertilize monthly with a 20-10-10 or similar high-nitrogen formula diluted ¼ teaspoon per quart of water.

OLEA See *Osmanthus*
OLIVE, SWEET See *Osmanthus*

ONCIDIUM
O. varicosum rogersii (dancing lady orchid)

Oncidiums bear great clusters of long-lasting delicate flowers, sometimes with 100 or more in bloom at once. *O. varicosum rogersii*, which blossoms in fall and winter, has bright yellow flowers up to 2 inches across with wide, flaring, skirt-shaped lips *(photograph, page 56).*

HOW TO GROW. Oncidiums do best in at least four hours of direct sunlight a day but should be shaded from hot midday rays by curtains or blinds. Night temperatures of 55° to 65° and day temperatures of 68° or higher are ideal. Pot in a mixture of 2 parts fir bark or shredded tree-fern fiber and 1 part coarse peat moss. Place the pot on a humidifying tray *(page 77).* Allow the potting medium to become moderately dry between thorough waterings during the growing season, from winter through late summer; while the plant is dormant in the fall, water only enough to keep from shriveling. Fertilize monthly during the growing season with a 20-10-10 or similar high-nitrogen formula diluted ¼ teaspoon per quart of water.

ONION, FALSE SEA See *Ornithogalum*
ORANGE See *Citrus*
ORCHID, CHRISTMAS See *Cattleya*
ORCHID, CLAMSHELL See *Epidendrum*
ORCHID, DANCING LADY See *Oncidium*
ORCHID, EASTER See *Cattleya*
ORCHID, LADY-OF-THE-NIGHT See *Brassavola*
ORCHID, LILY-OF-THE-VALLEY See *Odontoglossum*
ORCHID, MOTH See *Phalaenopsis*
ORCHID, NUT See *Achimenes*
ORCHID, SPIDER See *Brassia*

ORNITHOGALUM
O. arabicum (star-of-Bethlehem), *O. caudatum* (false sea onion), *O. thyrsoides* (chincherinchee)

These easy-to-grow bulb plants are notable for their long-lasting clusters of fragrant star-shaped flowers, which appear on a central stalk in winter and spring. *O. arabicum* produces six to 12 white 2-inch flowers with conspicuous black pollen-receiving pistils on a 1- to 2-foot stalk among slender 18-inch green leaves. *O. caudatum* bears a mass of 50 to 100 small white flowers with a green center line on each petal; the 18- to 36-inch flower stalk grows from a 3- to 4-inch bulb that is almost entirely out of the soil. *O. thyrsoides* has white or yellow 2-inch flowers on a 6- to 18-inch stalk; blossoms often last six weeks or more.

HOW TO GROW. These species do best in at least four hours of direct sunlight a day, night temperatures of 50° to 60° and day temperatures of 68° to 72°. Allow the soil to become slightly dry between thorough waterings and fertilize monthly during the growing season; do not water or fertilize while the bulbs are dormant. Pot or repot bulbs in early fall. Propagate during dormancy from the small bulbs that develop beside larger ones.

OSMANTHUS
O. fragrans, also called *Olea fragrans* (sweet olive)

The orange-blossom fragrance of sweet olives comes from clusters of almost unnoticeable four-petaled greenish white flowers, each about ³⁄₁₆ inch across, set among handsome leathery dark green leaves 3 inches long. Plants, which grow 2 to 3 feet tall, bloom continuously all year.

HOW TO GROW. Sweet olives thrive in bright sun or very light shade, night temperatures of 50° to 55° and day temperatures of 68° to 72°. Keep the soil moist and fertilize monthly. Propagate in summer from stem cuttings.

OXALIS
O. bowieana, also called *O. bowiei, O. purpurata bowiei; O. brasiliensis; O. cernua*, also called *O. pes-caprae* (Bermuda buttercup); *O. purpurea* 'Grand Duchess'

These charming bulb plants, which grow only 4 to 6 inches high, bear many satiny 1- to 1½-inch flowers among 2- to 4-inch cloverlike leaves during fall, winter and spring. The flowers of *O. bowieana* are purplish pink; *O. brasiliensis*, rosy red; *O. cernua*, yellow single or double; Grand Duchess, bright pink or white. Blossoms open only on sunny days and close at night and in cloudy weather.

HOW TO GROW. Oxalis does best in at least four hours of direct sunlight a day, night temperatures of 50° to 60° and day temperatures of 68° to 72°. Keep moist; fertilize monthly while the plants are growing. After the foliage withers, keep bulbs dry until fall. Propagate in fall from the small bulbs that develop beside larger ones.

P
PAINTED FEATHER See *Vriesia*

PAPHIOPEDILUM, formerly called CYPRIPEDIUM
P. callosum, P. hybrids

The varieties of these orchids that have mottled leaves are among the easiest orchids to grow indoors (those with clear green foliage require temperatures too cool for easy indoor culture). *P. callosum*, an outstanding species that blooms in spring and summer, bears single 4-inch blossoms on 10- to 15-inch-tall stalks. Their pale green petals have rosy purple tips and are warted and hairy along their upper edges; the pouch-shaped lip is brownish purple; and the large, leaflike outer sepals are white with purple lines. Hybrids usually grow less than 15 inches tall. They bear 3- to 5-inch flowers in colors ranging from white and yellow to rose, pink, green and brown, usually with several colors in one blossom *(photograph, page 55)*; individual flowers often last one to three months.

HOW TO GROW. Mottled-leaved paphiopedilums do best in partial shade; too much light produces yellowish leaves and fewer blossoms. Night temperatures of 65° to 70° and day temperatures of 75° or higher are ideal. Plant in a mixture of 4 parts fine fir bark and 1 part coarse sand. Place the pot on a humidifying tray *(page 77)*. Fertilize monthly with a 20-10-10 or similar high-nitrogen formula diluted ¼ teaspoon per quart of water.

PASSIFLORA
P. alato-caerulea, also called *P. pfordtii; P. caerulea; P. coccinea; P. edulis* (granadilla); *P. trifasciata* (all called passionflower)

Clinging by tendrils to trellises or stakes or trained to string around a window, passionflower vines display intriguing blossoms of 10 outer petals and an intricate inner crown among deeply lobed leaves. Recommended types that bloom in spring and summer are *P. alato-caerulea*, with fragrant purple, pink and white 4-inch flowers and smooth 4- to 6-inch leaves; *P. caerulea*, with fragrant 3- to 4-inch pink and purple flowers and smooth, 4- to 5-inch gray-green leaves; *P. coccinea*, with 4- to 5-inch scarlet flowers and coarse, oval 3- to 6-inch leaves; *P. edulis*, with 2½-

PASSIONFLOWER
Passiflora alato-caerulea

inch purple and white flowers and shiny 4- to 6-inch leaves; and *P. trifasciata*, with fragrant 1- to 1½-inch yellow-white flowers and 4- to 6-inch leaves, purple below and olive to bronze green with silvery pink markings above.

HOW TO GROW. Passionflowers do best in at least four hours of direct sunlight a day, night temperatures of 55° to 65° and day temperatures of 68° or higher. Keep soil moist; fertilize every two weeks during the growing season. When plants are resting, keep the soil slightly dry. Cut plants back to 6 inches in January to force branching. Propagate from stem cuttings or seeds at any time.

PASSIONFLOWER See *Passiflora*
PATIENT LUCY See *Impatiens*

PELARGONIUM
P. crispum, P. denticulatum, P. graveolens,
P. odoratissimum, P. tomentosum (all called scented-leaf geranium); *P. hortorum* (zonal geranium);
P. peltatum (ivy geranium)

Geraniums are among the most widely grown flowering pot plants in the world. The best strains for indoor gardens are varieties of *P. hortorum*, which vary from 3 inches to 3 feet in height and bear flower clusters up to 4 inches across in red, white, pink or lavender; most bloom from late winter through the following fall. The soft plush leaves are horseshoe shaped with concentric bands of white, cream, yellow, red or brown. Also widely grown indoors are the spring-blooming scented-leaved geraniums such as *P. crispum* (lemon-scented, violet-colored flowers); *P. denticulatum* (pine-scented, lavender flowers); *P. graveolens* (rose-scented, pinkish purple flowers); *P. odoratissimum* (apple-scented, white flowers); and *P. tomentosum* (peppermint-scented, white flowers). All of them grow 1 to 3 feet tall. Varieties of the trailing ivy geranium, *P. peltatum*, bear 2- to 3-inch clusters of white, pink, red or lavender flowers from late spring through fall.

HOW TO GROW. Geraniums do best in at least four hours of direct sunlight a day, night temperatures of 50° to 55° and day temperatures of 68° to 72°, although night temperatures may go up to 65°. Allow the soil to become moderately dry between thorough waterings. Fertilize every two weeks from March through October, monthly the rest of the year. Propagate from stem cuttings any time.

PENTAS
P. lanceolata, also called *P. carnea* (Egyptian star cluster)

These plants bear 4-inch clusters of ½-inch flowers; the hairy oval leaves, 3 to 4 inches long, are often deeply veined. The variety Orchid Star has rosy lavender flowers; other varieties have red, pink, lavender or white flowers. The upright, bushy plants, usually kept 12 to 18 inches tall by pinching off the tips of stems, bloom year round.

HOW TO GROW. Egyptian star clusters do best in at least four hours of direct sunlight a day, night temperatures of 50° to 65° and day temperatures of 68° or higher. Keep soil moist and fertilize every two weeks. Propagate from stem cuttings at any time.

PEPPER, ORNAMENTAL See *Capsicum*
PERMANENT WAVE PLANT See *Billbergia*

PETUNIA
P. hybrids

Petunias make fine indoor plants, even though they last but a single winter season. The blossoms, up to 4 inches across, are often fringed and double flowered, and come in colors ranging from white and pale yellow through pink

GERANIUM
Pelargonium hortorum 'Skies of Italy'

EGYPTIAN STAR CLUSTER
Pentas lanceolata 'Orchid Star'

and red, to blue and deep purple, with some varieties multicolored. Plants grow to 6 to 12 inches or taller.

HOW TO GROW. Petunias do best in at least four hours of direct sunlight a day, and day temperatures of 68° to 72°. Night temperatures during the winter must be 50° to 55°; if higher, flower buds will not form. Let the soil become slightly dry between thorough waterings. Fertilize every two weeks. The best winter-flowering plants come from seedlings started in midsummer, but garden plants, cut back and potted in September, often flower all winter indoors.

PHALAENOPSIS
P. amabilis, P. hybrids (all called moth orchids)

Widely used in bridal bouquets, these orchids bear flat, 3½- to 4-inch blossoms in white, pink, yellow or purple, often with spots or bars of contrasting colors. Dozens of flowers may bloom at a time on arching, often branching flower stalks 2 to 4 feet long. The foliage—five or six lustrous leaves up to 12 inches long and 2 to 3 inches wide—is rarely more than a foot high. Most of the modern white varieties are derived from *P. amabilis,* whose lips are tinged with yellow and spotted with red (*photograph, page 57*). Most species bloom in spring, though hybrids may blossom at any season and some bloom year round.

HOW TO GROW. Moth orchids do best in bright indirect or curtain-filtered sunlight, night temperatures of 65° to 75° and day temperatures of 75° or higher. Plant in a mixture of 3 parts fir bark to 1 part coarse peat moss and 1 part redwood chips. Place the pot on a humidifying tray (*page 77*) and keep the planting medium moist. Fertilize monthly with a 20-10-10 or similar high-nitrogen formula diluted ¼ teaspoon per quart of water. To encourage branching and flowers, cut off the flower stalks just below the bottom flower when the blooms have faded.

PHARBITIS See *Ipomoea*
PIGTAIL PLANT See *Anthurium*
PINEAPPLE See *Ananas*
PLUME, BRAZILIAN See *Jacobinia*
PLUME, SCARLET See *Euphorbia*
POCKETBOOK FLOWER See *Calceolaria*
POINSETTIA See *Euphorbia*
POMEGRANATE See *Punica*
POWDER PUFF See *Calliandra*
PRIMROSE See *Primula*
PRIMROSE, CAPE See *Streptocarpus*

PRIMULA
P. malacoides (fairy primrose, baby primrose),
P. obconica (obconica primrose),
P. polyantha (polyanthus primrose)

Three species of primroses bring a touch of spring to homes in winter. The most popular, the fairy primrose, bears clouds of pink, red or white flowers, an inch or less across, arranged in tiers on slender 8- to 10-inch stalks. Clusters of fragrant, slightly larger blossoms, up to 2 inches across, adorn the two other species—the obconica, which comes in red, pink, lavender and white (and has rough hairy leaves that may cause a skin rash), and the polyanthus, which is shorter and bears white, yellow, pink, red, lavender or purple flowers. Blossoming plants of all three species are usually bought from florists and discarded when flowering ends. Polyanthus primroses, however, can be transplanted into a shady garden to grow as perennials.

HOW TO GROW. Primroses do best in bright indirect or curtain-filtered sunlight, night temperatures of 40° to 50° and day temperatures of 68° or lower. Keep slightly moist; fertilize every two weeks. Plants can be started from seeds

PETUNIA
Petunia 'Star Joy'

FAIRY PRIMROSE
Primula malacoides

DWARF POMEGRANATE
Punica granatum nana

GRECIAN VASE PLANT
Quesnelia liboniana

CARDINAL FLOWER
Rechsteineria cardinalis

but require such cool growing conditions that propagation is best left to professionals.

PUNICA

P. granatum nana (dwarf pomegranate)

The pomegranate was known to the Romans as the apple of Carthage. *P. granatum nana,* a dwarf variety, grows no more than 15 inches tall. Its 1-inch bell-shaped orange-red flowers blossom year round, most profusely in spring and summer, and are followed by 2-inch edible fruit. A type called Chico bears carnation-like double flowers but no fruit.

HOW TO GROW. Pomegranates do best in at least four hours of direct sunlight a day, night temperatures of 55° to 60° and day temperatures of 68° to 72°. Keep the soil moist and fertilize every three or four months. Propagate from stem cuttings in summer.

Q

QUEEN'S TEARS See *Billbergia*

QUESNELIA

Q. humilis, Q. liboniana, Q. marmorata
(all called Grecian vase plant)

Quesnelias are bromeliads whose water-holding rosettes surround slender stalks topped by spikes of petallike bracts set with tiny flowers that may bloom any time. *Q. humilis,* 10 to 12 inches tall, bears rose-red bracts, purple flowers; *Q. liboniana,* 12 to 15 inches tall, has coral-red bracts with deep blue blossoms; *Q. marmorata,* 18 inches or taller, has rose bracts, blue flowers and maroon-mottled leaves.

HOW TO GROW. Quesnelias do best in bright indirect or curtain-filtered sunlight, night temperatures of 60° to 65° and day temperatures of 70° or higher. Pot in 2 parts peat moss to 1 part packaged potting soil and 1 part sharp sand or perlite; do not add lime. Keep moist; fertilize monthly. Keep the cup at the base of the leaves full of water. Propagate from shoots that appear at the base of plants.

R

RECHSTEINERIA

R. cardinalis, also called *Sinningia cardinalis* (cardinal flower); *R. leucotricha,* also called *S. leucotricha* (Brazilian edelweiss); *R. verticillata,* also called *S. verticillata* (double-decker plant)

These gesneriads, which grow 12 to 18 inches tall, make excellent long-blooming house plants, bearing 1- to 2-inch tubular flowers above hairy, 4- to 6-inch leaves. The red cardinal flower blooms most of the year if old stems are removed. Brazilian edelweiss has salmon-rose flowers; it blooms for one month any time between April and September. The double-decker plant blooms in winter.

HOW TO GROW. Rechsteinerias do best in bright indirect or curtain-filtered sunlight but can take direct sun in winter; cardinal flowers and Brazilian edelweiss also thrive under 14 to 16 hours a day of artificial light. Night temperatures of 65° to 70° and day temperatures of 75° or higher are ideal. Pot in 2 parts peat moss to 1 part packaged potting soil and 1 part sharp sand or perlite and place pots on a humidifying tray *(page 41).* Water from the bottom so that moisture does not touch the leaves or flowers. Allow the soil to become very slightly dry between thorough waterings and fertilize monthly during the growing season; reduce water and omit fertilizer the rest of the year. Propagate cardinal flower and double-decker plants from stem cuttings in late winter or early spring; all three species can be started from seeds at any time.

RHIPSALIDOPSIS See *Schlumbergera*
RHYNCHOSPERMUM See *Trachelospermum*

RODRIGUEZIA

R. venusta, also called *R. bracteata, Burlingtonia fragrans*

These miniature orchids bear arching 6-inch stalks of fragrant, 1½-inch blossoms in white or blush pink, each with a yellow oblong blotch on its lip *(photograph, page 58).* The flowers bloom at different times of the year, usually in summer and fall, amid slender 4- to 5-inch leaves.

HOW TO GROW. Rodriguezias do best in bright indirect or curtain-filtered sunlight, night temperatures of 55° to 65° and day temperatures of 68° or higher. Plant in a mixture of 2 parts fir bark or shredded tree-fern fiber and 1 part coarse peat moss, or mount vertically on a slab of tree fern. Place the pot on a humidifying tray *(page 77)* and keep the potting medium moist at all times. Fertilize monthly with a 20-10-10 or similar high-nitrogen formula diluted ¼ teaspoon per quart of water.

ROSA

R. chinensis minima, also called *R. roulettii*
(miniature roses)

Miniature roses grow well indoors, blooming abundantly all year. Their fragrant, penny- to quarter-sized flowers come in white and shades of pink, red and yellow, as well as blends, and are borne among tiny, five-leaflet leaves. The many varieties available range from 6 to 12 inches at maturity; some bloom when only 3 to 4 inches high.

HOW TO GROW. Miniature roses do best in at least four hours of direct sunlight a day, night temperatures of 50° to 65° and day temperatures of 68° or higher. Keep moist and fertilize every two weeks. To keep red spider mites from sapping strength from the plants, wash the leaves —especially the undersides—forcefully with clear water at least weekly. Propagate from stem cuttings at any time.

ROSE See *Rosa*
ROSE OF CHINA See *Hibiscus*
ROSEMARY See *Rosmarinus*

ROSMARINUS

R. officinalis (rosemary)

Rosemary, used for centuries in cooking, also makes a splendid window-sill plant. Its two-lipped violet-blue fragrant flowers, ½ to ¾ inch across, bloom in midwinter or early spring; the aromatic leaves, ¾ to 2 inches long, are dark green above and fuzzy white beneath. An excellent variety, *R. officinalis prostratus* (prostrate rosemary), can be kept under 15 inches tall by pinching off the tips of stems (the pinched-off tips can be used for seasoning).

HOW TO GROW. Rosemary does best in at least four hours of direct sunlight a day, night temperatures of 50° to 55° and day temperatures of 68° to 72°. Let the soil become moderately dry between thorough waterings; fertilize every two or three months. Propagate from stem cuttings when their tip ends are firm or from seeds at any time.

ROVING SAILOR See *Saxifraga*

RUELLIA

R. amoena, R. macrantha, R. makoyana
(trailing velvet plant)

Perhaps the finest ruellia for growing indoors is *R. macrantha,* a 2- to 3-foot plant that bears rosy pink bell-shaped 2-inch blossoms in winter among 4- to 6-inch oval leaves. The two other species bear tubular blossoms; the 2-inch crimson flowers of *R. amoena* bloom profusely year round atop wiry stems 18 to 24 inches tall; *R. makoyana,* a trailing plant, is more often grown for its soft olive-green foliage, which has prominent silvery violet veins and purple

DOUBLE PINK MINIATURE ROSE
Rosa chinensis minima

PROSTRATE ROSEMARY
Rosmarinus officinalis prostratus

RUELLIA
Ruellia macrantha

CORAL PLANT
Russelia equisetiformis

AFRICAN VIOLET
Saintpaulia 'Rhapsodie Series'

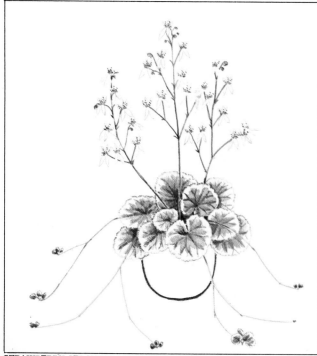

STRAWBERRY GERANIUM
Saxifraga stolonifera tricolor

undersides, than for its 1-inch, rosy red flowers, which bloom in fall and winter.

HOW TO GROW. Ruellias do best in bright indirect or curtain-filtered sunlight, night temperatures of 55° to 65° and day temperatures of 68° or higher. Pot in a mixture of 2 parts peat moss to 1 part packaged potting soil and 1 part sharp sand or perlite. Keep the soil moist and fertilize every two weeks during the growing season; reduce water and omit fertilizer while plants are resting. Old plants tend to get straggly, so many gardeners grow new ones from stem cuttings in spring or summer.

RUSSELIA
R. equisetiformis, also called *R. juncea*
(coral plant, fountain plant)

The bright green, arching branches of the coral plant, which bear 1- to 2-inch-long tubular scarlet flowers, may cascade out 3 feet or more across, making it a stunning choice for hanging containers. Plants bloom abundantly year round if given optimum growing conditions. The finely divided branches appear leafless at first glance but are actually covered with tiny scalelike leaves.

HOW TO GROW. Coral plants do best in at least four hours of direct sunlight a day, night temperatures of 50° to 55° and day temperatures of 68° to 72°. Let the soil become moderately dry between thorough waterings and fertilize every two weeks the year round. Propagate from stem cuttings taken during the summer.

S

SAGE, BLUE See *Eranthemum*

SAINTPAULIA
Many species and varieties called African violets

African violets are probably the most popular flowering house plants in America. Thousands of varieties of these gesneriads exist, and new hybrids are constantly being developed. Given proper care, today's varieties blossom continuously, bearing clusters of velvety 1- to 2-inch flowers in pink, blue or purple, as well as white and bicolors, all accented by conspicuous yellow pollen-bearing stamens. Flowers come in five-petaled single forms and many-petaled double forms; petal edges may be smooth, ruffled or frilled. Plants usually grow 4 to 6 inches tall, bearing flowers above rosettes of hairy 2- to 4-inch leaves that range from green to bronze, with some varieties mottled pink or white.

HOW TO GROW. African violets do best in bright indirect or curtain-filtered sunlight or in 14 to 16 hours of artificial light a day. Night temperatures of 65° to 70° and day temperatures of 75° or higher are ideal. Pot in 2 parts peat moss to 1 part packaged potting soil and 1 part sharp sand or perlite and place the pot on a humidifying tray *(page 41)*. Keep barely moist; fertilize monthly. Propagate named varieties from leaf cuttings or crown divisions any time. Propagate new varieties from seeds.

SAXIFRAGA
S. stolonifera, also called *S. sarmentosa, S. chinensis*
(strawberry geranium, strawberry begonia, roving sailor, mother-of-thousands)

Strawberry geraniums grow as dense 4- to 6-inch tufts of 1- to 1½-inch round, hairy, reddish green leaves with light veins and purplish red undersides. Wiry flower stalks rise up 9 to 12 inches from among the leaves, bearing clouds of tiny white flowers in summer. The species' common names derive from the way it sends out runners with new plants attached, in the manner of strawberry plants, which makes it attractive in hanging containers. *S. stolon-*

ifera tricolor, sometimes called Magic Carpet, is slightly smaller; its green-and-white leaves have pink edges and purplish rose undersides.

HOW TO GROW. Strawberry geraniums do best in light shade, night temperatures of 40° to 45° (though they will tolerate up to 60°) and day temperatures of 68° or lower. Let the soil dry slightly between thorough waterings. To encourage colorful foliage, fertilize sparingly, every three to four months. Propagate from runners *(page 97).*

SCHIZOCENTRON
S. elegans, also called *Haeria elegans, Heterocentron elegans* (Spanish shawl)

Spanish shawl, a creeping plant particularly suited to hanging containers, sends out an abundance of satiny, rosy purple, 1-inch flowers in late spring or early summer. Its dark green leaves are ½ inch long and diamond shaped.

HOW TO GROW. Spanish shawl grows best in partial shade, night temperatures of 50° to 55° and day temperatures of 68° to 72°. Keep soil moist and fertilize monthly. Propagate from stem cuttings or seeds at any time.

SCHLUMBERGERA
S. gaertneri, also called *Rhipsalidopsis gaertneri* (Easter cactus); hybrids of *S. gaertneri* and *Zygocactus truncatus* (hybrid Christmas cactus)

The names of these cacti, which are native to jungles rather than deserts, denote their blossoming season. The individual stem joints 1 to 1½ inches long, form arching, pendulous branches from whose tips hang satiny, many-petaled flowers. The Easter cactus bears starlike 1½-inch scarlet blossoms at the stem joints as well as at the stem ends. The Christmas cactus *(Zygocactus truncatus)* has clawlike stem joints and bears 3-inch-long hooded tubular pink, reddish, white or multicolored flowers. Hybrids of these two species have no claws; their flowers, also tubular but without hoods, come in lavender or purple as well as pink, red and white and may appear from December through February. All grow 1 to 1½ feet high.

HOW TO GROW. These cacti do best in bright indirect or curtain-filtered sunlight. Before blossoming, night temperatures must be about 55°. To ensure flowers, leave the plants outdoors from early fall until just before frost. Once the buds set, night temperatures of 60° to 70° and day temperatures of 70° or higher are ideal. Pot in a mixture composed of 2 parts peat moss to 1 part packaged potting soil and 1 part sharp sand or perlite. Keep the potting medium evenly moistened and fertilize every two weeks during the growing season but keep the mixture on the dry side and do not fertilize while the plants are resting. Propagate from seeds or from stem cuttings taken at any time except when the buds are setting.

SCILLA
S. sibirica (Siberian squill),
S. tubergeniana (Tubergenian squill)

Squills, familiar as early spring-flowering bulbs outdoors, are equally lovely as midwinter-blooming house plants, producing waxy bell-shaped flowers surrounded by smooth, straplike green leaves. Siberian squill bears ½- to 1-inch deep blue flowers on 6-inch spikes amid ½-inch-wide leaves that are 8 to 12 inches tall; the variety Spring Beauty, which grows about 10 inches tall, has 1- to 1½-inch blue blossoms. Tubergenian squill bears 1½-inch pale blue flowers that fade to white and grows about 6 inches high.

HOW TO GROW. Squills do best in full sun or light shade, night temperatures of 40° to 45° and day temperatures of 68° or lower. Pot new bulbs in early fall and put them in a

SPANISH SHAWL
Schizocentron elegans

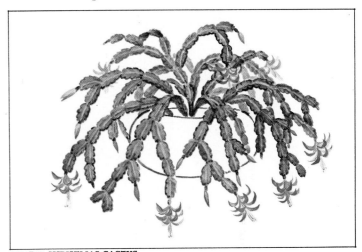
HYBRID CHRISTMAS CACTUS
Schlumbergera-Zygocactus hybrid

SIBERIAN SQUILL
Scilla sibirica 'Spring Beauty'

TOP: MEXICAN FLAME VINE
Senecio confusus

BOTTOM: CINERARIA
Senecio cruentus

GLOXINIA
Sinningia speciosa

cool dark place for eight to 10 weeks before bringing them into the light. Keep soil moist during active growth. Do not fertilize. After flowers fade and foliage withers, save the bulbs for planting in the garden in fall.

SCOTCH PURSE See *Malvaviscus*
SEA ONION, FALSE See *Ornithogalum*

SENECIO
S. confusus (Mexican flame vine); *S. cruentus,* also called *Cineraria grandiflora, C. hybrida* (cineraria); *S. mikanioides* (parlor ivy, German ivy)

These plants offer vivid color for indoor gardens, especially in winter and spring. The Mexican flame vine bears clusters of brilliant orange-red daisylike flowers 1½ inches across and may bloom occasionally through the year. Parlor ivy bears yellow flowers, only ⅓ inch across, in fragrant 1- to 3-inch clusters. Both can be kept small for use in hanging containers by pinching off the tips of stems. Mexican flame vines can be trained to a 3- to 4-foot trellis. Cinerarias have immense clusters of velvety flowers atop a dense growth of 3- to 4-inch leaves, green on top and purplish underneath. The blossoms, 1 to 4 or more inches across, may be white, pink, red, blue or purple with blue or white centers; some have concentric rings of varying colors.

HOW TO GROW. Mexican flame vines and parlor ivies do best in at least four hours of direct sunlight a day in winter and curtain-filtered sunlight the rest of the year; night temperatures of 50° to 55° and day temperatures of 68° to 72° are ideal. Keep moist and fertilize monthly. Cut back straggly plants after flowering to promote new growth. Propagate from stem cuttings. Cinerarias should be bought from florists and discarded after flowers fade. While in bloom, they do best in bright indirect or curtain-filtered sunlight, night temperatures of 40° to 45° and day temperatures of 68° or lower. Keep moist; do not fertilize.

SHRIMP PLANT See *Beloperone*

SINNINGIA
S. pusilla, S. speciosa (both called gloxinia)

The plants generally thougnt of as gloxinias are modern forms of *S. speciosa,* a tuberous-rooted Brazilian flower. The velvety bell-shaped blossoms of these free-flowing gesneriads range from 3 to 6 inches across and may be single, with five petal-like lobes, or double, with many lobes. They come in white, pink, deep red, lavender and purple, often edged or spotted with contrasting hues and are held slightly above the compact growth of velvety oval 5-inch leaves. The plants may blossom at any time and go through periods of growth and dormancy. A miniature gloxinia, *S. pusilla,* bears ½-inch violet flowers continuously all year.

HOW TO GROW. Gloxinias do best in bright indirect or curtain-filtered sunlight and can also be grown in 14 to 16 hours of artificial light a day. Night temperatures of 65° to 70° and day temperatures of 75° or higher are ideal. Set *S. pusilla* on a humidifying tray *(page 41).* Pot both species in 2 parts peat moss, 1 part packaged potting soil and 1 part sharp sand or perlite. Keep moist and fertilize monthly while the plants are growing. For *S. speciosa,* which has periods of dormancy, omit fertilizer when flowers fade, and reduce watering gradually, stopping completely when leaves wither; when new sprouts appear two to four months later, repot in a fresh mixture and begin watering and fertilizing again. Propagate both species from leaf cuttings, seeds or root divisions.

SINNINGIA See *Rechsteineria*

SLIPPERWORT See *Calceolaria*

SMITHIANTHA, formerly known as NAEGELIA
S. 'Carmel', *S. cinnabarina, S. zebrina* hybrids
(all called temple bells)

The bell-shaped 1½-inch-long flowers of these gesneriads come in white, pink, red, orange or yellow, often streaked or spotted inside with contrasting hues. They flower from late summer well into the winter. The heart-shaped, deep green leaves are often marbled red and purple and covered with a mat of red hairs. *S. cinnabarina* bears red, rose or orange-red flowers. *S. zebrina* hybrids are bushy plants, with yellow, pink and red-spotted blossoms. The hybrid Carmel bears red flowers with a red-spotted yellowish throat. All grow about a foot tall.

HOW TO GROW. Temple bells do best in bright indirect or curtain-filtered sunlight and can be grown under 14 to 16 hours of artificial light a day. Night temperatures of 65° to 70° and day temperatures of 75° or higher are ideal. Pot in 2 parts peat moss, 1 part packaged potting soil and 1 part sharp sand or perlite. Keep moist; fertilize monthly during the growing season. While the plants are dormant, moisten the soil just often enough to keep the scaly, thick underground stems (rhizomes) from dehydrating. Propagate by dividing the rhizomes after the blooming season or by taking leaf cuttings any time.

SOLANUM
S. pseudocapsicum (Jerusalem cherry, Cleveland cherry)

This 10- to 12-inch plant bears starlike ½-inch white flowers from July to September, followed by cherry-sized orange-scarlet or yellow fruit in November and December. Both grow in abundance among the plant's narrow, pointed 2- to 2½-inch dark green leaves. The colorful inedible fruit may cling to the plants for two months.

HOW TO GROW. Jerusalem cherries do best in at least four hours of direct sunlight a day, night temperatures of 50° to 55° and day temperatures of 68° to 72°. Allow the soil to become slightly dry between thorough soakings; fertilize monthly. Usually grown as an annual from seeds sown in February or March for fall fruiting, plants can be kept another year if cut back and repotted in spring. Pinch back the stem tips until late June to encourage thick growth.

SOPHROLAELIOCATTLEYA
Hybrids derived from *Sophronitis, Laelia* and *Cattleya*

These compact plants rarely grow more than a foot high but bear lavender to red flowers 4 to 7 inches across. Blossoms may appear at any season and the plants often bloom more than once a year. Among the many fine types are Falcon Westonbirt, Anzac Orchidhurst, Jewel Box and Miami (*photograph, page 56*).

HOW TO GROW. Sophrolaeliocattleyas do best in bright indirect or curtain-filtered sunlight, night temperatures of 55° to 65° and day temperatures of 68° or higher. Plant in 2 parts fir bark or shredded tree-fern fiber and 1 part coarse peat moss. Place the pot on a humidifying tray (*page 77*); let the mix dry slightly between thorough waterings. Fertilize monthly with a 20-10-10 or similar high-nitrogen formula diluted ¼ teaspoon per quart of water.

SPANISH SHAWL See *Schizocentron*

SPATHIPHYLLUM
S. clevelandii, also called *S. kochii; S.* 'Mauna Loa'

Spathiphyllums bear handsome, subtly fragrant leaf-shaped white flowers called spathes that closely resemble the blossoms of calla lilies. *S. clevelandii* blooms in sum-

TEMPLE BELLS
Smithiantha 'Carmel'

JERUSALEM CHERRY
Solanum pseudocapsicum

SPATHIPHYLLUM
Spathiphyllum clevelandii

mer and fall, producing waxy 3- to 4-inch flowers that turn apple green as they age. The hybrid Mauna Loa has 4- to 6-inch flowers that appear intermittently through the year. Both plants grow 12 to 18 inches tall and have shiny dark green leaves 8 to 10 inches long that rise on wiry stems and give the plants a striking appearance even when they are not flowering.

HOW TO GROW. Spathiphyllums do best in shade except in the winter, when they may receive curtain-filtered sunlight. Night temperatures of 60° to 65° and day temperatures of 70° or higher are ideal. Pot in a mixture of 2 parts peat moss, 1 part packaged potting soil and 1 part sharp sand or perlite. Keep the mix moist and fertilize every two to three months. Propagate by division at any time.

SPREKELIA
S. formosissima, also called *Amaryllis formosissima*
(Aztec lily, Jacobean lily, St.-James's-lily)

Each spring Aztec lilies send up single orchidlike flowers atop pink 12- to 18-inch stalks; usually these bulbs send up only one stalk, but occasionally they send up two. The deep red 4-inch blossoms may appear before, with or after the narrow 8- to 12-inch green leaves.

HOW TO GROW. Aztec lilies do best in at least four hours of direct sunlight a day, night temperatures of 60° to 65° and day temperatures of 70° or higher during their growing season from February to September, and 40° to 45° at night and 68° or lower when they are resting during the fall and early winter. Keep soil moist and fertilize monthly as long as the foliage is green; keep soil dry and do not fertilize while the plants are dormant. Repot every three to four years, planting bulbs so that the necks are visible above the soil. New plants can be propagated from small bulbs that develop next to the larger ones, but they will not reach flowering size for two or three years.

SQUILL See *Scilla*
STAR-OF-BETHLEHEM See *Ornithogalum*

STEPHANOTIS
S. floribunda (stephanotis, Madagascar jasmine)

Stephanotis, a long-time favorite in bridal bouquets, bears its exceedingly fragrant white blooms on handsome vines from May to October. The waxy tubular flowers, about an inch across, bloom in 4- to 6-inch clusters among leathery dark green 3- to 4-inch leaves. This vine may be woven through a small trellis, trained around the top of a window or grown as a bush-type plant by pinching off the tips of new stems.

HOW TO GROW. Stephanotis does best in at least four hours of direct sunlight a day, night temperatures of 60° to 65° and day temperatures of 70° or higher. Keep moist and fertilize monthly from March to October. Soil should be kept slightly on the dry side and fertilizer withheld from November through February. Propagate from stem cuttings or from seeds at any time.

STRELITZIA
S. reginae (strelitzia, bird-of-paradise flower)

Shaped like the heads of tropical birds, the multicolored 6-inch flowers of this exotic plant usually appear in summer and fall, occasionally at other times, on stout stalks above spear-shaped leaves about 3 inches wide and 12 to 15 inches long. Plants generally grow 2 to 3 feet tall, although a rare dwarf type, *S. reginae humilis,* grows to a height of only 18 inches.

HOW TO GROW. Strelitzias do best in at least four hours of direct sunlight a day, night temperatures of 50° to 55°

AZTEC LILY
Sprekelia formosissima

STEPHANOTIS
Stephanotis floribunda

STRELITZIA
Strelitzia reginae

and day temperatures of 68° to 72°. Allow the soil to become slightly dry between thorough waterings and fertilize every two weeks. Plants should be grown in large tubs and divided only when it is absolutely necessary; divisions often require two or three years to reach flowering size, and plants that are propagated from seed take five to 10 years to produce any flowers.

STREPTOCARPUS
S. rexii hybrids, *S. saxorum* (all called Cape primrose)

Named for their primroselike foliage and natural home near the Cape of Good Hope in South Africa, these gesneriads can be grown to blossom at any time of the year. Hybrids of *S. rexii* produce 2- to 5-inch trumpet-shaped blossoms in white, pink, rose, red, blue or purple, often with frilled edges and throats splashed with contrasting colors. Narrow stemless leaves, which are quilted and hairy, form ground-hugging rosettes 10 to 20 inches in diameter. An excellent strain is called Weismoor Hybrids. *S. saxorum,* a trailing species, bears 1½-inch-wide, trumpetlike lavender-blue flowers.

HOW TO GROW. Cape primroses do best in bright indirect or curtain-filtered sunlight and can be grown under 14 to 16 hours of artificial light a day. They thrive in night temperatures of 65° to 70° and day temperatures of 75° or higher. Pot in a mixture of 2 parts peat moss, 1 part packaged potting soil and 1 part sharp sand or perlite. Keep the mix moist; fertilize monthly during the growing season —year round for *S. saxorum,* which does not rest. When *S. rexii* hybrids cease blooming, give them only enough water to prevent the leaves from wilting. Repot when new growth starts—plants are usually dormant for two to three months. Propagate *S. rexii* by division when dormant or from seeds or leaf cuttings at any time; propagate *S. saxorum* from stem cuttings or seeds at any time.

STREPTOSOLEN
S. jamesonii, also called *Browallia jamesonii*
(orange streptosolen, orange browallia)

The orange streptosolen is a rambling plant valued for its great clusters of bright orange flowers about an inch across, which appear in winter and intermittently through the year among 1- to 2-inch oval leaves. Plants are well suited to hanging containers. If trained to a stake, they grow up to 3 feet tall in treelike forms with new growth trailing gracefully in the shape of an umbrella.

HOW TO GROW. Streptosolens do best in at least four hours of direct sunlight a day in winter, and in bright indirect or curtain-filtered sunlight in summer. Night temperatures of 50° to 55° and day temperatures of 68° to 72° are ideal. Keep soil moist and fertilize monthly. Propagate from stem cuttings at any time.

T

TABERNAEMONTANA See *Ervatamia*
TAILFLOWER See *Anthurium*
TANGERINE See *Citrus*
TEMPLE BELLS See *Smithiantha*

TETRANEMA
T. mexicanum, also called *Allophyton mexicanum*
(Mexican foxglove)

The Mexican foxglove bears ¼-inch pink to purple blossoms that look like little violets. The dainty, nodding flowers bloom year round atop 6- to 8-inch flower stalks, which rise from the center of a compact rosette of dark green, leathery leaves.

HOW TO GROW. Mexican foxgloves do best in partial

CAPE PRIMROSE
Streptocarpus 'Weismoor Hybrids'

ORANGE STREPTOSOLEN
Streptosolen jamesonii

MEXICAN FOXGLOVE
Tetranema mexicanum

BLACK-EYED-SUSAN VINE
Thunbergia alata

TILLANDSIA
Tillandsia cyanea

CONFEDERATE STAR JASMINE
Trachelospermum jasminoides

shade, night temperatures of 50° to 55° and day temperatures of 68° to 72°. Keep moist; fertilize every two weeks. Propagate any time by dividing old plants or from seeds.

THUNBERGIA
T. alata (black-eyed-Susan vine)

The black-eyed-Susan vine, treated as an outdoor annual in northern gardens, is actually a perennial vine well suited to growing indoors. Its 1- to 2-inch-wide flowers have black or dark purple centers and paper-thin white, buff, yellow or orange petals. The wiry stems grow about 2 to 4 feet long, bearing 1- to 2-inch-long leaves. The plants may be given a little trellis to climb on or allowed to cascade from a hanging container.

HOW TO GROW. Black-eyed-Susan vines do best in at least four hours of direct sunlight a day, night temperatures of 50° to 60° and day temperatures of 68° to 72°. Keep moist and fertilize every two weeks during the fall and winter growing season. When the vines become straggly, cut them off at the soil level and fresh growth will arise. Propagate from seeds in midsummer to have flowering-sized plants for winter blossoming.

TILLANDSIA
T. cyanea, T. lindenii

Most tillandsias grown as house plants have slender gray-green leaves that curve back at the ends and form loose rosettes; above the rosettes rise flower spikes that bear a single fragrant blossom at a time from fall through spring. *T. cyanea* produces a flat diamond-shaped pinkish red spike with deep blue flowers; it grows 8 to 10 inches tall and has 6-inch-long leaves. *T. lindenii* sends up a vivid pink paddle-shaped bract set with blue flowers; its rosette spreads 15 inches in diameter. Tillandsias comprise the largest genus of bromeliads, including the well-known air plant called Spanish moss.

HOW TO GROW. Tillandsias do best in bright indirect or curtain-filtered sunlight, night temperatures of 60° to 65° and day temperatures of 70° or higher. Pot in a mixture of 2 parts peat moss to 1 part packaged potting soil and 1 part sharp sand or perlite set over a layer of coarse drainage material such as pieces of broken clay flowerpots. Do not add lime. Keep moist and feed monthly with a quarter-strength fertilizer from fall through spring. Propagate from shoots that appear at the base of plants.

TOBACCO See *Nicotiana*

TRACHELOSPERMUM, also called RHYNCHOSPERMUM
T. asiaticum (Japanese star jasmine, yellow star jasmine), *T. jasminoides* (Confederate star jasmine, Chinese star jasmine)

These slow-growing vines, which have 1½- to 2½-inch-long shiny green leaves, produce fragrant starlike ½- to 1-inch flowers, generally in spring and summer. *T. asiaticum* has yellowish white flowers. *T. jasminoides* bears white flowers; a variety, *T. jasminoides variegatum*, has handsome green and white leaves with red markings. Plants can be trained on low trellises or grown as bushes by pinching off the tips of stems.

HOW TO GROW. Star jasmines do best in at least four hours of direct sunlight a day in winter, bright indirect or curtain-filtered sunlight the rest of the year. Night temperatures of 50° to 55° and day temperatures of 68° to 72° are ideal. Allow the soil to become slightly dry between thorough waterings. Fertilize every two to three months. Propagate from stem cuttings in fall or winter.

TREASURE FLOWER See *Gazania*

TRICHOCENTRUM
T. tigrinum

These miniature orchids, which rarely reach 6 inches in height, bear sweetly fragrant 2-inch flowers, one or two to a spike, in spring and early summer. The blossoms, yellow or yellow green, are thickly covered with purplish red spots, and have a widely flaring lip that is pure white except for a rosy red base (*photograph, page 58*). The thick, 4- to 5-inch-long leaves are green above and reddish underneath.

HOW TO GROW. *Trichocentrum* species do best in bright indirect or curtain-filtered sunlight, night temperatures of 55° to 70° and day temperatures of 68° or higher. They may be grown on a slab of tree fern or in a mixture of 2 parts fir bark or shredded tree-fern fiber and 1 part coarse peat moss. Place the pot on a humidifying tray (*page 77*) and keep the potting medium constantly moist. Fertilize monthly with a 20-10-10 or similar high-nitrogen formula diluted ¼ teaspoon per quart of water.

TRICHOSPORUM See *Aeschynanthus*

TROPAEOLUM
T. majus (common nasturtium)

These inexpensive annuals will blossom most of the winter on a sunny window sill. Their soft, fragrant 2-inch flowers, with few or many petals, come in white, yellow, orange, pink, scarlet, deep red and mahogany brown, appearing among shield-shaped 1½- to 2½-inch leaves. Bushy varieties grow 1 to 2 feet high; trailing or climbing types are attractive in hanging containers.

HOW TO GROW. Nasturtiums do best in at least four hours of direct sunlight a day, night temperatures of 40° to 55° and day temperatures of 68° or lower. Keep the soil moist and fertilize monthly. Seeds sown in late summer will produce fine flowering plants for the winter.

TULBAGHIA
T. fragrans, also called *T. pulchella* (fragrant tulbaghia); *T. violacea* (society garlic, violet tulbaghia)

Tulbaghias are bulb plants that bloom continuously throughout the year, displaying 20 to 30 sweetly scented ½-inch lavender flowers in clusters at the tops of 12- to 15-inch tall stalks. The arching leaves of *T. violacea* give off a garliclike odor when bruised.

HOW TO GROW. Tulbaghias do best in at least four hours of direct sunlight a day, night temperatures of 40° to 45° and day temperatures of 68° or lower. Keep the soil moist and fertilize monthly. Bulbs multiply rapidly and should be divided and repotted when they become overcrowded.

TULIPA
Several classes of large-flowered tulips

Familiar florists' pot plants in winter and spring, tulips range in color from white to cream, yellow, orange, pink, red, lavender blue, purple, brown, nearly black and even green. Professional tulip growers recognize 15 categories in this genus, varying from 3 inches to nearly 3 feet in height, with blossoms 1 to 7 inches across when open. Although most any tulip can be grown as a pot plant, the classes most easily grown are: single early, double early, Darwin, cottage, parrot and double late.

HOW TO GROW. Tulips bought in bud and bloom do best in bright indirect or curtain-filtered sunlight, night temperatures of 40° to 45° and day temperatures of 68° or lower. Keep the soil moist but do not fertilize. Once forced by florists for indoor blooming, bulbs are useless for further forcing and are difficult to propagate, but they may be

COMMON NASTURTIUM
Tropaeolum majus

FRAGRANT TULBAGHIA
Tulbaghia fragrans

PARROT TULIP
Tulipa 'Fantasy'

SCARBOROUGH LILY
Vallota speciosa

VELTHEIMIA
Veltheimia viridifolia

planted in the garden in cooler climates if the foliage is allowed to mature normally and the bulbs are kept dry until planting time in September.

TURK'S-CAP See *Malvaviscus*
TWELVE APOSTLES See *Neomarica*

U

URN PLANT See *Aechmea*

V

VALLOTA

V. speciosa (Scarborough lily)

This bulb plant has clusters of three to 10 scarlet flowers, 3 to 4 inches in diameter, atop 2-foot-tall stalks in late summer; white and salmon-pink varieties are rarer. Flower stalks are surrounded by 12- to 18-inch-long leaves.

HOW TO GROW. Scarborough lilies do best in at least four hours of direct sunlight a day, night temperatures of 50° to 55° and day temperatures of 68° to 72°. Keep the soil well moistened and fertilize monthly from spring until fall. After the flowers have faded, withhold fertilizer and water the plant sparingly so that the soil will stay slightly dry through the winter. Early each summer, wash away some of the old soil without disturbing the roots and replace it with fresh soil. Repot in fresh potting mixture every three or four years. Propagate in early summer from the small bulbs that develop beside the larger ones.

VELTHEIMIA

V. viridifolia, also called *V. undulata;*
V. capensis, also called *V. glauca*

Two species of veltheimias serve as handsome winter-flowering bulb plants. *V. viridifolia* produces clusters of 50 to 60 long-lasting 1-inch flowers that are pinkish purple with yellow speckles. They bloom at the top of flower stalks 1 to 2 feet tall. The leaves grow 12 to 14 inches long. *V. capensis* produces green-tipped pink flowers.

HOW TO GROW. Veltheimias do best in at least four hours of direct sunlight a day except when flowering, when they should have bright indirect or curtain-filtered sunlight. Night temperatures of 40° to 60° and day temperatures of 72° or lower are ideal. Pot so that the top third of the bulb is out of the soil. Keep the soil barely moist until growth starts in fall, then keep constantly moist and fertilize monthly during the growing season. When the foliage dies down in the summer, keep the soil dry and omit fertilizer. Propagate in spring by dividing the bulbs.

VELVET PLANT, TRAILING See *Ruellia*
VIOLET, AFRICAN See *Saintpaulia*
VIOLET, ARABIAN See *Exacum*
VIOLET, FLAME See *Episcia*

VRIESIA

V. guttata, V. 'Mariae' (painted feather),
V. splendens (flaming sword)

Vriesias are popular bromeliads noted either for the exotic markings of their vase-shaped leaf rosettes or for their brilliantly colored flower clusters. Two species combine both: *V. guttata* bears bright pink paddle-shaped clusters of petallike 1- to 2-inch bracts set with pale yellow flowers from late winter to early summer; gray-green leaves are covered with small maroon spots. *V. splendens,* which blooms in spring and summer, has sword-shaped clusters of 1- to 2-inch fiery red bracts with yellow flowers, and blue-green leaves with deep purplish crossbars. A summer-blooming variety with plain green leaves but startling 1-

to 2-inch orange-red and yellow bracts and yellow flowers is the hybrid Mariae. All grow about a foot tall.

HOW TO GROW. Vriesias do best in bright indirect or curtain-filtered sunlight, night temperatures of 55° to 65° and day temperatures of 65° or higher. Pot in 2 parts peat moss to 1 part packaged potting soil and 1 part sharp sand or perlite. Set over a layer of drainage material, such as coarse gravel. Keep the mix moist and the cup formed by the leaf rosette full of water; fertilize monthly. Propagate from shoots that appear at the base.

W

WAXMALLOW See *Malvaviscus*
WAXPLANT See *Hoya*
WIDOW'S-TEAR See *Achimenes*

Y

YESTERDAY, TODAY AND TOMORROW See *Brunfelsia*

Z

ZANTEDESCHIA
Z. aethiopica minor, Z. 'Apricot Sunrise Hybrids',
Z. elliottiana (golden calla), *Z. rehmannii* (pink calla)
(all called calla lily)

Calla lilies are easy-to-grow bulb plants whose blooms flaunt rolled and flaring 4- to 6-inch waxy single petals called spathes. Rising from the base of each spathe is a pencil-shaped spike, or spadix, bearing the plant's tiny true flowers. Thick leaves, up to 8 inches long and 5 inches wide, are shaped like arrowheads and frequently bear white markings. *Z. aethiopica minor,* an 18-inch-high variety, has 4-inch white flowers that bloom year round. Other types may be planted at any time of year to bloom in about two months; they will continue to bloom at two- or three-month intervals if allowed to rest after each blooming. These types include *Z. elliottiana,* which grows up to 24 inches tall and bears 6-inch yellow flowers; and two 12- to 18-inch tall types, *Z. rehmannii,* with 4-inch pink flowers, and Apricot Sunrise Hybrids, with pink, red or yellow blossoms.

HOW TO GROW. Calla lilies do best in direct sunlight except at midday when they should be given bright indirect or curtain-filtered sunlight. Night temperatures of 50° to 65° and day temperatures of 68° or higher are ideal. Keep the soil thoroughly wet at all times; fertilize monthly during the growing season. Withhold moisture after the flowering stops. Propagate by division of tuberous roots in late summer or early fall.

ZEPHYRANTHES
Many species and hybrids commonly known as zephyr lily, flower of the west wind

Zephyr lilies are charming, easy-to-grow bulb plants. Each slender 6- to 8-inch flower stalk bears a single upward-facing blossom about 2 inches across in pink, yellow, white, or apricot. Blossoming may occur at any time, and it is not uncommon to have two or more crops of flowers during a year. The firm grasslike foliage grows 8 to 12 inches long.

HOW TO GROW. Zephyr lilies do best in at least four hours of direct sunlight a day, night temperatures of 40° to 45° and day temperatures of 68° or lower. Keep moist; fertilize monthly while plants are growing. After flowers and foliage wither, stop watering for about 10 weeks to let the plant rest, then renew watering and fertilizing. The plant will blossom again in about 10 weeks. Propagate from the small bulbs that develop beside larger ones.

ZYGOCACTUS See *Schlumbergera*

VRIESIA
Vriesia 'Mariae'

GOLDEN CALLA LILY
Zantedeschia elliottiana

ZEPHYR LILY
Zephyranthes rosea

Appendix

Characteristics of 149 house plants

Listed below for quick references are the varieties illustrated in Chapter 6 and on pages 55-58.

	FLOWER COLOR					OTHER TRAITS					PLANT HEIGHT			LIGHT				NIGHT TEMP.			BLOOMING SEASON			
	White	Yellow-orange	Pink-red	Blue-purple	Multicolor	Fragrance	Colorful foliage	Decorative fruit	Climbing	Trailing	Under 1 foot	1 to 2 feet	Over 2 feet	Direct sun	Indirect or filtered sun	Shade	Artificial light	40° to 50°	50° to 60°	60° to 70°	Spring	Summer	Fall	Winter
ABUTILON MEGAPOTAMICUM VARIEGATUM (flowering maple)			•						•			•	•				•			•	•	•	•	•
ACALYPHA HISPIDA (chenille plant)			•									•	•	•					•	•	•	•	•	•
ACHIMENES 'CHARM' (magic flower)			•							•			•			•				•		•		
AECHMEA FASCIATA (urn plant)				•		•						•			•					•		•		
AESCHYNANTHUS PARVIFOLIUS (lipstick plant)				•						•		•	•	•	•				•	•		•		
AGAPANTHUS 'PETER PAN' (agapanthus)				•								•		•				•				•		
ALLAMANDA CATHARTICA WILLIAMSII (allamanda)		•							•			•	•						•	•	•	•	•	
ANANAS COMOSUS VARIEGATUS (pineapple)			•		•	•	•					•	•			•			•	•		•	•	
ANGRAECUM DISTICHUM (angraecum orchid)	•				•					•			•				•		•	•	•	•	•	•
ANTHURIUM SCHERZERIANUM (flamingo flower)			•							•			•			•			•	•	•	•	•	•
APHELANDRA SQUARROSA LOUISAE (zebra plant)		•								•			•			•				•			•	
ARDISIA CRISPA (ardisia)	•		•					•				•			•				•		•			
AZALEA 'ALBERT-ELIZABETH' (azalea)			•									•		•		•			•		•			•
BEGONIA SEMPERFLORENS (wax begonia)			•							•	•		•			•			•		•			
BELOPERONE GUTTATA 'YELLOW QUEEN' (shrimp plant)		•									•		•			•			•					
BILLBERGIA 'FANTASIA' (billbergia)			•		•						•		•					•				•		
BOUGAINVILLEA 'BARBARA KARST' (bougainvillea)			•					•				•							•	•	•	•	•	•
BRASSAVOLA NODOSA (lady-of-the-night orchid)	•	•			•					•			•			•			•	•		•		•
BRASSIA CAUDATA (spider orchid)			•	•	•					•			•			•			•		•	•		
BROWALLIA SPECIOSA MAJOR (browallia)				•					•			•			•			•		•	•		
BRUNFELSIA CALYCINA (yesterday, today and tomorrow)			•	•							•		•			•			•	•	•	•	•
CALCEOLARIA HERBEOHYBRIDA 'MULTIFLORA NANA' (pocketbook flower)		•								•			•		•				•		•			
CALLIANDRA INEQUILATERA (pink powder puff)			•		•					•	•					•			•	•			•
CAMELLIA JAPONICA 'DEBUTANTE' (common camellia)			•								•		•			•			•			•	•
CAMPANULA ISOPHYLLA ALBA (white Italian bellflower)	•						•	•			•		•			•			•			•	•
CAPSICUM ANNUUM CONOIDES (ornamental pepper)	•					•			•		•		•						•			•	•
CARISSA GRANDIFLORA NANA COMPACTA (Natal plum)	•			•		•				•		•			•			•	•	•	•	•	•
CATTLEYA LABIATA (cattleya orchid)	•	•	•							•		•			•			•	•		•	•	
CESTRUM NOCTURNUM (night-blooming jasmine)	•			•	•					•		•			•			•	•		•		
CHIRITA LAVANDULACEA (chirita)				•						•	•			•			•		•			•	
CHRYSANTHEMUM FRUTESCENS (marguerite)		•								•		•			•	•		•		•	•	•	
CHRYSANTHEMUM MORIFOLIUM (florists' chrysanthemum)		•								•		•			•			•			•	•	
CITRUS TAITENSIS (Otaheite orange)	•			•	•					•	•			•			•			•	•		
CLERODENDRUM THOMSONAE (glory bower)			•					•			•		•			•			•			•	
CLIVIA MINIATA (Kafir lily)		•									•		•			•			•	•			
COFFEA ARABICA (Arabian coffee)	•			•	•					•		•			•			•	•			•	
COLUMNEA 'YELLOW DRAGON' (columnea)		•						•			•		•		•		•	•	•	•	•	•	
CRINODONNA CORSII (crinodonna)			•		•					•	•			•			•			•	•		
CRINUM 'ELLEN BOSANQUET' (crinum)			•		•					•	•	•			•			•		•	•		
CROCUS 'PICKWICK' (crocus)				•					•		•			•			•						•
CROSSANDRA INFUNDIBULIFORMIS (firecracker flower)		•								•	•			•			•		•	•	•	•	
CRYPTANTHUS 'IT' (earth star)	•				•					•	•					•		•		•			
CUPHEA IGNEA (cigar plant)			•							•	•		•			•		•	•	•	•		
CYCLAMEN PERSICUM GIGANTEUM (cyclamen)			•		•					•	•			•			•	•				•	•
CYMBIDIUM 'MINUET' (cymbidium orchid)			•							•	•		•			•			•			•	•
DAPHNE ODORA (winter daphne)			•		•			•			•		•			•			•				•
DENDROBIUM LODDIGESII (dendrobium orchid)			•	•			•			•		•			•			•	•			•	
DIPLADENIA AMOENA (dipladenia)			•						•				•	•			•			•	•	•	
DYCKIA FOSTERIANA 'SILVER QUEEN' (dyckia)		•	•		•				•		•	•	•	•			•			•		•	
EPIDENDRUM COCHLEATUM (clamshell orchid)				•	•		•			•		•			•	•	•		•	•	•	•		•

Plant	FLOWER COLOR					OTHER TRAITS					PLANT HEIGHT			LIGHT				NIGHT TEMP.			BLOOMING SEASONS			
	White	Yellow-orange	Pink-red	Blue-purple	Multicolor	Fragrance	Colorful foliage	Decorative fruit	Climbing	Trailing	Under 1 foot	1 to 2 feet	Over 2 feet	Direct sun	Indirect or filtered sun	Shade	Artificial light	40° to 50°	50° to 60°	60° to 70°	Spring	Summer	Fall	Winter
EPIPHYLLUM HERMOSISSIMUS (orchid cactus)					●							●			●		●							●
EPISCIA 'EMBER LACE' (episcia)			●				●		●	●					●		●			●	●	●	●	
ERANTHEMUM NERVOSUM (blue sage)				●								●		●		●			●	●				●
ERVATAMIA DIVARICATA PLENA (butterfly gardenia)	●				●							●	●	●					●	●				●
EUCHARIS GRANDIFLORA (Amazon lily)	●				●							●			●				●	●	●	●	●	●
EUPHORBIA PULCHERRIMA 'ECKESPOINT C-1' (poinsettia)			●									●		●					●	●				●
EXACUM AFFINE 'MIDGET' (Arabian violet)				●		●					●				●					●	●	●	●	●
FELICIA AMELLOIDES (blue marguerite)				●								●		●					●		●	●		
FORTUNELLA MARGARITA (Nagami kumquat)	●				●			●				●		●					●		●			
FUCHSIA 'PINK CLOUD' (fuchsia)			●									●	●	●					●		●			
GARDENIA JASMINOIDES VEITCHII (gardenia)	●				●							●	●	●					●	●	●	●		
GAZANIA 'SUNSHINE HYBRIDS' (gazania)					●					●	●			●					●		●			
GELSEMIUM SEMPERVIRENS (Carolina jasmine)		●				●			●	●	●	●		●	●				●		●			
GLORIOSA ROTHSCHILDIANA (glory lily)					●							●	●	●	●					●		●		
GLOXINERA 'ROSEBELLS' (gloxinera)			●								●				●		●			●	●	●	●	
GUZMANIA MONOSTACHYA (guzmania)					●		●				●				●					●	●	●		
HAEMANTHUS MULTIFLORUS (blood lily)			●								●			●					●			●		
HELIOTROPIUM ARBORESCENS (common heliotrope)			●		●	●					●	●	●	●					●		●	●	●	●
HIBISCUS ROSA-SINENSIS (Chinese hibiscus)			●									●	●	●					●		●	●	●	●
HIPPEASTRUM 'FIRE DANCE' (amaryllis)			●									●		●					●		●			
HOYA CARNOSA (waxplant)	●				●				●	●		●		●	●				●		●	●		
HYACINTHUS 'KING OF THE BLUES' (hyacinth)			●		●						●			●	●	●		●			●			
HYDRANGEA MACROPHYLLA (common bigleaf hydrangea)			●									●			●			●			●			
HYPOCYRTA NUMMULARIA (goldfish plant)			●							●		●			●		●			●	●	●	●	●
IMPATIENS 'SCARLET BABY' (patient Lucy)			●								●			●	●	●				●	●	●	●	●
IPOMOEA 'EARLY CALL' (morning glory)			●						●			●	●						●			●		
IXORA COCCINEA (flame-of-the-woods)			●					●				●		●						●	●	●	●	●
JACOBINIA SUBERECTA (jacobinia)			●									●		●						●		●		
JASMINUM POLYANTHUM (jasmine)	●				●				●	●		●			●				●		●			●
KALANCHOE BLOSSFELDIANA 'TETRA VULCAN' (kalanchoe)			●								●			●					●					●
KOHLERIA AMABILIS (kohleria)			●				●				●				●					●	●	●	●	
LACHENALIA PENDULA (Cape cowslip)			●								●				●			●			●			●
LAELIA FLAVA (laelia orchid)		●										●		●	●			●	●					●
LAELIOCATTLEYA 'EL CERRITO' (laeliocattleya orchid)		●										●			●				●					●
LANTANA CAMARA (common lantana)					●	●					●	●	●	●						●		●	●	●
LANTANA SELLOWIANA (trailing lantana)			●	●						●		●	●	●						●	●	●	●	●
LILIUM LONGIFLORUM 'CROFT' (Easter lily)	●				●							●			●			●	●		●			
LOBULARIA MARITIMA FLORE PLENO (double sweet alyssum)	●				●				●	●	●			●					●		●	●	●	●
MALPIGHIA COCCIGERA (holly malpighia)			●					●			●			●	●	●				●		●		
MALVAVISCUS ARBOREUS PENDULIFLORUS (Turk's-cap)			●										●	●						●	●	●	●	
MANETTIA INFLATA (firecracker vine)					●				●			●			●	●				●	●	●	●	●
MAXILLARIA TENUIFOLIA (maxillaria orchid)					●	●					●								●	●		●		
MUSCARI ARMENIACUM (grape hyacinth)			●	●							●					●		●			●			●
NARCISSUS 'KING ALFRED' (daffodil)		●									●				●			●			●			●
NARCISSUS 'SOLEIL D'OR' (narcissus)		●									●				●			●	●		●			●
NEOFINETIA FALCATA (neofinetia orchid)	●				●						●				●				●	●	●		●	
NEOMARICA GRACILIS (Apostle plant)					●	●						●			●					●				●
NICOTIANA ALATA GRANDIFLORA (flowering tobacco)		●				●						●			●	●				●		●		
NIDULARIUM REGELIOIDES (nidularium)			●				●	●			●				●					●	●	●	●	●
ODONTOGLOSSUM PULCHELLUM (lily-of-the-valley orchid)					●	●					●			●	●			●	●	●				●

	Flower Color					Other Traits					Plant Height			Light				Night Temp.			Blooming Seasons			
	White	Yellow-orange	Pink-red	Blue-purple	Multicolor	Fragrance	Colorful foliage	Decorative fruit	Climbing	Trailing	Under 1 foot	1 to 2 feet	Over 2 feet	Direct sun	Indirect or filtered sun	Shade	Artificial light	40° to 50°	50° to 60°	60° to 70°	Spring	Summer	Fall	Winter
ONCIDIUM VARICOSUM ROGERSII (dancing lady orchid)		●										●		●	●				●	●			●	●
ORNITHOGALUM CAUDATUM (false sea onion)	●				●							●	●		●					●				●
OSMANTHUS FRAGRANS (sweet olive)	●				●							●	●	●	●				●		●	●	●	●
OXALIS PURPUREA 'GRAND DUCHESS' (oxalis)			●							●	●			●					●				●	●
PAPHIOPEDILUM CALLOSUM 'BALINESE DANCER' (paphiopedilum orchid)			●		●		●					●			●	●								
PASSIFLORA ALATO-CAERULEA (passionflower)			●	●					●			●	●	●					●	●		●	●	
PELARGONIUM HORTORUM 'SKIES OF ITALY' (geranium)		●				●					●	●		●					●		●	●	●	
PENTAS LANCEOLATA 'ORCHID STAR' (Egyptian star cluster)				●								●		●					●			●	●	
PETUNIA 'STAR JOY' (petunia)			●							●		●		●					●					
PHALAENOPSIS AMABILIS (moth orchid)	●											●	●		●				●	●				
PRIMULA MALACOIDES (fairy primrose)		●								●		●		●			●							●
PUNICA GRANATUM NANA (dwarf pomegranate)		●						●			●		●					●			●	●	●	
QUESNELIA LIBONIANA (Grecian vase plant)			●								●			●				●			●	●		
RECHSTEINERIA CARDINALIS (cardinal flower)		●								●		●				●			●			●	●	
RODRIGUEZIA VENUSTA 'ANN' (rodriguezia orchid)			●	●						●		●						●	●			●	●	
ROSA CHINENSIS MINIMA (double pink miniature rose)		●							●		●		●				●	●		●	●	●	●	
ROSMARINUS OFFICINALIS PROSTRATUS (prostrate rosemary)			●		●	●				●		●		●				●			●	●	●	●
RUELLIA MACRANTHA (ruellia)		●									●		●				●	●				●	●	
RUSSELIA EQUISETIFORMIS (coral plant)		●							●		●	●					●		●	●	●	●		
SAINTPAULIA 'RHAPSODIE SERIES' (African violet)		●									●				●		●		●	●	●	●	●	●
SAXIFRAGA STOLONIFERA TRICOLOR (strawberry geranium)	●				●		●	●					●		●	●		●			●			
SCHIZOCENTRON ELEGANS (Spanish shawl)		●	●							●				●		●		●	●			●	●	
SCHLUMBERGERA-ZYGOCACTUS HYBRID (Christmas cactus)		●							●		●		●				●	●						●
SCILLA SIBIRICA 'SPRING BEAUTY' (squill)		●							●		●	●	●		●			●						
SENECIO CONFUSUS (Mexican flame vine)		●				●	●			●	●	●			●				●	●	●	●		
SENECIO CRUENTUS (cineraria)		●		●						●	●			●		●		●				●	●	
SINNINGIA SPECIOSA (gloxinia)		●								●			●	●		●		●	●	●	●	●		
SMITHIANTHA 'CARMEL' (temple bells)			●		●					●				●		●		●				●	●	
SOLANUM PSEUDOCAPSICUM (Jerusalem cherry)	●				●			●		●				●				●				●	●	
SOPHROLAELIOCATTLEYA 'MIAMI' (sophrolaeliocattleya orchid)		●							●				●			●		●	●					
SPATHIPHYLLUM CLEVELANDII (spathiphyllum)	●				●		●			●			●	●	●			●				●	●	
SPREKELIA FORMOSISSIMA (Aztec lily)		●							●				●			●	●				●			
STEPHANOTIS FLORIBUNDA (stephanotis)	●				●		●	●		●			●	●			●			●	●	●		
STRELITZIA REGINAE (strelitzia)			●					●	●				●			●			●	●	●		
STREPTOCARPUS 'WEISMOOR HYBRIDS' (Cape primrose)		●							●			●		●	●		●						
STREPTOSOLEN JAMESONII (orange streptosolen)		●						●			●		●			●	●	●	●	●	●	●	
TETRANEMA MEXICANUM (Mexican foxglove)			●					●			●		●		●		●	●	●	●	●	●	
THUNBERGIA ALATA (black-eyed-Susan vine)			●			●	●		●		●		●			●						●	
TILLANDSIA CYANEA (tillandsia)			●	●					●			●		●				●	●		●		
TRACHELOSPERMUM JASMINOIDES (star jasmine)	●				●		●	●		●	●	●	●			●			●	●	●	●	
TRICHOCENTRUM TIGRINUM (trichocentrum orchid)			●	●	●				●				●			●		●	●	●			
TROPAEOLUM MAJUS (common nasturtium)		●			●				●		●			●			●	●			●	●	●	
TULBAGHIA FRAGRANS (fragrant tulbaghia)			●			●					●		●			●	●			●	●	●	●	
TULIPA 'FANTASY' (parrot tulip)			●							●		●	●			●	●		●				
VALLOTA SPECIOSA (Scarborough lily)		●									●		●			●			●			●		
VELTHEIMIA VIRIDIFOLIA (veltheimia)			●						●		●	●			●	●						●	
VRIESIA 'MARIAE' (vriesia)			●						●		●		●			●	●			●			
ZANTEDESCHIA ELLIOTTIANA (golden calla lily)		●			●				●		●	●	●			●	●	●	●	●	●		
ZEPHYRANTHES ROSEA (zephyr lily)			●						●		●		●		●				●	●	●	●	

Picture Credits

The sources for the illustrations that appear in this book are listed below. Credits for pictures from left to right are separated by semicolons, from top to bottom by dashes. Cover—Leonard Wolfe. 4—Keith Martin courtesy James Underwood Crockett; Leonard Wolfe. 6—Evelyn Hofer courtesy Mark Twain Memorial. 11,13,14,15—Drawings by Vincent Lewis. 17—Evelyn Hofer. 18 through 21—Costa Manos from Magnum. 22,23—Paul Slaughter. 24—Ted Streshinsky. 25,27,29,32,33—Drawings by Vincent Lewis. Credits for pages 34,35,36 are for photographs only. 34 —Top, New York Public Library Picture Collection—Bibliothèque Nationale, Paris; Hunt Botanical Library Collection, Carnegie-Mellon University, Pittsburgh, Pa. 35—Hunt Botanical Library Collection, Carnegie-Mellon University, Pittsburgh, Pa.; Bettmann Archive—Hunt Botanical Library Collection, Carnegie-Mellon University, Pittsburgh, Pa.; New York Public Library Picture Collection. 36—New York Public Library Picture Collection except bottom center left Staatsbibliothek, Berlin Bildarchiv (Handke). 38,40,41,42 —Drawings by Vincent Lewis. 44—Peter Gautel courtesy Badisches Landesmuseum, Karlsruhe. 46,48,50,51,52,53 —Drawings by Vincent Lewis. 55—Property of American Orchid Society Inc. except right second from top Phil Brodatz. 56—Rutherford Platt except bottom left property of American Orchid Society Inc. 57—Phil Brodatz; property of American Orchid Society Inc. except third from top Don Richardson. 58—Property of American Orchid Society Inc. except top left Orchid Jungle. 60,61—Drawings by Vincent Lewis. 62,63,64—Illustrations by Rebecca Merrilees. 66 —By Gracious Permission of Her Majesty, Queen Elizabeth II. 70,71,73,75,77—Drawings by Vincent Lewis. 81,82, 83—Bob Peterson. 84,85—Gene Daniels from Black Star. 86—Iris August. 87—Barry August—Iris August. 88—Richard Jeffery. 91,93,94,95,97—Drawings by Vincent Lewis. 98 through 151—Illustrations by Allianora Rosse.

Acknowledgments

For their help in the preparation of this book, the editors wish to thank the following: Airguide Instrument Company, Chicago, Ill.; Mrs. Iris August, Bayshore, N.Y.; Podesta Baldocchi, San Francisco, Calif.; Mrs. Ernesta Drinker Ballard, Executive Director, Pennsylvania Horticultural Society, Philadelphia, Pa.; Mrs. Robert I. Ballinger Jr., Villanova, Pa.; Mrs. Pearl Benell, President, American Begonia Society, Whittier, Calif.; Theodore W. Bossert, Curator of Portraits, Hunt Botanical Library, Carnegie-Mellon University, Pittsburgh, Pa.; Mr. and Mrs. William Crane, New York City; Mr. and Mrs. Warren F. Cressy, Falls Village, Conn.; Mrs. Edith Crockett, Librarian, Horticultural Society of New York, New York City; Mrs. Muriel C. Crossman, Librarian, Massachusetts Horticultural Society, Boston, Mass.; Gene Daniels, Camarillo, Calif.; Marie Eaton, Seattle African Violet Club, Seattle, Wash.; Mr. and Mrs. David Eisendrath, Brooklyn, N.Y.; Mrs. Wanda Elin, Fullerton, Calif.; Audre Fiber, Fiber Jehu, Inc., New York City; The Gazebo, New York City; Miss Marie Giasi, Librarian, Brooklyn Botanic Garden, Brooklyn, N.Y.; The Green Thumb, New York City; Dr. Arthur Grove, Houston, Texas; Miss Elizabeth Hall, Senior Librarian, Horticultural Society of New York, New York City; Ben Heller, New York City; Mrs. Hugh Hencken, Newton, Mass.; Mr. and Mrs. Harold Howard, Los Angeles, Calif.; Mr. and Mrs. Paul Lee, San Diego, Calif.; Emory Leland, Seattle, Wash.; Mark Marko, Monrovia Nurseries, Azusa, Calif.; Ronnie Nevins, Fullerton, Calif.; New York Botanical Garden Library, Bronx, N.Y.; Mrs. Thelma O'Reilly, La Mesa, Calif.; Mrs. Henry Parish II, Hadley-Parish, Inc., New York City; Mrs. Ruth Pease, Judging Course Director, American Begonia Society, Los Angeles, Calif.; Walter Pease, Past President, American Begonia Society, Los Angeles, Calif.; Mrs. William Piel Jr., New York City; Plantamation, Inc., New York City; Mr. and Mrs. Herbert H. Plever, Jamaica, N.Y.; Mrs. Diane Powers, San Diego, Calif.; Sylvania Lighting Center, Danvers, Mass.; Charles Tagg, Past President, American Begonia Society, Fullerton, Calif.; Mrs. Alma Wright, Editor, *Gesneriad Saintpaulia News*, Knoxville, Tenn.; Rudolf Ziesenhenne, Nomenclature Director, American Begonia Society, Santa Barbara, Calif.

Bibliography

Ballard, Ernesta D., *Garden in Your House*. Harper & Row, 1958.

Brooklyn Botanic Garden, *Gardening in Containers*. Brooklyn Botanic Garden, 1958.

Brooklyn Botanic Garden, *Handbook on Propagation*. Brooklyn Botanic Garden, 1965.

Brooklyn Botanic Garden, *House Plants*. Brooklyn Botanic Garden, 1965.

Brooklyn Botanic Garden, *Plants & Gardens: Gardening Under Artificial Light*. Brooklyn Botanic Garden, 1970.

Cherry, Elaine, *Fluorescent Light Gardening*. Van Nostrand Reinhold Company, 1965.

Cruso, Thalassa, *Making Things Grow*. Alfred A. Knopf, Inc., 1969.

Elbert, George and Edward Hyams, *House Plants*. Funk & Wagnalls, 1968.

Everett, Thomas, *How to Grow Beautiful House Plants*. Arco Publications, 1953.

Fennell, T. A. Jr., *Orchids for Home and Garden*. Holt, Rinehart and Winston, 1959.

Free, Montague, *All About African Violets*. The American Garden Guild and Doubleday & Company, Inc., 1951.

Free, Montague, *All About House Plants*. The American Garden Guild and Doubleday & Company, Inc., 1946.

Free, Montague, *Plant Propagation in Pictures*. The American Garden Guild and Doubleday & Company, Inc., 1957.

Graf, Alfred Byrd, *Exotic Plant Manual*. Roehrs Company, 1970.

Kains, M. G., *Plant Propagation*. Orange Judd Publishing Company, 1931.

McDonald, Elvin, *World Book of House Plants*. The World Publishing Company, 1963.

McDonald, Elvin, *Complete Book of Gardening Under Lights*. Doubleday & Company, Inc., 1965.

Moore, Harold E., *African Violets, Gloxinias and Their Relatives*. The Macmillan Company, 1957.

Nehrling, Arno and Irene, *Propagating House Plants*. Hearthside Press, 1962.

Northern, Rebecca Tyson, *Home Orchid Growing*. Van Nostrand Reinhold Company, 1962.

Rector, Carolyn, *How to Grow African Violets: A Sunset Book*. Lane Books, 1962.

Schuler, Stanley, *1001 House Plant Questions Answered*. Van Nostrand Reinhold Company, 1963.

Selsam, Millicent E., *How to Grow House Plants*. William Morrow and Company, 1960.

Sunset Books, *How to Grow House Plants*, Lane Books, 1968.

Sutcliffe, Alys, *House Plants for City Dwellers*. E. P. Dutton & Co., Inc., 1964.

Wilson, Helen Van Pelt, *African Violet Book*. Hawthorn Books, Inc., 1970.

Index

*Numerals in italics indicate an
illustration of the subject mentioned*

abutilon, *102, chart* 152
Acacia, *18*
Acalypha, 102, chart 152
Achania. See Malvaviscus
Achimenes, 12, *102, chart* 152
Acid-loving plants, 69
Acidity, correction of, 47
Adam's-apple. *See Ervatamia*
Adaptability to environment, 25
Aechmea, 16, *17,* 67, *103, chart*
152
Aerosol sprays, 72
Aeschynanthus, 103, chart 152. *See
also* Basketvine
African lily, blue. *See Agapanthus*
African violets, 7, 10, 11, 12, 13, *24,
25,* 41, 49, 72, 73-74, 101; light
preferences of, 26, 28, 29, 30, 31;
prize-winning, 80, *81, 82, 83;*
propagation of, 70, 89, 93, 96-97;
temperature requirements of, 41,
42, 43; watering, 33, 38, *chart* 63.
See also Saintpaulia
Agapanthus, 103-104, *chart* 152
Agathaea. See Felicia
Air circulation, of, 43, 70; in
photosynthesis, 27; in rooting
medium, 92; in seed germination,
99; in soil, 32, 45
Air layering, *98*
Air plants, 12, 45. *See also* Orchids,
epiphytic
Alcohol, *chart* 64-65, 72
Algae, green, 49, *chart* 62
Allamanda, 104, chart 152
Allophyton. See Tetranema
Alloplectus. See Hypocyrta
Alyssum. See Lobularia
Amarcrinum. See Crinodonna
Amaryllis. See Hippeastrum
*Amaryllis formosissima. See
Sprekelia*
Amazon lily. *See Eucharis*
Ammonium sulfate, 69
Ananas, 104, chart 152. *See also*
Pineapple
Angraecum, 55, 60, *104, chart* 152
Angraecum falcatum. See Neofinetia
Anthers, *13*
Anthurium, 105, chart 152
Aphelandra, 105, chart 152
Aphids, 15, *chart* 64-65, 71, 72
Apostle plant. *See Neomarica*
Arabian violet. *See Exacum*
Aramite, *chart* 64-65
Ardisia, 105, chart 152
Artificial light, uses of, 7, 10, 16, *17,
18,* 28-31, *29,* 78, 82, 86, 89, *chart*
152-154
Aspidistra, 9
Aster. *See Felicia*
Atomizer, 40, 79
August, Mrs. Iris, 86, *87*
Azalea, *18,* 22, *23, 24, 25,* 39, 41, 47,
48, 69, 71-72, 92, 95, 101, 105, *106,
chart* 152

banking, for display, 16, *18-19*
Barbados cherry. *See Malpighia*
Bark, fir tree, 60, 61, 79
Basketvine, 54. *See also
Aeschynanthus*
Baths, *chart* 64-65, 70-*71,* 72
Beefsteak plant. *See Acalypha*
Beer, *chart* 64-65
Bégon, Michel, *34*
Begonia, 6, 7, 9, 10, 11, 15, *24, 25,* 26,
30, *34,* 72, 74, 79, *106, chart* 152;
prize-winning, 80, *84, 85;*
propagation of, 90, 92, 94, 95, 96,
99
Begonia, strawberry. *See Saxifraga*
Bellflower. *See Campanula*
Beloperone, 106-107, *chart* 152
Bengal lily. *See Crinum*
Bermuda buttercup. *See Oxalis*
Bermuda lily, 47
Billbergia, 107, chart 152
Bird-of-Paradise flower. *See Strelitzia*
Black-eyed-Susan vine. *See
Thunbergia*
Blood lily. *See Haemanthus*
Blooming seasons, 10, 11, *chart* 152-
154
Blue sage. *See Eranthemum*
Botrytis blight, *chart* 64-65
Bottom watering. *See* Saucer watering
Bougainvillea, 35, *107, chart* 152
Bracts, *13*
Brassavola, 54, 55, *107, chart* 152. *See
also* Lady-of-the-night orchid
Brassia, 57, *108, chart* 152
Brazilian edelweiss. *See Rechsteineria*
Brazilian plume. *See Jacobinia*
Bromeliads, 11-12; characteristics of,
12, *13;* fertilization of, 13; inducing
bloom of, 67; propagation by offsets
of, 97; soil requirements of, 45;
specialization in, 12
Browallia, 108, chart 152
Browallia jamesonii. See Streptosolen
Browallia, orange. *See Streptosolen*
Brunfels, Otto, *35*
Brunfelsia, 35, *108, chart* 152
Bud eyes, 73
Bulbs, winter-flowering, 41, 73
Burlingtonia. See Rodriguezia
Bushes, 8
Buttercup, Bermuda. *See Oxalis*
Butterfly gardenia, 8. *See also
Ervatamia*
Buying plants, *14*-15, 78

Cactus, Christmas, 10, 76-77. *See
also Schlumbergera*
Cactus, Easter. *See Schlumbergera*
Cactus, orchid, 76. *See also
Epiphyllum*
Cactus, queen-of-the-night. *See
Epiphyllum*
Calceolaria, 9, 37, *108,* 109, *chart* 152
Calla. *See Zantedeschia*
Calliandra, 73, 74, 98, *109, chart* 152
Camellia, 8-9, 42, 53, 74, 98, 101, *109*-
110, *chart* 152
Campanula, 110, chart 152
Cape cowslip. *See Lachenalia*
Cape jasmine. *See Gardenia*
Cape primrose. *See Streptocarpus*

Capsicum, 31, *110, chart* 152
Carbon dioxide, 26, 27
Cardinal flower. *See Rechsteineria*
Care of house plants, day-to-day, 10,
60, 61, 67-79; baths, 70-71; feeding,
68-70; inspection, 67-68; outdoor
care in summer, 73-76; pest and
disease control, *chart* 64-65, 71-73;
during resting periods, 76-77
Carissa, 31, *110, chart* 152
Carnations, 9, 30
Carolina jasmine, 8. *See also
Gelsemium*
Cattleya, 55, 76, 79, 110-111, *chart*
152
Central heating, 10, 12; microclimate
variations in, 12
Cestrum, 111, *chart* 152
Chameleon plant. *See Brunfelsia*
Charcoal granules, 40, 51, 79
Chenille plant. *See Acalypha*
Cherry, Barbados. *See Malpighia*
Cherry, Cleveland. *See Solanum*
Cherry, Jerusalem. *See Solanum*
Cherry pie. *See Heliotropium*
Chincherinchee. *See
Ornithogalum*
Chirita, 111, *chart* 152
Chlorinated water, 37
Chlorophyll, 25-26, 27
Chloroplasts, *27*
Christmas cactus, 10, 76-77. *See also
Schlumbergera*
Christmas orchid. *See Cattleya*
Chrysanthemum, 23, *24, 25,* 26, *112,
chart* 152
Cigar plant. *See Cuphea*
Cineraria, 9, *22,* 23, 48. *See also
Senecio*
Citrus, 8-9, 31, 74, *112, chart* 152. *See
also* Lemon; Lime; Orange
Clamshell orchid, *58.* *See also
Epidendrum*
Clay pots: fertilizer salts on, 49, *chart*
63; green algae on, 49, *chart* 62;
porosity of, 49; scrubbing, 49, 59;
soaking, 50, 59; weight of, 49. *See
also* Pots
Clerodendron. See Clerodendrum
Clerodendrum, 8, 16, *112*-113, *chart*
152
Climbing lily. *See Gloriosa*
Clivia, 113, chart 152
Coffea, 113, chart 152
Coffee, Arabian. *See Coffea*
Cold, protection from, *15*
Colonna, Fabio, *35*
Columnea, 35, *113*-114, *chart* 152
Conservatories, 6, 7, 9, 28
Containers, *11,* 45, 47, *48,* 50-51, 77;
decorative, *48,* 50, 77; roll-around
plant box, *11*
Copperleaf. *See Acalypha*
Coral plant. *See Russelia*
Cordyline terminalis, 29
Cowslip, Cape. *See Lachenalia*
Crape jasmine. *See Ervatamia*
Crinodonna, 54, *114, chart* 152
Crinum, 114, chart 152
Crocus, 9, *114*-115, *chart* 152
Crossandra, 26, *115, chart*
152
Crossbreeding, 90

Crown rot, 37, *chart* 64-65
Crowns, definition of, 96
Cryptanthus, 115, *chart* 152
Cuphea, 115-*116*, *chart* 152
Cuttings, 15, 47, 89, 90-96; leaf, *93*, 96;
  pot prepared for, *91*, *93*, *95*; rooting,
  47, 94-96; stem, 90-94, *91*, 95; vein,
  94
Cyclamen, *6*, *7*, *18*, *20-21*, 26, 37, 41,
  43, 72, *116*, *chart* 152
Cyclamen mites, *chart* 64-65, 71, 72
Cymbidium, 54, *55*, 116, *chart* 152
Cypripedium. See Paphiopedilum

daedalacanthus nervosus. See
  Eranthemum
Daffodil. *See Narcissus*
Daisy, blue. *See Felicia*
Daisy, Boston. *See Chrysanthemum*
Daisy, gerbera, *23*
Daisy, kingfisher. *See Felicia*
Daisy, Paris. *See Chrysanthemum*
Dancing lady orchid. *See Oncidium*
Daniels, Gene, 80, 84, *85*
Daniels, Nettie, 80, 84, *85*
Daphne, 97, 101, 116-*117*, *chart* 152
Darkness, period of, 28, 31, 78
Datura, 9
De Bougainville, L.A., *35*
Decay, 37
Decorating with plants, 16-23, 48
Dehumidifiers, 86
Dendrobium, *57*, 117, *chart* 152
De Vriese, W. H., *34*
Diammonium phosphate, 69
Dicofol, *chart* 64-65, 72
Dipladenia, *117*, *chart* 152
Dipstick, *50*, 51-52
Disease, 7, *chart* 64-65; isolation from,
  63, 72-73; resistance to, 54
Displaying plants, *48*, *88*, 89
Division, propagation by, 96-97
Dormancy, 32-33, 59, 69-70, 73, 76, 86
Double-decker plant. *See*
  Rechsteineria
Drafts, cold, 43
Drainage, 46, 50-52, 60, 61; layer, 48,
  50-51, 52, 59; for hanging plants, *75*
Dust, 70
Dyckia, 117-*118*, *chart* 152

earth star. *See Cryptanthus*
Easter cactus. *See Schlumbergera*
Easter lily, 8, *24*, *25*, 47, 66, 67. *See
  also Lilium*
Easter orchid. *See Cattleya*
Edelweiss, Brazilian. *See*
  Rechsteineria
Egyptian star cluster. *See Pentas*
Electric eye, 89
Elfin herb. *See Cuphea*
Epidendrum, *58*, 118, *chart* 152. *See
  also* Clamshell orchid
Epiphyllum, *118*, *chart* 153. *See also*
  Orchid cactus
Epiphytes, 12. *See also* Orchids,
  epiphytic
Episcia, 97, *118*-119, *chart* 153
Eranthemum, 119, *chart* 153
Ervatamia, 8, *119*, *chart* 153
Ethylene gas, 67

Eucharis, 119-*120*, *chart* 153
Euphorbia, *120*, *chart* 153. *See also*
  Poinsettia
Exacum, *120*, *chart* 153

faded flowers, removing, 63, 68
Families of flowering plants, 12, *13*.
  See also Bromeliads; Gesneriads;
  Orchids
Feeding, 7-8, 68-70; begonias, 84;
  foliar, 75; gloxinias, 86; orchids, 79.
  See also Fertilizer
Felicia, 120-*121*, *chart* 153
Ferbam, *chart* 64-65
Ferns, 7, 8, 9, 16, *17*
Fertilization, 13
Fertilizer: acid, 69; for African
  violets, 82, 83; chemical, 68; excess,
  consequences of, *chart* 62; forms of,
  69; ingredients, 68-69; lack of, *chart*
  63; for orchids, 79; organic, 68;
  salts, build-up of, 32, 38, 49, *chart*
  63; for specific plants, 10
Fertilizer salts, 32, 38, 49, *chart* 63
Fir tree bark, 60, 61, 79
Firecracker flower. *See Crossandra*
Firecracker vine. *See Manettia*
Flame bush, Trinidad. *See Calliandra*
Flame-of-the-woods. *See Ixora*
Flame vine, Mexican. *See Senecio*
Flame violet. *See Episcia*
Flaming sword. *See Vriesia*
Flamingo flower. *See Anthurium*
Fleur d'amour. *See Ervatamia*
Flies, white, *chart* 64-65
Flower color, *chart* 152-154
Flower of the west wind. *See*
  Zephyranthes
Flower shows: prize-winning entries,
  80, *81-87*
Flowering maple. *See Abutilon*
Flowering tobacco, 8. *See also*
  Nicotiana
Foliage, 10, 14, 78, *chart* 152-154
Foliage plants, 16
Foliar feeding, 75
Fortunella, 31, *121*, *chart* 153. *See also*
  Kumquat
Fountain plant. *See Russelia*
Foxglove, Mexican. *See Tetranema*
Fragrance, 8, 9, *charts* 152-154
Fruit, 8, 31, *charts* 152-154
Fuchs, Leonhard, *36*
Fuchsia, 9, *36*, 42, 101, *121*-122, *chart*
  153
Fungi, 72
Fungicide, *chart* 64-65, 96
Fungus leaf spot, *chart* 64-65

gardenia, 8, 26, 47, 48, 69, 79, 122,
  chart 153; propagation of, 90, 92
Gardenia, butterfly, 8. *See also*
  Ervatamia
Garlic, society. *See Tulbaghia*
Gaza, Teodoro, *36*
Gazania, *36*, *122*, *chart* 153
Gelsemium, 8, 122, *123*, *chart* 153. *See
  also* Carolina jasmine
Geranium, 9, *24*, *25*, 26, 28, 49, 72, 79,
  90. *See also Pelargonium*
Geranium, ivy, 16

Geranium, jungle. *See Ixora*
Geranium, strawberry, 97. *See also*
  Saxifraga
Gerbera, *23*
German ivy. *See Senecio*
Germination, seed, 98-99
Gesneriads, 11-12; characteristics of,
  12, *13*; humidity requirements of,
  41; propagation by leaf cuttings of,
  93; soil for, 45; specialization in, 12
Gift plants, *24*, *25*
Gloriosa, *123*, *chart* 153. *See also*
  Glory lily
Glory bower. *See Clerodendrum*
Glory lily, 73. *See also Gloriosa*
Gloxinera, *123*, *chart* 153
Gloxinia, *6*, *7*, 10, 11, 12, 42, 43, 67-
  68; under artificial light, 29, 30, 31;
  dormant period of, 33, 69, 73, 76;
  prize-winning, 80, *86*, *87*;
  propagation of, 93, 96, 99. *See also*
  Sinningia
Goldfish plant. *See Hypocyrta*
Granadilla. *See Passiflora*
Grape hyacinth. *See Muscari*
Grape juice, *chart* 64-65
Gravel, 11, 33, 41, 48, 50, 74
Gray-mold blight, *chart* 64-65
Grecian vase plant. *See Quesnelia*
Green scum, *chart* 62
Greenhouses, 8, 9, 28; glass-jar, 99;
  instant, 18; window, *88*, 89
Growing medium: for each kind of
  plant, 45; for orchids, 45, 60;
  standard mixture, 46-47
Guzmania, *124*, *chart* 153

haemanthus, *124*, *chart* 153
Haeria. See Schizocentron
Hanging baskets, 47; drainage from,
  75
Heaths, African, 9
Heliotrope, 9. *See also Heliotropium*
Heliotropium, 124-*125*, *chart* 153. *See
  also* Heliotrope
Heterocentron. See Schizocentron
Hibiscus, 8, 10, 48, 53, 59, 73, 98, *125*,
  chart 153
Hippeastrum, *125*, *chart* 153
Holly, miniature. *See Malpighia*
Holly, Singapore. *See Malpighia*
Holly malpighia. *See Malpighia*
Honeysuckle fuchsia. *See Fuchsia*
Hortensia, 9
Hoya, 8, 73, *125*-126, *chart* 153
Humidifying tray, 39-40, *41*, 43, 77,
  79
Humidity, 7, 10, 25, 39-41, 89; for
  African violets, 82; in containers,
  11, 48; contribution of plants to, 40,
  41, 49; controlling, *41*, 86; for
  gloxinias, 86; increasing of, by
  misting, *40-41*, 61, 77, 79;
  increasing of, with plant trays, 39-
  40, *41*, 43, 77, 79; lack of, 7, 10,
  chart 62; measuring, 14, 40, 41; for
  orchids, 12, 60, 77, 78-79; variations
  within houses of, 12; varying needs
  for, 12
Hyacinth, *6*, *7*, 8, 9, 73, 101. *See also*
  Hyacinthus
Hyacinth, grape. *See Muscari*

Hyacinthus, 8, *126*, *chart* 153. *See also* Hyacinth
Hydrangea, 6, 7, *126*, 127, *chart* 153
Hydrogen, 27
Hygrometer, 14, 40, *41*
Hypocyrta, *126*, 127, *chart* 153

immersion, watering by, *32*, 37, 38
Impatiens, 74, 90, *127*, *chart* 153
Indoor gardens, 7, 8-9, 16, *17*, *18-19*
Inga. *See Calliandra*
Insecticide, *chart* 64-65, 72
Insects, 7, 68; isolation of plants infested by, 72-73; pollination by, 13; signs of, 62, *chart* 64-65, 68; washing off of, 70, 76
Inspection, root, 52
Ipomoea, *127*, *chart* 153
Iris, 9
Iris, walking, 8, 96. *See also Neomarica*
Ivy, 9
Ivy, English, 92
Ivy, German. *See Senecio*
Ivy, parlor. *See Senecio*
Ixora, *128*, *chart* 153

Jacobinia, *128*, *chart* 153
Jasmine, 8, 9, 73, 97. *See also Jasminum*
Jasmine, Cape. *See Gardenia*
Jasmine, Carolina, 8. *See also Gelsemium*
Jasmine, crape. *See Ervatamia*
Jasmine, day-blooming. *See Cestrum*
Jasmine, Madagascar, 8. *See also Stephanotis*
Jasmine, night-blooming. *See Cestrum*
Jasmine, star, 8. *See also Trachelospermum*
Jasmine, willow-leaved. *See Cestrum*
Jasminum, *128-129*, *chart* 153. *See also* Jasmine
Jungle geranium. *See Ixora*
Justicia magnifica. *See Jacobinia*
Justicia nervosa. *See Eranthemum*

kafir lily. *See Clivia*
Kalanchoe, *129*, *chart* 153
King's-crown. *See Jacobinia*
Knocking out, *52*, 53
Kohleria, *129*, *chart* 153
Kumquat, 31. *See also Fortunella*

lachenalia, *130*, *chart* 153
Lady-of-the-night orchid, 55. *See also Brassavola*
Lady's-eardrop. *See Fuchsia*
Laelia, *56*, *130*, *chart* 153
Laeliocattleya, 16, *17*, *57*, 67, *130-131*, *chart* 153
Lantana, 26, 48, *130*, 131, *chart* 153
Layering, propagation by, 89; air, *98*; soil, 97-98
Leaf cuttings, propagation by, *93*, 96;

leaf wedges, *95*, 96; mailing of, *69*; vein cuttings, *94*, 96
Leaf mold, 45-46, 47
Leaf spot, fungus, *chart* 64-65
Leaves, in photosynthesis, 27
Leland, Emory, 80, *82*, 83
Lemon, 8, 31, 74. *See also Citrus*
Leopard lily. *See Lachenalia*
Libonia. *See Jacobinia*
Lice, plant, 15. *See also* Aphids
Light, 7, 10, 13, 16, *17*, 18, 25-31, 43, 68, 77, 78, 89, 99; artificial, 10, 28-31, *29*, 89; different kinds of, 26; fluorescent, 16, *17*, 18, *29*, 30, 82; fluorescent fixture, *29*; incandescent, 28-29, 30; insufficient, consequences of, 28, *chart* 62; lighted planters, 16-*17*, 30-31; needs of individual plants, 12, 13, 25, 26, 28, 30, 31, 77, 78, *chart* 152-154; and photosynthesis, 25-26, 27, 29; sunlight, variations in, 10, 12, 26; supplemental illumination, 29-30; too much, consequences of, 28, *chart* 62
Light energy, in photosynthesis, 27
Light meter, 26
Lighted planters, 16, *17*, 30-31
Lilium, 8, 47, *66*, *67*, *131*, *chart* 153. *See also* Easter lily; Madonna lily
Lily. *See Lilium*
Lily, Amazon. *See Eucharis*
Lily, Aztec. *See Sprekelia*
Lily, Bengal. *See Crinum*
Lily, Bermuda, 47
Lily, blue African. *See Agapanthus*
Lily, blood. *See Haemanthus*
Lily, calla. *See Zantedeschia*
Lily, climbing. *See Gloriosa*
Lily, Easter, 8, *24*, *25*, 47, *66*, *67*. *See also Lilium*
Lily, glory, 73. *See also Gloriosa*
Lily, Jacobean. *See Sprekelia*
Lily, Kafir. *See Clivia*
Lily, leopard. *See Lachenalia*
Lily, madonna, 47, *66*, 67
Lily, milk-and-wine. *See Crinum*
Lily, St.-James's. *See Sprekelia*
Lily, Scarborough. *See Vallota*
Lily, zephyr. *See Zephyranthes*
Lily of the Nile. *See Agapanthus*
Lily-of-the-valley orchid, 58. *See also Odontoglossum*
Lime, 74. *See also Citrus*
Limestone, ground, 47
Lipstick plant. *See Aeschynanthus*
Lobelia, 28
Lobularia, *132*, *chart* 153
Location, selection of, 26-28

madagascar jasmine, 8. *See also Stephanotis*
Madonna lily, 47, *66*, 67
Magic flower. *See Achimenes*
Malathion, *chart* 64-65, 72
Malpighi, *36*
Malpighia, *36*, *132*, *chart* 153
Malvaviscus, *132-133*, *chart* 153
Mandevillea. *See Dipladenia*
Manettia, *133*, *chart* 153
Maple, flowering. *See Abutilon*
Marble chips, 79

Marguerite. *See Chrysanthemum*
Marguerite, blue. *See Felicia*
Maxillaria, *58*, *133*, *chart* 153
Maximum-minimum thermometer, 14, *42-43*
Mealy bugs, 15, 62, *chart* 64-65, 71, 72
Mexican flame vine. *See Senecio*
Microclimates, 12-14, 42
Milk-and-wine lily. *See Crinum*
Misting, 40-41, 61, 77, 79
Mites, 15, *chart* 64-65, 70, 71-72
Morning glory. *See Ipomoea*
Moss, Spanish, 12
Moth orchid. *See Phalaenopsis*
Mother-of-thousands. *See Saxifraga*
Muscari, *133*, *chart* 153
Mystacidium. *See Angraecum*

naegelia. *See Smithiantha*
Narcissus, 73, *134*, *chart* 153
Nasturtium, 8. *See also Tropaeolum*
Natal plum. *See Carissa*
National societies, 12, 80
Nematanthus. *See Hypocyrta*
Neofinetia, *57*, 134, *chart* 153
Neomarica, 8, 96, *134*, *chart* 153. *See* Walking iris
Nerium. *See Ervatamia*
Nero's-crown. *See Ervatamia*
Nicot, Jean, 34
Nicotiana, 8, *34*, *135*, *chart* 153
Nicotine sulfate, *chart* 64-65
Nidularium, *135*, *chart* 153
Nitrogen, *chart* 62, 68, 69, 83
Nopalxochia. *See Epiphyllum*
Nut orchid. *See Achimenes*

odontoglossum, *58*, 135, 136, *chart* 153
Offsets, propagation from, 97
Olea. *See Osmanthus*
Olive, sweet. *See Osmanthus*
Oncidium, *56*, 136, *chart* 154
Onion, false sea. *See Ornithogalum*
Orange, 8, 68, 74. *See also Citrus*
Orchid, cattleya, *55*, 76, 79. *See also Cattleya*
Orchid, Christmas. *See Cattleya*
Orchid, clamshell, 58. *See also Epidendrum*
Orchid, dancing lady. *See Oncidium*
Orchid, Easter. *See Cattleya*
Orchid, lady-of-the-night, 55. *See also Brassavola*
Orchid, lady's-slipper, 28
Orchid, laeliocattleya, 67. *See also Laeliocattleya*
Orchid, lily-of-the-valley, 58. *See also Odontoglossum*
Orchid, moth. *See Phalaenopsis*
Orchid, nut. *See Achimenes*
Orchid, spider. *See Brassia*
Orchid cactus, 76. *See also Epiphyllum*
Orchid monkeys, 49
Orchids, 7, 11-12, 16, *17*, 54, *55-58*, 77, 101; characteristics of, 12, *13*; day-to-day care of, *60-61*, 77-79; epiphytic, 12, 49, 59, 79;

monopodial, *60*-61; repotting of, 59-61, *60, 61;* reproductive system of, 12, *13;* requirements of, 12, 41, 45, 59-61, 77-79; specialization in, 12; sympodial, 60-*61;* terrestrial, 12, 79
Organic matter, 45, 46-47
Ornamental pepper. *See Capsicum*
Ornithogalum, 136, chart 154
Osmanthus, 136-137, chart 154
Outdoor plants, 11
Outdoor summer care, 73-76, 77
Ovary, 13
Overwatering, 31, 32, 51, *chart* 62, 72
Ovules, 13
Oxalis, 136, 137, chart 154
Oxygen, 26, 27

Painted feather. *See Vriesia*
Palms, 9
Paphiopedilum, 55, 137, chart 154
Papyrus, 9
Parlor ivy. *See Senecio*
Passiflora, 137-138, chart 154. *See also* Passionflower
Passionflower, 79. *See also Passiflora*
Pasteurizing soil, 46
Patient Lucy, 26. *See also* Impatiens
Peat moss, 33, 45-46, 47, 60, 61, 74, 79, 92
Pelargonium, 138, chart 154. *See also* Geranium
Pentas, 138, chart 154
Pepper, ornamental. *See Capsicum*
Perlite, 11, 33, 40, 41, 43, 47, 48, 51, 79, 92
Permanent wave plant. *See Billbergia*
Pesticides, *chart* 64-65, 72, 75
Pests, 15, 62, *chart* 64-65, 71-73
Petals, *13*
Petunia, 138-139, chart 154
pH level, 47
Phalaenopsis, 16, *17, 57,* 60, 139, *chart* 154
Pharbitis. See Ipomoea
Philodendron, 16, 92
Phosphorus, 68, 69, 83
Photosynthesis, 25-26, *27*
Phyllocactus. See Epiphyllum
Pigtail plant. *See Anthurium*
Pinching back, 68, *73*
Pineapple, 12. *See also Ananas*
Pistil, 12, *13*
Plant lice, 15. *See also* Aphids
Planters, lighted, 16-*17,* 30-31
Plastic, clear, *33,* 92, 99
Plastic pots, 49; shapes of, 49; weight of, 49; waterlogging in, 49. *See also* Pots
Plum, Natal. *See Carissa*
Plume, Brazilian. *See Jacobinia*
Plume, scarlet. *See Euphorbia*
Pocketbook flower. *See Calceolaria*
Poinsett, Joel Roberts, *34*
Poinsettia, 7, *24, 25,* 31, *34, 42. See also Euphorbia*
Pomegranate, 7. *See also Punica*
Pores, leaf, *27*
Pot-bound plants, 54, *Chart 63,* 68
Potash, 83
Potassium, 68, 69
Pots, 8, 45, 47-50, 59, 99; clay, 49, 50, 59; plastic, 49; shapes of, 50, 59;

sizes of, 47, 49
Potting, *51,* 52-53; inserting wick, *38;* orchids, 60,61
Potting mixture, 45, 46-47, 51, 52, 59, 60, 92, 99
Powder puff. *See Calliandra*
Primrose, 7, *18-19, 20-21,* 26, 41, 43, 49. *See also Primula*
Primrose, Cape. *See Streptocarpus*
Primula, 139-140, chart 154. *See also* Primrose
Propagation, 15, 89-99; by air layering, *98;* from leaf cuttings, *93;* from runners, *97;* from seeds, 77-78, 86; from stem cuttings, *91;* of begonias, by leaf sections, *95;* of begonias, by vein cuttings, *94*
Protection, wrapping for, *15*
Pruning, *53,* 59, 68
Punica, 140, chart 154
Pyrethrum, *chart* 64-65, 72

Queen Charlotte Sophia, *36*
Queen-of-the-night cactus. *See Epiphyllum*
Queen's tears. *See Billbergia*
Quesnelia, 140, chart 154

Rechsteineria, *140,* chart 154
Red spider mites, 15, *chart* 64-65, 70, 71-72
Removing plant from pot, *52,* 53
Repotting, 53, 54-61, 68; correct time for, 59; of orchids, 59-61; root examination during, *52,* 53, 54; size of pot for, 59; need for, 53, 54, 59, 68
Reproduction, sexual, 89, 90, 98-99
Reproduction, vegetative: advantages of, 90; of bulbs, 89; by division, 96-97; by layering, 97-*98;* by leaf cuttings, 89, 90, *93;* by offsets, 97; reliability of, 90; by root cuttings, 90; by runners, 89, *97;* by stem cuttings, 90, *91;* variety of methods of, 89-90
Reproductive system, 12, *13*
Rest periods, nightly, 28, 31, 78
Resting period, 11, 32-33, 76-77
Rhipsalidopsis. See Schlumbergera
Rhizome, *61*
Rhynchospermum. See Trachelospermum
Rieger begonia. *See Begonia*
Rodriguezia, 58, 141, chart 154
Root hairs, *27*
Root pruning, 53
Root rot, 32, 45, 46, 49, *chart* 64-65
Rooting, 94-96; hormone, 91, 92, 94, 98; medium, 92; powder, 91, 92, 94, 98; supplies for, 92-94
Roots, how to examine, *52,* 54-59
Rosa, 141, chart 154. *See also* Rose
Rose, 71-72. *See also Rosa*
Rose of China. *See Hibiscus*
Rosemary. *See Rosmarinus*
Rosmarinus, 141, chart 154
Rotenone, *chart* 64-65, 72
Roving sailor. *See Saxifraga*
Rubber plant, 16
Ruellia, 141-142, chart 154
Runners, propagation from, *97*

Russelia, 142, chart 154

Sage, blue. *See Eranthemum*
Saintpaulia, 25, *142,* chart 154. *See also* African violet
Sand, 40, 43, 47, 92
Saucer watering, *32,* 37, 38
Saxifraga, 142-143, chart 154. *See also* Strawberry geranium
Scales, *chart* 64-65
Scarlet plume. *See Euphorbia*
Schizocentron, 143, chart 154
Schlumbergera, 143, chart 154. *See also* Christmas cactus
Scilla, 143, 144, chart 154
Scotch purse. *See Malvaviscus*
Sea onion, false. *See Ornithogalum*
Seeds, 13, 77-78, 98-99
Self-watering devices, 39
Senecio, 144, chart 154. *See also* Cineraria
Sepals, *13*
Shards, 48, 49, 50, 51, 59, 60, 61
Shrimp plant. *See Beloperone*
Shrubs, 9, 10
Silicone coating, 49
Singapore holly. *See Malpighia*
Sinningia, 144, chart 154. *See also* Gloxinia, *Rechsteineria*
Slipperwort. *See Calceolaria*
Slugs, *chart* 64-65
Smithiantha, 145, chart 154
Snails, *chart* 64-65
Societies, national, 12, 80
Society garlic. *See Tulbaghia*
Soil, 45-47; depth of, for bulbs, 49; level of, *46,* 51, 52, 59; pasteurizing of, 46; for seedlings, 99; for specific plants, 10; structure of, 46
Solanum, 145, chart 154
Sophrolaeliocattleya, 56, 145, chart 154
Spanish moss, 12
Spanish shawl. *See Schizocentron*
Spathiphyllum, 145-146, chart 154
Sphagnum moss, 11, 47, 51, 75, 92, 94, 99
Sphagnum peat moss, 47
Spider mites, 15, *chart* 64-65, 71-72
Spider orchid. *See Brassia*
Sprekelia, 146, chart 154
Squill. *See Scilla*
Staging, 11, 16, *18-19,* 48
Stamens, 12, *13*
Star cluster, Egyptian. *See Pentas*
Star jasmine, 8. *See also Trachelospermum*
Starches, 26, 27
Stem cuttings, 90-94, *91;* pot prepared for, *91, 93, 95*
Stem rot, *chart* 64-65
Stephanotis, 8, *146,* chart 154
Stigma, *13*
Stones, 50-51
Strawberry begonia. *See Saxifraga*
Strawberry geranium, 97. *See also Saxifraga*
Strelitzia, 36, 146-147, chart 154
Streptocarpus, 147, chart 154
Streptosolen, 147, chart 154
Sugars, 26, 27
Sun scorch, *chart* 63

Sunlight. *See* Light
Supplements, soil, 46
Sweet olive. *See Osmanthus*

tabernaemontana. *See Ervatamia*
Tailflower. *See Anthurium*
Tangerine. *See Citrus*
Temperature, air, 7, 25, 41-43; day, 41, 42; during vacation care, 33; factors affecting, 41; measuring of, 14, 42-43; night, 18, 41-42; *chart* 152-154; outdoors, 74, 75; protection from abrupt change of, 15; varied preferences for, 11, 12, 41, 42, 86
Temperature, water: for baths, *chart*
Temperature, water: for baths, *chart* 64-65, 70-71, 72; for misting, 40; for watering, 33-37, *chart* 63
Temple bells. *See Smithiantha*
Terrestrial orchids, 12
Tetradifon, *chart*, 64-65
Tetranema, 147-148, chart 154
Thermometer, maximum-minimum, 14, 42-43
Thunberg, Carl Peter, *35*
Thunbergia, 35, 148, chart 154
Ti log, 29
Tillandsia, 148, chart 154
Timer, automatic, 30, 89
Tobacco, flowering, 8. *See also Nicotiana*
Tomatoes, 30
Top pruning, *53*
Top watering, 32, 37-38
Trachelospermum, 8, 148, chart 154
Transpiration, 41, 51
Trays, humidifying, 39-40, *41,* 43, 77, 79
Treasure flower. *See Gazania*

Tree-fern fiber, 60
Trees, miniature, 7, 8
Trichocentrum, 58, 149, *chart* 154
Trichosporum. See Aeschynanthus
Trinidad flame bush. *See Calliandra*
Tropaeolum, 8, *149, chart* 154
Tropical plants, 10, 12, 43
Tulbaghia, 149, chart 154
Tulip, 41, 73, 89. *See also Tulipa*
Tulipa, 149-150, chart 154. *See also* Tulip
Turning plants, 68, 74, 82
Turk's-cap. *See Malvaviscus*
Twelve Apostles. *See Neomarica*

urn plant. *See Aechmea*

Vacation care, *33*
Vallota, 150, chart 154
Vein cuttings, propagation by, *94, 96*
Veltheimia, 150, chart 154
Velvet plant, trailing. *See Ruellia*
Ventilation, 78, 79
Vermiculite, 92
Vines, 7, 8, 89
Violet, African. *See* African violet; *Saintpaulia*
Violet, Arabian. *See Exacum*
Violet, flame. *See Episcia*
Violets, 9
Vriesia, 34, 67, *150-151, chart* 154

Walking iris, 8, 96. *See also Neomarica*
Washing plants, *chart* 64-65, *70-71,* 72, 76

Water: chemical content of, 37; in photosynthesis, 26, 27; temperature of, 33-37, 40, *chart* 63, *chart* 64-65, 70, 71, 72. *See also* Watering
Water gauge, dipstick, *50,* 51-52
Water-softening devices, 37
Watering 7-8, 25, 31-39, 43, 46, 68; African violets, *82;* begonias, 84; frequency of, 32; insufficient, consequences of, *chart* 26; methods of, 32, 37-39, 46; of orchids, 60, 77, 79; overwatering, consequences of, 31-32, 45, *chart 62,* 72, 79; time of day for, 33, 72; varying with life cycle, 32-33, 39, 76; varying with pot size and type, 39, 49, 51; varying with weather. *See also* Drainage; Water
Wax begonia. *See Begonia*
Waxmallow. *See Malvaviscus*
Waxplant, 8. *See also Hoya*
White flies, *chart* 64-65
Wick watering, 38, 39
Widow's-tear. *See Achimenes*
Window gardens, 16, *18-19, 20-21*
Window greenhouse, *88,* 89
Woody-stemmed plants, 73; pruning of, *53*
Wrapping, protective, *15*

yesterday, today and tomorrow. *See Brunfelsia*

Zantedeschia, *151, chart* 154
Zebra plant. *See Aphelandra*
Zephyranthes, 151, chart 154
Zineb, *chart* 64-65